THE  CT

Dean J. DeFino

B L O O M S B U R Y

NEW YORK • LONDON • NEW DELHI • SYDNEY

Bloomsbury Academic
An imprint of Bloomsbury Publishing Inc

1385 Broadway   50 Bedford Square
New York   London
NY 10018   WC1B 3DP
USA   UK

www.bloomsbury.com

Bloomsbury is a registered trade mark of Bloomsbury Publishing PLC

First published 2014

© Dean J. DeFino, 2014

Library of Congress Cataloging-in-Publication Data
DeFino, Dean J.
The HBO effect / Dean J. DeFino.
pages cm
Includes bibliographical references and index.
ISBN 978-1-4411-8043-8 (hardback)– ISBN 978-0-8264-2130-2 (paperback) 1.
Home Box Office (Firm) I. Title.
PN1992.92.H66D44 2013
302.23–dc23
2013029934

ISBN: HB: 978-1-4411-8043-8
PB: 978-0-8264-2130-2
ePDF: 978-1-6235-6521-3
ePub: 978-1-6235-6127-7

Typeset by Fakenham Prepress Solutions, Fakenham, Norfolk NR21 8NN
Printed and bound in the United States of America

THE HBO EFFECT

for Whitney

next time,
a love poem

CONTENTS

ACKNOWLEDGMENTS

This book would not exist without the help and support of dozens of people.

I would like to take a moment to thank a few by name. Thanks to Barbara Solomon, Stanley Solomon, Matt Longabucco, Dorothy Brophy, Jame Richards, and Fran Hannigan for their thoughtful responses to early drafts of this work. Thanks to the folks at Bloomsbury: especially Katie Gallof, who has been an enthusiastic advocate for this project from the start. Thanks to Iona College for supporting the research and writing of this book through fellowship leave. And thanks most of all to my family—Whitney, Iris and Will—for endless patience, constant encouragement, and unconditional love.

there, or shared any of the same experiences as the show's characters. It just hung from a hook among the other gimcracks that go for Christmas finery. Twenty-five percent off, with the purchase of a tree. But how had it gotten there to begin with? How had *The Sopranos* achieved this particular level of iconic status? How had the story of an anxious sociopath with mother issues, produced sporadically over seven years by a premium cable channel with a subscription base of no more than 30 percent of American households managed to bring its cultural weight to bear on a Christmas ornament? Was this the fate of all pop culture in the postmodern age, from the teen heartthrob to the "great works" of American television? And if so, should I expect to find a *Masterpiece Theater* frisbee on some other wall?

These are the questions one ponders while stuck waiting in line, trying to avoid other nagging ones like, "Why am I wasting my money on this thing?" But the longer I thought about these other seemingly profound questions, the more pointed that nagging one became. I am no collector of camp or kitsch, nor was this a simple fan impulse. I know what it is like to be an unembarrassed fan, to hoard *Trailer Park Boys* DVDs, and to anticipate every new Bob Dylan recording, despite his voice sounding every day more like a torn snare drum. But this was something else. True, I have been a devotee of HBO since college, when I wasted untold hours in dorm rooms dulling my senses with the network's seemingly endless stream of mediocre Hollywood fluff. Like so many, I have followed the parade of original programs it began turning out in the 1990s. Years before discovering the ornament, I had already begun publishing work on HBO and teaching an undergraduate course called "The HBO Effect." But not until that Black Friday had I truly begun to grapple with the meaning of that phrase, and to really assess the impact HBO has had upon me, upon American television, and upon popular culture.

The purpose of this book is to try to account for that impact. Over the past decade and a half, HBO has been identified as the wellspring of a new "Golden Age" in American television. Prior to the launch of their original series *Oz* in 1997, *Sex and the City* in 1998, and *The Sopranos* in 1999, the network was viewed primarily as a supplier of uncensored movies, sports programming, and stand-up comedy specials. HBO was barely mentioned outside of industry publications such as *Broadcasting and Cable* and *Multichannel News*, and even those references focused on the network's innovative business model, rather than its programming. To date, the only book-length *history* of HBO is George Mair's *Inside*

HBO (1988), which deals almost exclusively with industry and front office issues, and, as its subtitle states, *The Billion-Dollar War Between HBO, Hollywood, and the Home Video Revolution*. But since the late 1990s, television critics and scholars have been clamoring to assess HBO's growing catalog of original series, miniseries, documentaries and feature films,[1] and debating the legitimacy of the network's most famous tagline, "It's Not TV: It's HBO."[2]

Over time, a consensus seems to have emerged concerning the terms of HBO's legacy to contemporary television: its innovations in the delivery of television programming (via subscription, satellite, multiplexing); its expansion of "acceptable" content (sex, violence, profanity); its transformation of conventional genres (crime, western, comedy); its branding strategies; and its fostering of creativity in a medium notoriously averse to risk. In the pages that follow, I will consider each of these effects. But I will also look at other less-visible ways HBO and its programming reflect and influence the culture, such as the ways its original programs challenge the conventional notions of "realism" and political bias. These will not only give us a clearer picture of the HBO effect, but a better sense of its contours and nuances.

It can sometimes be difficult to see the relationship between cause and effect. The great Roman writer, Ovid, understood this. When he set about compiling the myths of the ancient world in *Metamorphoses*, he organized them around the theme of change, or metamorphosis, because in the end that is what all stories are about. Something changes. A cause leads to an effect. In myth, those changes often occur for mysterious reasons. Was it pride or reason that convinced Eve to eat the apple? Why did Zeus take the form of a swan when he raped Leda? The Ovid line quoted at the head of this chapter is taken from one of the most bizarre myths in all of *Metamorphoses*: the story of Hermaphroditus, whose name is the source of the word, "hermaphrodite." At one level, the myth recounts a simple cause-and-effect chain: Hermaphroditus refuses the sexual advances of a water nymph (cause), so she curses him with another set of genitals (effect); he then curses her sacred spring (cause), so that all who bathe in it become bisexual (effect). I said it was bizarre. But the myth speaks to the limit of simple causal understanding, which often confuses the *what* for the *why*. Why does the nymph choose this particular curse, and *why* does Hermaphroditus make innocent bathers bear the brunt of his revenge?

Similar questions arise when thinking about the bizarre logic of HBO merchandising, from "Famiglia" ornaments (*The Sopranos*), to "Imp" iPhone covers (*Game of Thrones*), "Let's hug it out, Bitch" mouse pads (*Entourage*), "Team Nucky" t-shirts (*Boardwalk Empire*), "Shmohawk" hoodies (*Curb Your Enthusiasm*), Kenny Powers bobbleheads (*Eastbound and Down*), and "blood bath" shower gels (*True Blood*): Why these things? What do they "mean," and to whom? Such cheap novelties are merely a few of the visible links in a chain of cause and effect that, when pulled, reveals others hidden just below the surface. The more we uncover, the easier to trace where they come from and where they lead. So let us begin by pulling on those we can easily see. Here we will only glance them, but in the chapters to follow we will scrutinize them in much more detail.

Cause and effect

The HBO effect can be seen in the remarkable history of innovations and "firsts" that helped to shape the network, particularly in its early years. When cable entrepreneur, Chuck Dolan, launched the service in 1972, it became the first successful commercial venture in "pay" television, though the idea for subscription-based programming had been around since the earliest days of television, and several experimental systems had been tried over the previous three decades. Commercial cable systems had been in operation since the late 1940s, delivering broadcast signals to customers outside of the signal range, but HBO's success would signif- icantly increase the value of these existing systems by allowing them to offer exclusive content. In 1975, under the management of Gerald Levin, HBO became the first commercial television service to beam its signal via satellite, so moving cable and over-the-air broadcast from the age of the local and regional to the national and global. With success, HBO drew the attention of its network competitors, who in turn directed the attention of federal regulators to them. But while the broadcast networks and the smaller cable operators cowered to the regulatory authority of the Federal Communications Commission (FCC), Levin and HBO used the enormous resources of their parent company, Time, Inc., to successfully sue the federal agency over regulatory restrictions that made too fine a distinction between "pay" cable services and programming broadcast over the public airwaves. Many industry observers saw them as a sort of David to the broadcasters' Goliath.

No doubt HBO's success owes a great debt to the vision of men like Chuck Dolan and Gerald Levin, but it owes an equal or greater one to its deep-pocketed corporate parent, to the deregulatory efforts of the Nixon, Ford and Reagan administrations and—as I will outline in the next chapter—to a cloud of utopian rhetoric that had surrounded discussions of cable's future since the mid-1960s. In short, HBO was as much a by-product of its time as a product of a few men's imaginations. And, as we will see, its extraordinary financial and creative successes have been born from, nourished by, and shaped by the conditions of that time far more than any business plan or innovation.

Another often-noted marker of the HBO effect has been the relaxation of television content restrictions; or, the increased allowance of sex, violence, and swearing on TV. HBO has always tried to distinguish itself from its competitors by offering what others could not. And because the pay service is not bound by the same FCC restrictions as broadcasters who use public airwaves, the easiest way for HBO to distinguish itself has been through explicit content. In 1977, HBO featured comedian George Carlin's first stand-up special, including the infamous "Seven Words You Can Never Say on Television" routine that had landed Carlin in hot water with the FCC a few years prior. Since then it has made a business of defying the conventions of television content. In the 1980s, many people subscribed to HBO specifically for the R-rated movies and comedy specials. And with the introduction of high-quality series such as *Oz* and *The Sopranos* in the 1990s, HBO also became known for its graphic, realistic depictions of violence. As the general public has become more tolerant of relaxed content standards—thanks in large part to the success of HBO original programming—we have seen something of a bleed-over into broadcast and basic cable. Take, for example, the use of obscenities. In the 1990s, cultural critics worried about the use of the words "dick" and "asshole" on NBC's *NYPD Blue*. Now viewers are likely to encounter all seven of Carlin's "dirty words" in any given episode of FX's popular late-night comedy, *It's Always Sunny in Philadelphia*. In fact, a recent study shows that, between 2005 and 2010 alone—while HBO was achieving record viewer numbers—overall incidents of scripted profanity on broadcast and basic cable television increased by nearly 70 percent, with the largest increase for bleeped-out uses of the word "fuck": from 11 incidences in 2005, to 276 in 2010.[3] And while HBO is not the sole reason for this more relaxed attitude toward obscenity on television, as we will see in Chapter 3, it has had a significant impact on the ways "dirty words" are used in service to realism (especially in drama) and irony (especially in comedy).

Of course, "graphic content" is only one of the ways HBO has impacted contemporary television. In its celebrated original series, the network has introduced a level of narrative, character, and thematic sophistication that has spread across the channel spectrum. Later chapters will look at specific programs that have adopted what has come to be known as the "HBO style." For the moment it is enough to try to imagine the Machiavellian sociopath Vic Mackey of FX's *The Shield*, or the self-loathing narcissist Don Draper of AMC's *Mad Men* without Tony Soprano as a template. Or the brooding strangeness of *Desperate Housewives* and the mythical complexity of *Lost* without the existential dark of *Six Feet Under* and the enormous scale and bravado of *The Wire*. In *30 Rock*, Tina Fey does a postmodern turn on the "have it all" feminism of *The Mary Tyler Moore Show*, but her character Liz Lemon owes an equal debt to the women of *Sex and the City*, who put off romance for career in their twenties, only to face the consequences of that decision in their thirties and forties. Contemporary television still makes plenty of room for beautiful people leading lives of steamy romance and manufactured crisis (*Grey's Anatomy*; *Pretty Little Liars*), or wacky domestic sitcoms where the dads are lovably oblivious and moms and kids roll their eyes with tolerant affection (*The Middle*; *Suburgatory*). But what about the growing number of unsympathetic characters whose stories are compelling not because they allow us to escape into a fantasy of wish fulfillment and order, but because they reflect (albeit *in extremis*) the frustrating messiness of real life (*Rescue Me*; *Breaking Bad*)? Or the darker vein of contemporary sitcoms that give the lie to so-called "family values"(*Arrested Development*; *It's Always Sunny in Philadelphia*)? As we will see in later chapters, each of these owes a direct debt to HBO.

When we talk about HBO's "original programming," we tend to mean scripted dramas and comedies. But the bulk of programming produced by the network has been in the areas of sports and documentary. HBO's longest-running series are all sports programs—*HBO World Championship Boxing*, *Wimbledon Tennis*, *Inside the NFL*—and the network has remained the perennial home of boxing since launching its satellite service in 1975 with a live telecast of Muhammad Ali and Joe Frazier's "Thrilla in Manila." In the late 1970s, HBO began supplementing its movie and sports schedule with documentaries produced in-house, and has since cemented its reputation as the patron of the form, providing financial support and an audience for countless filmmakers, who in turn have provided the network with a steady stream of awards and critical praise. Of course, not everyone has had unmitigated praise for HBO's sports and documentary programming. Boxing writers and fans frequently complain that HBO's stranglehold on the sport has drastically narrowed the field of fighters who gain the spotlight, and effectively turned HBO from an exhibitor into a promoter.[4] Despite the great debt scores of documentary filmmakers owe to HBO, many complain that a sort of "house style" has come to dominate the form, and that, given HBO's dominance in the field, other outlets that might have served as providers in the past (PBS, BBC) are now less likely to do so. Though few would argue that HBO's dominance in these fields constitutes a monopoly (since it does not actively prevent others from entering the market), many are left to wonder whether the negative effects of HBO patronage might outweigh the positive.

Monopolistic or not, HBO is certainly known for its aggressive and transformative business tactics. As a service that has always relied on Hollywood movies to fill its broadcast schedule, it could not help but have a broad impact upon the movie business. Decades before Napster sent the music industry into a tailspin, HBO took on Hollywood, forcing struggling studios to tie their fortunes to the "Home Box Office" with sweetheart contracts that offered blocks of films at steep discounts, and movie financing deals that guaranteed exclusive rights to television broadcast *and* a percentage of the theatrical box office. And when HBO expanded to a 24–hour service in the early 1980s, it helped fill the balance of the programming schedule by making their own movies, more cheaply than, and outside of, the incestuous culture of the Hollywood studios. HBO Films was launched in 1983 with *The Terry Fox Story*, and has since produced more than 200 films and miniseries, making it one of the most prolific and award-winning independent film studios of all time. Just as HBO changed the way movies are seen, it has had a significant impact upon how they are made.

Some critics have gone further to suggest that, thanks to the quality of original films, miniseries and series produced by HBO and its imitators at networks like Showtime, Starz, AMC, FX, and USA, television has superseded cinema as the pre-eminent narrative medium of our time. By attracting some of the biggest talents in film and television (Steven Spielberg, Alan Ball, Larry David, David Milch, Martin Scorsese, Aaron Sorkin) and giving them absolute freedom to work, HBO has indeed made television a destination for the sort of mature, satisfying stories once relegated to independent and "art" cinema. And because long-form television narrative allows for a complexity of character and plot unavailable to the shorter-form feature film, talented writers, directors and producers may now find television work more appealing and fulfilling than film work.

HBO has been a magnet for established television talent attracted by the relative freedom from content restrictions and broadcast networks' emphasis on quantity over quality. David Chase, who had a successful career as a writer and producer on such series as *The Rockford Files* and *Northern Exposure* long before creating *The Sopranos*, landed seren- dipitously at HBO after shopping the mob drama to all of the broadcast networks. He soon realized that working for HBO allowed him more time and freedom to develop the visual and narrative details of the show, without any studio bosses looking over his shoulder. Alan Ball used his Oscar for best screenplay (*American Beauty*, 1999) to escape what he characterized as sitcom hell (he had written previously for *Grace Under Fire* and *Cybill*), into the welcoming arms of HBO, where he was given total creative control over *Six Feet Under*, then *True Blood*. *Seinfeld* co-creator, Larry David, brought HBO's longest-running scripted series, *Curb Your Enthusiasm*, to the network because he wanted to avoid the grinding 22–episode seasons and frequent clashes with network censors he had experienced at NBC. David Milch (*NYPD Blue*) and David Simon (*Homicide: Life on the Street*) brought *Deadwood* and *The Wire* to HBO because their obsessive, idiosyncratic, detail-oriented working methods abraded with the "best practices" of the broadcast networks.

While HBO has drawn on established talent, it has also been a proving ground for young writers, producers and directors who have since spread their talents—and aspects of the so-called "HBO style"— across the channel spectrum. As we will see in Chapter 3, this influence is felt particularly in HBO's comic programming, but it is also evident in drama. Take, for example, Todd A. Kessler, who wrote and produced more than 20 episodes of *The Sopranos* before leaving HBO to co-create another series about amoral characters with sociopathic tendencies: FX's *Damages*. Or James Manos Jr, who got his start as a producer for HBO Films (*The Positively True Adventures of the Alleged Texas Cheerleader-Murdering Mom*, 1993), then worked on the first season of *The Sopranos* before being brought in by the FX network to consult on the freshman season of *The Shield*: a series with an acknowledged debt to *The Sopranos* for its unsympathetic lead character, dark criminal themes, and graphic content. Manos would then go on to create, write and produce the still-darker, still-more-graphic *Dexter* for Showtime, starring Michael C. Hall, previously known for his iconic role in another HBO series, *Six Feet Under*. Much of *Dexter* has been written and directed by people Manos knew from his HBO days.

Perhaps the ultimate example of the diaspora of HBO talent is Matt Weiner, who worked his way up the ranks in the *Sopranos* writers' room, eventually becoming executive producer, all the while developing another series intended for HBO under the tutelage of *Sopranos* creator, David Chase. Though neither Weiner nor Chase were successful in their attempts to sell the show to HBO, they did manage to interest a small basic cable network that was hoping to do what HBO had done a decade earlier: supplement its slate of Hollywood films with distinctive original programming. The network was AMC, and the show was *Mad Men*. Again with the help of Chase, Weiner prepared *Mad Men* while still working on *The Sopranos*, which allowed AMC to premiere the series only a month after the mob hit took its final bow. The timing was intentional: AMC and Weiner hoped to draw in all of those cut-adrift *Sopranos* fans. It also allowed Weiner to lure over several writers, producers and directors from the earlier series. And the gambit paid off. Although the audience for *Mad Men* remains significantly smaller than that of *The Sopranos* in its prime, it has dominated the Emmy awards since its premiere season, and is frequently listed among the greatest series in the history of television.

A quality brand

The most significant measure of the HBO effect is the way it has helped to give shape to that otherwise ill-defined term, "quality TV." The meaning of quality TV has evolved over time, leaving some contemporary critics to debate whether any generally accepted definition exists, or can exist.[5] In the 1970s, quality TV referred almost exclusively to sitcoms like *All in the Family*, *The Mary Tyler Moore Show*, and *M*A*S*H*, which reflected shifting social values regarding race, class, gender, and politics. In the 1980s, it meant long-form serial dramas, with overlapping, multi-episode story arcs (*Hill Street Blues*, *St Elsewhere*, *LA Law*), and increasingly complex characterization. These features certainly carry over into contemporary definitions of quality TV, but several others have emerged, including verisimilitude, moral ambiguity, psychological realism, and narrative irresolution. Here HBO has truly distinguished itself, through epics of social and moral disintegration (*The Sopranos*; *The Wire*) and epic revisions of history (*Deadwood*; *Rome*) and myth (*True Blood*; *Game of Thrones*); through domestic melodramas that ruthlessly dissect "family values" (*Six Feet Under*; *Big Love*) and comedies that dive gleefully into the chasm that separates Hollywood from the "real world" (*The Larry Sanders Show*; *Curb Your Enthusiasm*).

In at least two respects, however, the definition of quality TV seems not to have changed over time. First, we tend to think of it as aspirational, driven at least in part by some high cultural impulse to make television "better." As we will see in the next chapter, television has long been susceptible to this quasi-utopian impulse despite, or perhaps because it has so long been denigrated as a medium for cheap, uninspired, and repetitious entertainment. Nostalgic conversations about quality TV often point to the literary bona fides of writers from television's first "Golden Age" in the 1950s and early 1960s—especially Paddy Chayefsky (*Playhouse 90*) and Rod Serling (*The Twilight Zone*)—ignoring or forgetting the many vapid programs that were the usual daily fare. Film scholars with a penchant for later series like *Twin Peaks* and *The Singing Detective* have often attempted to use the criteria of so-called "art cinema" to elevate them above "boob tube" banalities.[6] But from *Mary Tyler Moore* to *Mad Men*, "quality" has always been more about branding than aspiration. It is no coincidence that contemporary notions of "quality" television did not begin to emerge until the early 1970s, when television networks first began tracking audiences using demographic data (age, race, gender, class, geography), and developing programming aimed at high-value demographic groups like white, educated, professional middle-class women (at whom *Mary Tyler Moore* was aimed). Nor that it began to take its current shape in the 1980s and 1990s when, thanks to the deregulation of the cable industry, broadcasters were forced to compete for that high-value demographic with an increasing number of basic cable networks.

This market-based approach certainly does not preclude the possibility of "better" television. But it does make the fate of such programming susceptible to shifts in the marketplace, especially for networks that rely upon anxious advertisers who demand both quality and quantity of audience. Each television season, less than half of new series survive, and many more never make it out of development because programmers and advertisers remain unconvinced that the ratio of costs to potential ratings will fall in their favor, and because broadcast and basic cable networks cannot afford to have their shows run at a loss. HBO's subscription model offers more liberty, since subscriber loyalty is based on overall satisfaction with the movies, sports, and original content provided by the service, rather than individual programs. But even HBO feels the pressure to produce "hit" series (*Sex and the City*; *The Sopranos*; *Game of Thrones*), if for no other reason than to subsidize lower-performing, though critically acclaimed programs that "elevate the brand" (*The Wire*; *In Treatment*; *Treme*). And given these natural advantages, expectations are high. When HBO released *Oz* and *Sex and the City* at the tail end of the twentieth century, critics seemed mainly interested in the frank dialogue and full frontal nudity. With *The Sopranos*, they spied an underdog worthy of championing, which *Curb Your Enthusiasm* and *Six Feet Under* only confirmed. With *Deadwood* and *The Wire*, they saw HBO traveling into the deep, dangerous waters previously traversed only by great works of literature and art. But by the time *Big Love* was launched, *Six Feet Under* took its final bow, and rumors of *The Sopranos'* demise were confirmed, critics had already begun complaining about a drop-off in the quality of new programs, and wondering how HBO would keep its behemoth, recklessly speeding ship from running headlong into an iceberg. As Tony Soprano tells his consigliore, Silvio Dante, it's not easy being on top: "Every decision you make affects every facet of every other fuckin' thing…. And in the end you're completely alone with it all."

The second consistent feature of quality TV is the importance of audience loyalty. Quality TV is also often "appointment TV." Unlike the sort of nebulous programming we watch simply because it is on and we happen to be sitting in front of the television, "quality" series—especially dramas—typically demand a commitment to their detailed and constantly evolving stories, from week to week, season to season. Not surprisingly, cult film studies and television studies both came into their own in the mid-1980s, thanks in large part to the proliferation of home video, which not only allowed viewers to watch at their leisure, but to scrutinize—with pause, reverse, fast-forward, etc.—in a way that had been previously impossible through regular television and theatrical viewing. As viewers, we are partly compelled by a sense of identification, of belonging, of the sort of ritual sublimation that we associate with "cult" cinema and television. These are shows we champion, collect on home video for convenient and repeated viewing, and reference in daily interactions with fellow viewers. They become part of our social milieu, in some cases even a litmus test ("What kind of a person doesn't like *The Wire?*").

Ironically, what attracts many viewers—that sense of belonging to an exclusive group who are "in the know"—tends to limit, or at least segment the audience. For example, when ratings for Fox's *The Simpsons* exploded in its sophomore season, early fans drawn to its broad satire and pervasive pop cultural references often sneered at the sort of viewers who sported "Bartmania" t-shirts and spouted catchphrases like "Don't have a cow, man!" Similarly, fans of *The Sopranos* who marveled at the brilliant ways the series played upon their sympathies and antipathies— one minute Tony is crying about a childhood trauma in his therapist's office, the next he is killing his cousin with a shotgun—openly scorned those who tuned in to see who got "whacked," to hear Paulie "Walnuts" Gualtieri rant about some perceived slight, and to catch the occasional glimpse of a stripper at the Bada Bing. The most successful "quality" series play to both high- and low-brow constituencies without offending or dismissing either, but it is a tough balance to maintain.

Here again HBO has a significant advantage. Ad-driven networks struggle to be identified as sources of quality programming, by whatever terms their audiences may define "quality" (whether neurotic mobsters or naked women). But mere membership in the culture, or perhaps the cult of HBO is a guarantee of quality TV, because HBO has made *itself*, not just its programming, the very brand of "quality." Television networks like NBC or AMC struggle to make successful "quality" series, occasionally producing a masterpiece on the scale of *The West Wing* or *Breaking Bad*, but HBO... well, "It's not TV; It's HBO." Rather than striving to meet some standard of "quality television," it claims to redefine both "quality" and "television."

Many would argue that this is a hollow boast.[7] But whatever the real merits of HBO's claim to being something *other than* television, it speaks to the two traits that have allowed HBO to remain out front of its competitors and imitators for the past four decades: its tenacity and adaptability. While some entities maintain their positions of power for long periods of time by neutralizing their competition and buying influence (General Motors, McDonalds), others take risks and adapt to shifting market conditions (Texas Instruments, Apple). And the brand that is able to get out in front of others has the distinct advantage of setting the terms or serving as a template for competitors. There are of course disadvantages (Apple's investments in research and development far exceed those of other companies who simply follow their lead), but it guarantees that one's brand is always part of the conversation (any smartphone is inevitably compared to the iPhone). HBO's long-time competitor, Showtime, has tried strategies to mirror HBO (boxing, stand-up comedy) and others to distinguish itself (its original series in the 1990s and early 2000s were mostly either gay-themed dramas or science fiction), but despite the success of its Mixed Martial Arts programming and series like *Dexter* and *Weeds*, it remains under HBO's long shadow.

Companies endure to the extent that they adapt to change, and what makes a company adaptable is its ability to see opportunity where others see threat. Take, for example, the home video revolution of the 1980s. Hollywood saw it as a direct threat to theater-based cinema, and broadcast networks worried that advertisers would refuse to pay for expensive commercials that viewers could simply skip over with a fast-forward button. So they did what big companies averse to change always do: they tried to stop it by putting the manufacturers of videocassette recorders out of business. They sued, most notably in what would become one of the landmark cases in the history of intellectual property law, *Sony v. Universal Studios* (1984). The studios lost. But HBO saw home video as a double opportunity: to expand its reach into the home video business, and to expand its service by inviting subscribers to record movies and programs they might otherwise have missed. Because HBO was able to adapt to this shift, it now draws a sizable portion of its revenues from the home video market. For example, *Game of Thrones* recouped its entire $60 million first season budget in the first week of DVD and Blu Ray sales.

Contemporary television viewers equipped with digital video recorders and web-based broadcasting options have forced ad-driven networks to find more effective ways to advertise their sponsors' goods and services, from product placements and banner ads to interactive links that exploit the Internet connectivity of "smart" TVs. Of course, HBO has no sponsors to please. It deals directly with its subscribers. But the network has found itself in an increasingly competitive market, with the ready availability of web video sites (YouTube, Vimeo), an increasing number of "cable-cutters" who prefer to watch television via *a la carte* services (iTunes, Hulu Plus), and web-based companies venturing into original series of a quality comparable to HBO (Netflix's *Lilyhammer*, *House of Cards* and *Hemlock Grove*).

HBO has distinguished itself from conventional television by embracing rather than mitigating risk. As a premium service reliant on subscriber dollars, HBO must continue to offer what cannot be found elsewhere. This does not mean that the network throws away the mold with each new series or documentary or feature film. There are patterns to be found, and in the pages that follow we will discover many of them. Although HBO is less likely than its network competitors to clone successful formulas until revenue potential has been exhausted (think of the endless stream of competition-based reality shows, medical romances, forensic science dramas, and family and workplace sitcoms that fill out primetime broadcast network schedules), HBO is certainly not averse to revisiting old successes, whether it be New Jersey mob stories (*The Sopranos*; *Boardwalk Empire*), tales of urban destitution (*The Wire*; *Treme*), or meditations on American ascendancy (*From the Earth to the Moon*; *Band of Brothers*; *The Pacific*; *John Adams*). But unlike other networks, which often market their programs as the audio-visual equivalent of comfort food—some familiar sensation to help fill the void—HBO's brand promises challenge, surprise, and a heightened experience. As HBO's own advertisements make clear, its programming is meant to be "provocative," "bold," and "groundbreaking." And if recent ventures are any indication, the network continues to believe its own ads. In only the past few years, HBO has premiered its most ambitious and expensive series in genres both familiar (the period drama, *Boardwalk Empire*) and new to the network (the fantasy drama, *Game of Thrones*). It has evolved beyond the male, middle-aged perspective defined its programming in such popular series as *The Sopranos* and *Curb Your Enthusiasm*, seeking out more feminine (*Enlightened*) and youthful (*Girls*) points of view. It has produced some of its most politically engaged features (*Recount*; *Game Change*) and documentaries (*Ghosts of Abu Ghraib*; *Terror in Mumbai*). It has even bought the film and television rights to the complete works of William Faulkner. And in a nod to the age of convergence media, when "television" has less to do with a living room appliance than a catalog of available programming, it has launched HBOGo, a service that allows HBO subscribers to access its content from anywhere in the United States using any web-enabled device. In the last chapter of this book, we will consider whether HBO actually has prepared itself for this brave new world, but one thing is certain: it has never resisted change before.

The big picture

Of course, there is a big difference between HBO embracing its messaging, and the critic accepting its claims, especially when the critic's natural inclination should be to doubt and to question. Given the title of this book, one might reasonably expect me to claim that, beginning with *The Sopranos*—or maybe *Oz* or *The Larry Sanders Show*—HBO ushered in a new "Golden Age" of American Television. There would certainly be some justification in doing so. HBO *has* had a marked effect on the way we think about television, and especially the standards of "quality" television. But its impact has been neither pervasive, nor absolute. What was television like *before* all of those Sunday dinners with Livia Soprano (*The Sopranos*) and cosmopolitans with Carrie Bradshaw (*Sex and the City*); before grieving with the Fisher clan (*Six Feet Under*), swearing with Al Swearengen (*Deadwood*), and facing a Nazi siege in the Ardennes forest with Easy Company on Christmas Day 1944 (*Band of Brothers*)? It is hard to remember. But in one way, at least, television remains what it has always been: a mixed bag. During HBO's peak creative period in the early 2000s, other networks thrived on innocuous network sitcoms (*Friends, According to Jim*) and reality shows (*Survivor, Fear Factor*), and even the great Home Box Office was not ashamed to stoop to such gratuitous trifles as *The Mind of a Married Man, G-String Divas* and *Cathouse*.

In nearly any generation, one can find "key" works of television to support the notion of a "Golden Age," just as any baseball season will have its winning streaks and no-hitters, despite the cruel tendency of statistics to balance out in the end. But the larger problem with this sort of epochal thinking is that it tends to eclipse the old with the new, the failures with the successes. This is especially true of television, "a medium without a past."[8] Although boutique cable outlets like Nick and Night and TV Land offer "classic" shows in syndication, the survival of networks depends upon a careful balance of the familiar with the new. This is typically achieved by putting a novel twist on an old formula, giving the *impression* of something original while still appealing to pre-established sensibilities. To some extent, this is true of film and literature as well. Only a small fraction of the total number of movies viewed by American film and television audiences in any given year are older than a decade, and those are almost entirely relegated to boutique "classic" television networks like TCM and AMC. At the same time, contemporary fiction far outsells literary "classics." Though the vast majority of contemporary narrative is built upon familiar genre and character conventions, it seems "new" because of variations in setting, tone, language, and theme. The "classics" of film and literature remain culturally enshrined in well-established canons and scholarly work, but as a culturally disparaged form, television is largely unprotected. True, "television studies" has emerged as a serious discipline over the past three decades, with an exponential growth in the number of books, blogs, and college courses devoted to the subject. But most of this work endorses the sort of "Golden Age" fallacy that damns many worthy programs to the dustbin of history. Scholars and critics tend to cherry-pick pre-contemporary programs such as *I Love Lucy*, *The Twilight Zone*, *The Mary Tyler Moore Show*, and *Hill Street Blues* to lay the framework for a definition of quality TV, but otherwise distain any programs before *Twin Peaks* or *Seinfeld* as mere entertainments. Little wonder HBO received virtually no scholarly attention prior to the launch of *The Sopranos*, which critics hailed for its "cinematic" and "literary" qualities. Or to put it another way, its "Not TV"-ness.

Critical accounts of HBO often read like a tale of two networks: the first a cable/satellite maverick that transformed the way television is transmitted and sold, and the second an independent studio that, through original series and films, has transformed the creative boundaries of television. But these are merely two sides of the same coin. HBO has profited because it is willing to take risks, and it has always tried to give its subscribers something they could not find elsewhere, from championship boxing and exclusive Hollywood movies to not-safe-for-television stand-up comedians and scripted series. Those profits have made it possible to take further risks that, when successful, raise subscriber numbers, award tallies, and brand perception. Television is a business, but to suggest that money breeds mediocrity unfairly damns the whole enterprise. After all, it would be hard to imagine William Shakespeare, or Pablo Picasso, or Bob Dylan having produced the sheer volume of brilliant work that is their legacy had they only sought artistic immortality, rather than the respectability, freedom and love they hoped money would buy. Critics and fans of HBO seem far less interested in questions of profit and market share than the entertainment, aesthetic, and philosophical merits of beloved programs, probably because they find the money questions too tedious, too crass, or too messy. But to accurately measure HBO's impact on contemporary television, one must acknowledge perhaps its most important example: that high quality and high profits not only *can* co-exist but—in the realm of television at least—they *must* co-exist. For what is "quality" but another form of currency? And when critics endorse the notion that HBO fostered a new "Golden Age" in American television, they are contributing to the gold standard of that currency, whether or not they wish to talk about money. In the end, the only real difference between HBO the Titan of Industry and HBO the Patron of Quality Television is a difference of perspective. Any fair account of the HBO effect must therefore be willing to look at its subject from multiple points of view.

Or as Tony Soprano would say, "Think: the big fuckin' picture."

The pilot episode of *The Sopranos* opens with a shot of Tony sitting in an empty reception room, staring anxiously at a statue of a naked woman. Tony is in the mid-background, his face framed by the legs of the statue in the extreme foreground. He glares at it from below, a mixture of erotic tension and childlike fear in his eyes. It is in many ways the perfect image to frame Tony's story. A man defined by the patriarchal values of the Mob—stamina, fealty, predation—Tony is surrounded on all sides by

FIGURE 1.1 A sense of perspective: Tony in the waiting room. *The Sopranos*, HBO

women who threaten his autonomy: his hateful and overbearing mother Livia, his moralizing but morally-compromised wife Carmela, and his by turns nurturing, clinical, and sexy psychiatrist, Dr Melfi, whom he is waiting to see for the first time as the series begins. The hour of screen time that follows this scene is filled with the detailed backstory of Tony's business and personal relationships, acts of grotesque violence, and frequent references to the deteriorating mental state that brought him to Dr Melfi in the first place. We see the plotting of his mother and jealous uncle against him, his struggles with members of his crew, altercations with his wife and children, a full-blown panic attack, and even a therapeutic revelation having to do with a dream of some ducks who had recently taken up residence in Tony's swimming pool. In all, at least 12 plots and subplots, enough stories for half a dozen episodes of any other series.

The episode closes with yet another summary image: a long, slow zoom out from a bird's eye view—or duck's eye view—of Tony's suburban backyard as guests at his son's thirteenth birthday party are called inside to eat, leaving the expansive yard and swimming pool where the ducks once lived as empty as the reception room where the series began. As the image fades and the end titles roll, we hear the voice of Nick Lowe, singing his plaintive version of "The Beast in Me," a song about a man who struggles with his animal nature. The image and the song speak volumes about the emptiness and crisis in Tony's life, the hollow success and constant threat of failure. Suddenly the jumble of stories and characters from the past hour seems to come clearly into focus, violent soap opera gilt in tones of tragedy. It is the sort of moment for which the series will become known, in which the most banal of scenes resounds with meaning and significance, and we imagine the story of this lone man as another, much larger one about the fragile state of mankind, and the burdens under which we all suffer.

Or so it seems.

It is immensely satisfying to take the long view of any story, no matter how sordid. Though the edges may look ragged and chaotic up close, with distance they seem smoother and interconnected. We draw general conclusions to avoid the messiness of having to account for the ragged edges of things, the incoherence, the gaps, and lapses. The same can be true of the close-up view, where every detail seems fraught with significance. With enough critical attention and cleverness we can imagine we see the universe in a grain of sand. Yet the "big fuckin' picture" Tony

Soprano refers to requires not only the long- and the close-up view, but a willingness to acknowledge, even embrace the ragged, the incoherent, the gaps, and the lapses. These, too, are part of the picture. Despite the opening and closing images of the pilot episode of *The Sopranos*, and despite how finely-crafted and well-acted this and every other episode is, the series is a dark and cluttered thing, filled with frustrations and unsatisfied expectations, in which nothing can be reduced to a single meaning (is Tony a sociopath or a man in crisis?), no one is redeemed (death is the only meaningful change any character undergoes), and stories end rather than being resolved. Order is illusion, whether in the long view or up close. For evidence of that fact, we need only look at the controversial closing scene of the series finale, where an ordinary moment of domestic calm in a diner builds unbearable tension out of thin air, only to cut to black. It is the sort of thing that makes us wonder why the series ever saw the light of day, much less earned the dubious honor of a collectible Christmas ornament.

Yet it did succeed beyond anything cable television had ever seen: a series that drew comparable ratings to the prestige productions of the major networks, though it was only available to a far smaller audience of paying subscribers; that introduced new idioms into the vernacular, new characters into the pantheon of great American fiction, and new directions for the crime genre; that established a run of more than a decade, during which HBO received more critical and popular attention, and more Emmy and Peabody nominations than any other network on television. When describing the impact of any cultural phenomenon, one always faces the danger of confusing its real effect with its "time capsule" value: how it helps to shape and/or challenge mainstream culture, versus how it embodies our highest achievements and aspirations. *The Sopranos* is an exceptional case, in that it does both. As the most successful series in HBO's history, it is the poster child for the high-quality, challenging, exclusive programming that can only be offered by HBO, due to its enormous economic resources, its creative freedoms, and a business model that demands boldness; not just as an ideological value, but as a necessity to its survival in an increasingly diverse and competitive marketplace. An extraordinary artistic achievement, *The Sopranos* is the direct result of a number of measured choices made over the course of the network's history, a by-product of the brand that has become synonymous with the brand itself. *The Sopranos is* HBO, at its best: the culmination of a mythic, monolithic master narrative about a network that rose from the obscurity of a small Pennsylvania cable system in 1972 to become one of the most valuable and influential networks in the history of television.

This book is certainly interested in that master narrative. In the following chapters, we will explore the ways that industrial conditions helped shape HBO, and how HBO subsequently transformed pay and cable television from a quasi-utopian ideal to an enormously profitable business built on exclusivity and influence. We will consider the ways HBO exploited its content freedoms and, as a matter of course, expanded the bounds of television content and form. We will analyze the impact of scheduling, demography, and distribution models on the content, scale and narrative ambitions of programming produced and aired by HBO. And we will reflect upon the ways HBO's past success translates into the age of convergence media, whether it has changed the rules so much as to threaten its own place in the game, or built up reserves in talent, treasure and ingenuity to ensure its future, and its future impact on what may soon no longer be called "television." But we will also look at the ragged edges and the gaps: the competing, sometimes contradictory, swirl of forces surrounding HBO's creation; the ideological assumptions that feed into HBO programming; the largely unexamined heritage of its comedic programs; its radical take on serial narrative; its impact on representations of gender; and some of the more subtle ways it has impacted television production methods. If the HBO effect can in part be assessed using criteria one might find in any self-help book or management guide—assertiveness, adaptability, risk-taking—it can also be seen in those things that have made HBO truly unique.

Examining these less apparent effects requires taking up new perspectives. It is easy to mistake critical work for a sort of scientific method in the pursuit of some objective truth, but really the process is about the willingness to see through a fresh set of eyes. Indeed, the great lesson of a medium like television is that there can be no objective truth, only the form we give it. Images and words are chosen, then shaped, and ordered to produce a certain, necessarily subjective effect. "Realism" is never truly "real," any more than "truth" is ever really "true." They are at best equivalences, approximations, virtual realities, and truths. But media, and especially audio-visual media like television, encourage us to perceive "reality" in ways not possible without the aid of their framing, recording and editing devices, giving shape and definition to "truths" and artistic visions unavailable through ordinary sensory perception.

In 1990, Voyager 1 sent back its famous photograph of earth from 4 billion miles away. At the time, astronomer and popular author Carl Sagan commented that it looked like nothing more than a "pale blue dot" or "mote of dust" in an endless expanse of space: what he took for a stark reminder of our "responsibility to deal more kindly and compassionately with one another and to preserve and cherish … the only home we've ever known."[9] The extreme long view of the photograph showed us just how remote and isolated we are. According to Sagan, the vastness of enveloping space only made our human struggles seem more profound and meaningful because those struggles truly were "all there is" for those who have only known life on that tiny dot.

But one need not travel to the edge of the galaxy to sense this sort of profound connection. The television camera works as well. I think of a particularly haunting scene from the popular 1970s sitcom, *M*A*S*H*, in which actor Gary Berghoff struggles in the role of Corporal Radar O'Reilly to read a simple, 20-word announcement: "Lieutenant Colonel… Henry Blake's plane… was shot down… over the Sea of Japan. It spun in … there were no survivors" ("Abyssinia, Henry" 3:24). Berghoff had been given the lines to read only moments before the scene was shot (in one take), and his reaction is not an actor's performance at all, but a display

FIGURE 1.2 Radar O'Reilly, *M*A*S*H*, Twentieth Century Fox/CBS

of personal grief over the departure of a beloved character and cast member (McLean Stevenson, who played Henry Blake, decided to leave the show at the height of its popularity). In that moment when the worlds of fiction and reality overlap, his grief seems universal, not because it is authentic, but because it connects to our own. As viewers of the show, we have come to love Henry/Stevenson as much as Radar/Berghoff, and feel his loss just as intensely.

It should come as no surprise, then, that the series' broadcast network, CBS, received hundreds of letters expressing those viewers' outrage and grief. But so it is with truly great television. Like the fixed image of the "pale blue dot," it seems "true" because it is contained in a finite, framed moment rather than moving in and out of view and lingering indefinitely, as it tends to do in "real" life. In effect, the very artifice of the fiction that surrounds the moment lends it truth and power.

Knowledge, indeed wisdom, begins with critical perception: the ability to analyze and categorize data. And media capable of shaping that data can be remarkable tools of critical perception. Although narrative media like television are primarily concerned with shaping that data to prompt certain sensory impressions (we wonder why Radar looks gut-punched at the beginning of the scene) and emotions (our sense of loss is underscored and amplified by the montage of funny Henry Blake moments that follows the reading of the announcement), they can also make us think: about loss, about our place in the universe, and about the power of images generally. This is perhaps the defining mark of great works of art, including "quality" TV. Most of the critical work written on HBO programming is directly or indirectly about *how* and *what* it makes us think. Is *Sex and the City* feminist, post-feminist, or anti-feminist? Why do we sympathize with Tony Soprano? Do HBO's Second World War miniseries (*Band of Brothers*; *The Pacific*) endorse the heroic notion of a so-called "Greatest Generation"? To literary critics like myself, these are the sorts of questions we use to prove the value and durability of a text. After all, "great" works of narrative reveal more than who did what to whom, and why. They plumb the social, psychological, and spiritual depths of our existence. The fact that we are now asking these questions of television programs indicates just how much the medium has evolved. Or at least, how our perspectives on the merits of television have evolved. And HBO has been a big part of that evolution.

****

But only a part.

Let me be clear: this book does not argue that television begins or ends with HBO, nor that all roads lead to *Rome*, or *The Sopranos*, or *Curb Your Enthusiasm*, or *Boardwalk Empire*. Nor does it make the case that the most recent "Golden Age" of quality TV eclipses what came before. Quite the contrary. By locating some of the ways HBO impacts the history of American television and popular culture (its global impact being a topic requiring at least another book), I mean to suggest that it is itself a by-product of that long history, not some aberration. That is precisely what makes the story of HBO and its effect so compelling. It is not a novelty, but a manifestation of something immanent to television and popular culture generally. This is precisely why HBO has so long endured and dominated.

Of course, we cannot predict the future based on past successes. Though HBO's moment in the sun has lasted longer than one might reasonably expect in the ever-changing world of entertainment media, it remains to be seen how much longer it will last, and whether the impression it has left will fade quickly or persist. It is easy to mistake the finite for the infinite, whether imagining the history of mankind while looking at a photograph of the earth from 4 billion miles away, or writing a book that considers the impact of a modern media giant. At 5 or 6 billion miles, even the dot disappears, and the blackness itself becomes "all there is." And regardless of how big or small, ragged or smooth the images I project of HBO in these pages, surely none will reveal the whole picture.

2 A GREAT NOTION

Once you get into this great stream of history, you can't get out.
RICHARD NIXON[1]

Sometimes I have a great notion to jump in the river and drown.
LEADBELLY, "GOODNIGHT IRENE"

We tend to mark the history of ideas by moments of revelation: Newton being whacked on the head by a falling apple; Einstein observing a clock tower from a street car; Archimedes running naked through the streets of Syracuse shouting "Eureka!" But if the value of an idea is measured by its durability, many of the most enduring are those that accrue over time, such as democracy, drama, and human flight. Though far less lofty, the idea of Home Box Office falls into this latter category. Although the concept was not fully developed until about a year before the service was launched in 1972, that concept drew heavily upon notions of cable television, pay television and satellite television that had been around since as early as the 1930s and 1940s, and grew out of cultural debates that played out in the popular press and the halls of government and academia in the 1950s and 1960s. In this chapter I want to look carefully at the lines of connection between these often-competing ideas and perspectives, and how they coalesce and are finally transformed by the idea of HBO. My intent is not simply to place the origins of HBO in an historical context, but to suggest the many ways it directly or indirectly invested itself in its times.

By way of introduction to this discussion of HBO's appearance and early development in the 1970s, I want to begin with another, more bizarre but parallel narrative of the time: the strange claim that Richard Nixon, and not Al Gore, created the Internet.

Creation myths

At least that is how Nixon's Chief of Staff, H. R. Haldeman, tells it in Michael Medved's 1979 book, *The Shadow Presidents*, in which he briefly sketches unrealized plans for a national two-way communication network of computers connected by coaxial cables to every television in America. It was to be the signature accomplishment of the Nixon administration, one that would trump even Eisenhower's national highway system because it would create a virtual America built upon the principle of instant connectivity. "Just as Eisenhower linked up the nation's cities by highways so that you could get there," says Haldeman, "the Nixon legacy would have linked them by cable communications so you wouldn't have to go there."[2] In 1979, a decade and a half before the emergence of the World Wide Web as we know it, Medved would liken the plan to George Orwell's "Big Brother." But in his book he fails to mention that the Nixon plan for a "Wired Nation," as Haldeman calls it, had actually been part of a wide-ranging public discussion for at least a decade.

Since Internet pioneer J. C. R. Licklider first described the potential for a network of computers "connected to one another by wide-band communication lines,"[3] then began to develop such a system for the Department of Defense in the early 1960s,[4] and media theorist Marshall McLuhan first popularized the idea of a technologically-linked "global village" in such widely-read books as *The Gutenberg Galaxy* (1962) and *Understanding Media* (1964), the notion of a broadband multimedia communication system had been working its way into the popular consciousness. And because of its remarkable potential for rapid and high-volume information delivery, coaxial cables—those stiff, round, ubiquitous cords that now connect countless televisions and computers, which most of us simply refer to as "cable"—were the "wide-band communication lines" at the center of those discussions. Unlike telephone lines, coaxial cables are heavily insulated and shielded against electrical interference. That, and the relative thickness of their solid copper cores, make them ideal for carrying large amounts of data over long distances. By the 1960s, "cable" was already a proven technology. AT&T had begun laying thousands of miles of coaxial in 1941 to improve telephone signal quality and range, then to link television transmitters, and small independent cable antenna systems had been operating since 1948 to extend the over-the-air signal range of broadcast television to remote areas. Several factors had prevented the technology from eclipsing over-the-air communications, including enormous overhead costs and a tangled web of regulatory issues. But by the mid-1960s, the medium was getting attention from a number of interest groups, who saw the potential for its expanded channel capacity and two-way capability to radically change the nature of communication.

Studies were commissioned by government agencies and non-profit foundations to assess cable's potential, while articles began appearing in government, academic and popular publications, extolling the virtues of the medium. One such piece, published in *The Nation* in 1970 and titled "The Wired Nation," was clearly a model for the plan Haldeman later described. Written by Ralph Lee Smith while working as a research assistant for the Sloan Commission on Cable Communications, and expanded into a popular book the following year, "The Wired Nation" describes an "information highway" constructed of coaxial cables, computers, and television sets, "a communication center of a breadth and flexibility to influence every aspect of private and community life."[5] Even the wording of Haldeman's description sounds as though it is directly cribbed from Smith. Here is "The Wired Nation": "In the 1960s, the nation provided large federal subsidies for a new interstate highway system to facilitate and modernize the flow of automotive traffic in the United States. In the 1970s, it should make a similar national commitment for an electronic highway system to facilitate the exchange of information and ideas." Smith's book marks the climax of what would be known as the "Blue Sky" period of cable history, defined by an almost utopian optimism for the medium, where even the President of the United States came to believe in its ability to transform American society. But more on that later.

At about the time Nixon and Smith were hashing out plans for their virtual highways, another scheme was being hatched in the New York offices of one of the world's largest media companies. And though it was certainly less ambitious than these others, it would have a profound and far more immediate impact upon media history. The man with the plan was Charles "Chuck" Dolan, a cable pioneer who got his start in television when he and his wife launched a business in their Cleveland, Ohio home supplying college football highlight reels to television stations all over the country. Dolan eventually sold the company to one of his New York customers, and had his first brush with cable success after founding Sterling Communications and introducing a service called

Teleguide: a cable-based in-room hotel visitor's guide, the precursor to the contemporary "hotel channel." On the back of that success, Dolan bought the franchise rights to wire lower Manhattan for cable, and formed Sterling Manhattan Cable in 1965. He took on a partner to cover the enormous set-up and operational costs: print media giant Time, Inc., which had recently begun diversifying a media portfolio, which already included several broadcast television stations. In the late 1960s, the FCC introduced a rule forbidding cross-ownership of cable and broadcast systems, so Time abandoned broadcast for cable because the company saw a greater potential for growth. However, increasingly burdensome content restrictions from the FCC, cost overages in the millions of dollars, and anemic subscription numbers all contributed to a growing pessimism at Time. Each new loan to Dolan earned Time a greater share of the company, but it was merely a bigger piece of a failing enterprise. The company tried to sell, but there were no takers. Then Dolan came up with his next Big Idea: a subscription-based cable channel devoted entirely to uncut Hollywood films and exclusive sports programming, which would be transmitted via microwave signal to participating cable systems.

Dolan originally pitched the idea as "The Green Channel." And though the Time board worried that they might be throwing good money after bad, they took a gamble on what they hoped would be a game changer. The financial risks were relatively small. Cable systems were expensive to build and maintain, but with a content delivery service, resources would be entirely focused upon securing that content and attracting an audience through existing cable systems. Though the Sterling Cable project had hardly been a rousing success, it had proven that people were willing to pay for premium content. Ironically, the service could not be carried over the Sterling Manhattan system due to a provision against pay television in the franchise agreement. So on November 8, 1972—one day after the re-election of would-be Internet pioneer Richard Nixon—Dolan's newest enterprise, renamed Home Box Office, went live for the first time to 365 subscribers of the Service Electric cable system in Wilkes-Barre, Pennsylvania.

The first broadcast was a 1970 film adaptation of Ken Kesey's 1964 novel, *Sometimes a Great Notion*, directed by and starring Paul Newman. It is the saga of a family of independent loggers in Oregon who face all of their foes—from the rising river to the local labor union—with a bitter laugh and their grammatically-dubious family motto, "Never Give

FIGURE 2.1 Paul Newman as Hank Stamper, *Sometimes a Great Notion*, Universal Pictures, 1970

a Inch." Accounts of the early history of HBO often highlight the irony of this choice, considering the significant challenges that the venture faced early on, from fickle federal regulators and indifferent affiliates to hostile studios and high "churn" rates ("churn" describes the number of subscribers lost each billing period to cancelled subscriptions). Even the weather seemed to war against them. On the inaugural day of HBO service, much of western Pennsylvania was still underwater from Hurricane Agnes, and its high winds blew the receiving dish off of the Wilkes-Barre affiliate office just before the initial broadcast. Technicians had to be dispatched to the roof to hold it in place. Meanwhile, HBO's president—a Time executive named J. Richard Munro, whom the board installed as part of its deal with Dolan—sat in an epic traffic jam on the George Washington Bridge, missing the entire launch. *Sometimes a Great Notion* was followed by a National Hockey League game between the New York Rangers and the Vancouver Canucks, then a few months later by Chuck Dolan's exit from the company to run a struggling cable operation in Long Island called Cablevision, then three years later by the launch of HBO and the entire television industry into the satellite age.

The story of HBO's origins has become one of the archetypal narratives in the history of television, partly because Dolan's project would have such a deep and lasting impact upon the medium, and partly because of the inherently sexy way it taps into the spirit of rugged individualism at the center of American frontier mythology. It is a story of innovation, adaptability, willfulness, big risk, and even bigger reward. And it has the air of a creation myth, the birth of a great enterprise. When we gloss the history of HBO, we tend to reference a series of firsts: first successful subscription television network, first to offer continuous commercial broadcast via satellite, first to encrypt its signal, first to broadcast in high definition, first to multiplex, etc. But creation myths serve the believer and the agnostic differently. For the believer, they offer primal evidence of the power of ideals; sacred spaces marked by sanctuaries, monuments, and commemorative plaques; and heroes in the form of pioneers, revolutionaries, and visionaries. But for the agnostic, they offer something just as valuable: insight into the values, fears, and desires of the culture surrounding them.

Like Nixon's borrowed vision of a "Wired Nation," the idea for and eventual success of HBO speaks to a world that had begun to think of media in entirely different ways. Industrial notions of print, radio, cinema, and television would soon give way to content delivery systems, distributed networks, and media conglomerates. While once coaxial cable systems served simply to extend the range of broadcast signals, now "cable" meant both a parallel form of television and a generic system for the delivery of information. In the 1960s, print empire Time Inc. adopted the corporate mantra, "We are in the information business," and in the 1970s funded the creation of a "home box office" that would later distinguish itself with the slogan, "It's Not T.V.: It's HBO." But that distinction should have been clear from the start. The media world was changing with the wider world itself, and though the two-way communication network envisioned by Smith would take two decades to emerge, HBO would prove to be not only a by-product of that change, but an important agent.

HBO's initial impact upon the emerging media environment came in the areas of cable, satellite and pay-TV, and would constitute the first and perhaps biggest ripples of the HBO effect. Though Dolan's plan had none of the techno-utopian grandiosity of "The Wired Nation," and though he had no more invented the idea of a subscription-based pay television service delivered via cable than Richard Nixon or Ralph Lee Smith created the Internet, he was uniquely positioned to exploit others' unrealized ambitions for the medium. The Home Box Office, like the Information Superhighway that would eventually emerge in the 1990s, was simply an idea whose time had come.

Blue skies

Though the early days of Sterling Cable and Home Box Office would be marked by struggle, Dolan and Time Inc. had gotten into the cable television business at what would turn out to be a fortuitous time in its history, a period when regulatory battles in Washington met a strain of optimistic rhetoric about the future of cable, which came to be known as "Blue Sky."[6] Commercial cable systems had been in operation in America since the late 1940s, when a few independent entrepreneurs—many of them appliance salesmen looking to take advantage of the first boon in American television sales—extended over-the-air broadcast signals to communities outside their range by connecting networks of coaxial cables to large, well-placed antennae. Hence the original designation of cable systems as Community Antenna Television (CATV). And provided they were not being used to pull in distant signals that exceeded the range of local television stations, they remained largely under the radar of the FCC. Some members of the Commission even questioned whether they had regulatory jurisdiction over cable systems, since they did not technically operate on the public airwaves that the FCC had been established to protect. But as the number of cable systems increased, and major technological improvements made the importation of distant signals inevitable, the FCC was forced to consider the "problem" of cable. Their actions would shine a light on the burgeoning industry.

In 1965 and 1966, the FCC passed a number of regulations that effectively put the brakes on the growth of cable by imposing crippling content and carriage restrictions on existing cable providers. The two most onerous, both imposed in 1965, were known as "must carry" and "distant signal." The first required cable providers to carry local broadcast signals on their service, which consumed a great deal of their bandwidth. The second required the 100 largest cable providers to prove that the importation of distant signals was "in the public interest." Aspects of these rules would dog the cable industry well into the 1980s. The FCC also effectively froze licensing applications in the mid-1960s. In fact, Chuck Dolan's Sterling Manhattan Cable company was only able to acquire its license through a grandfather clause.

Halting cable's growth gave the FCC breathing room to consider its fate, but while the wheels of bureaucracy made their slow and deliberate turns, and the three major broadcast networks (ABC, CBS, and

NBC) lobbied against the cable industry in Washington, a number of media scholars, consumer advocates, cable entrepreneurs, educational reformers, and members of such disparate groups as the conservative RAND Corporation and the liberal American Civil Liberties Union were beginning to argue that cable offered a solution to many of the industrial and cultural problems that broadcast television had helped to create and/or exacerbate: the lowering of cultural standards, the demoralizing spread of consumerism, the centralization of power and resources among a small corporate elite, and so on. Less a specific set of plans or goals for the deployment of cable technology than a general sense of approbation for the potential of the medium, their "Blue Sky" rhetoric shared a great deal in common with that of the emerging Internet decades later. It described a culture of connectivity and access, an open marketplace of ideas and consumer goods, and an opportunity to streamline what had become an increasingly cumbersome telecommunications network.

Though their motives differed, and their politics were often diametrically opposed, "Blue Sky" cable advocates shared a belief in cable's potential and, just as importantly, the power of the marketplace to realize that potential. There were the cable operators and industry representatives—men such as Irving B. Kahn, Chief Executive Officer (CEO) of Teleprompter, and E. Stratford Smith, who served as General Counsel to the National Cable Television Association—arguing that cable brought healthy competition to a stagnant television business. There were public access activists, from industry insider Fred Friendly to civic groups like the Urban Institute, who saw in cable the potential for progressive social change. There were educational television advocates, including the National Education Association, Fred "Mister" Rogers and Senator John Pastore (D-RI), whose arguments for the Corporation for Public Broadcasting (CPB) and Public Broadcasting Services (PBS) rarely mentioned cable but clearly shared the "Blue Sky" commitment to a fundamental transformation of American television. There were academics and members of the intellectual elite who, under the influence of cybernetics theorist Norbert Weiner and media guru Marshall McLuhan, called for a wholesale shift in the way we think about media, and others who expressed increased hostility toward industry and governmental attempts to regulate cable, which hampered what Prof. Donald R. LeDuc called "this vital evolutionary process."[7] Perhaps most significant to the regulatory fight were the various studies enjoined by government agencies, such as President Johnson's Task Force on

Communications Policy, which in its 1968 Report envisioned cable "transforming the realm of communication,"[8] and the dozen or so reports commissioned by the Ford Foundation and carried out by the RAND Corporation, which advocated strongly for the dissolution of the existing broadcast infrastructure and its wholesale replacement with a more efficient, high-volume national cable system referred to as "wired city television."

The most influential of these studies came from the Commission on Cable Communications, established by the Alfred P. Sloan Foundation in 1968. Its report, published in book form in 1970 under the telling title, *On the Cable: Television of Abundance*, strongly advocated for the active development of cable systems across the country to break up the oligopoly of the three broadcast television networks. Television, the report asserted, was the largest, most powerful communications network ever conceived, but its banal content betrayed its promise. The report argued that cable, with its massive potential to expand the number of available channels, not only offered the possibility of increased competition, but "particularity": that is, the ability to gear programming to the tastes of smaller groups. Television could specialize, localize in ways that it had never been able to under the limitations of the broadcast system. This argument would greatly appeal to the FCC, which had been formed in 1934 with the primary purpose of protecting local programming (initially on radio). The Sloan report would remain the principle document of the "Blue Sky" period, and lead Ralph Lee Smith to bring a still broader vision of cable to light in "The Wired Nation."

While working for the Commission, Smith came into regular contact with a group of young access advocates whose desire to democratize American television had sprung from the countercultural movements of the 1960s. Many were members of a New York-based "alternative media think tank" called the Raindance Corporation—in ironic reference to the conservative RAND Corporation—who saw themselves as "a source of ideas, publications, videotapes and energy providing a theoretical basis for implementing communication tools in the project of social change."[9] Raindance was comprised primarily of video artists and underground journalists inspired by the introduction of inexpensive portable video cameras in the late 1960s, who produced direct cinema documentaries for local public access channels, including Sterling Manhattan Cable. They also published *Guerilla Television*, a how-to guide for like-minded folks looking to use "low-cost portable video-tape cameras, video cassettes, and cable television" to "design alternate television networks that favor portability and decentralization."[10] But most importantly, they published the groundbreaking journal, *Radical Software* (1970–4), which promoted ideas about alternative television that combined their interests in cybernetics, ecology and new media: ideas that would have a profound impact on "The Wired Nation."

Though rooted in 1960s counterculture, the Raindance group— Frank Gilette, Paul Ryan, Ira Schneider, Louis Jaffe, Beryl Korot, Phyllis Gershuny and Michael Shamberg—were not garden-variety hippies or radicalized social protestors. If anything, they represented a repudiation of the failure of 1960s counterculture. In the short span of a few years, the social activism of the New Left and the civil disobedience of the Students for a Democratic Society gave way to the violent revolutions of the Weather Underground and the Black Panthers; Altamont followed on the heels of Woodstock; and the psychotropic drugs, priapic rituals, and communalism of the Hippies and Ken Kesey's Merry Pranksters devolved into the silly theatricality of the Yippies and the madness of the Manson Family. By the early 1970s, that counterculture had degenerated into a Madison Avenue brand to sell bell-bottoms, arena rock shows, and three million copies of Charles Reich's woefully naïve Age of Aquarius paean, *The Greening of America*,[11] to suburban kids and their anxious parents. In the wake of this commodification, something new had begun to rise from the ashes of the ideology-driven top-down, anti-establishment, back-to-the-garden protest movement: a pragmatic, bottom-up, technology-friendly mindset inspired by the whole systems theories of Norbert Weiner and Buckminster Fuller, and the do-it-yourself spirit of *Popular Mechanics* and *Sunset* magazines.

This spirit was perhaps best exemplified by former Merry Prankster, Stewart Brand's ubiquitous *Whole Earth Catalog*: "a Low Maintenance, High Yield, Self Sustaining, Critical Information Service" published regularly from 1968 to 1974 and occasionally after; an expansive, continually revised, collection of advertisements for and reviews of books and products for pragmatic environmentalists, tech geeks, and anyone else seeking "access to tools" that sold hundreds of thousands of copies, that won the National Book Award in 1972, and that Steve Jobs later described as "sort of like Google in paperback form."[12]

At this point, a sensible person might ask, What does all of this "Blue Sky" rhetoric—not to mention the *Whole Earth Catalog*—have to do with HBO? After all, cable deregulation was the direct result of business-friendly Nixon administration policies, not some turn-of-phrase in the Sloan Commission report or the countercultural version of the L.L. Bean catalog (which Stewart Brand used as a model for the *Whole Earth Catalog*). HBO has never been about idealism, neither of the RAND nor the Rainbow variety. Cable was simply a means to an end, an available content delivery system. If *Radical Software* and the *Whole Earth Catalog* offered "access to tools" (the motto printed just below the title of Brand's massive DIY directory) for those who shared the belief that "information wants to be free," HBO has always been about *exclusive* access for those willing to pay a *premium*. While HBO programming often directly addresses issues near and dear to 1960s counterculture—free speech, sexual liberation, even politics—this has less to do with an ideological disposition than the freedom it enjoys from the censorship restrictions of the FCC. The audience finds graphic sex, speech, and violence on HBO because, until fairly recently, they could not find it elsewhere. And while the links between cyber-culture and the technophile progressives of *Radical Software* have been well established,[13] the MIT hackers and Silicon Valley Deadheads who eventually gave us the personal computer and the Internet would have been lucky to get a job logging tapes at HBO. In short, there is nothing utopian about Home Box Office. But the "Blue Sky" optimism of Smith and the Sloan Foundation, the "appropriate technology" ethos of *Radical Software* and the *Whole Earth Catalog*, and the market opportunism of HBO all share three key values. And as we will see, each of these would not only be essential to HBO's success, but its ongoing legacy.

To begin with, *all* of the rhetoric of these groups, whether born of pure commercial interest or some latter-day hippie back-to-the-land impulse, is market-based. While early debates over radio in the 1920s and television in the 1930s included fervent arguments for making them public institutions, by the 1960s the logic of the marketplace had taken over completely, and other than a few gestures at public broadcasting, that logic has remained largely unchallenged. Whether subscribing to a premium television service or purchasing a countercultural catalog, people trade in the currency of that marketplace.

Second, all of these parties saw technology as a tool, rather than as an end in itself. As a tool, we judge television not for what it *is* (an appliance, an over-the-air signal, *I Love Lucy*), but what it *does* (communication, entertainment, content delivery). True, use of a tool is a tactic endorsement of it—we cannot make television or build our own computer without becoming part of each technology's history—but the groups involved also seemed to intuitively understand Marshall McLuhan's famous dictum, "the medium is the message"[14]: that we can only know what we have made by its effect. HBO's success was built upon three technologies—television, cable, and satellite—each of which it fundamentally changed, not by inventing new devices, but by transforming the way that we think about each of them. It's not satellite, it's not cable, it's not pay-TV, or even TV for that matter: it's HBO.

Which leads us to the third point of connection: the network. Whether imagining an ecosystem, an information highway, or a pay television system, each of these parties envisioned a decentralized, non-linear, integrated structure, through which the whole is built not on a monolithic hierarchy—the food chain, the electromagnetic spectrum, the television station—but a series of evolving and expanding potentialities. An interactive and endlessly branching hypertext, rather than a fixed and linear text. Later chapters will go into this idea in greater detail—including HBO's place within a linear corporate structure—but for now suffice it to say that the HBO model of a television "network" was something very new in 1972. Whereas the old "broadcast" model was about maximizing the range and coverage of its signal by building a fixed infrastructure, HBO was able to move more nimbly through the same landscape, from one self-selecting system and subscriber to another. While broadcasters built empires out of towers and cables, HBO adapted itself to the conditions of the market. More on this shortly.

"Blue Sky" rhetoric ran up against predictable industrial and political realities in the early 1970s, some of which were, at least in part, the direct legacy of "Blue Sky." For example, though the deregulatory fervor of the "Blue Sky" documents, which argued for innovation and competition, played right into the Nixon administration's pro-business agenda, Nixon merely shed the regulations, making no provisions for the small-scale entrepreneurs who had created the cable business in the first place. The enormous costs associated with building and operating cable systems left the majority of smaller systems at the mercy of large multiple service operators (MSOs) eager to buy them up: companies such as Teleprompter, Cox Cable, Comcast and ATC (which would merge with Time, Inc. in 1979). An oligopoly similar to that enjoyed by the three broadcast networks was a logical, inevitable outcome. And with the resources of these MSOs directed at the immediate task of increasing their holdings and extending their reach, very little attention was being given to developing more innovative programming. For the most part, cable systems remained antenna services, albeit much larger, more efficient, and with a greater signal range than ever imaged by early CATV entrepreneurs.

But the "Blue Sky" legacy goes beyond its part in opening the cable markets to increasingly larger and fewer media conglomerates. By drawing attention to the dearth of educational, cultural, and public access television, it played an indirect but important role in the creation of the CPB and PBS. More directly, it helped bring about the cable-based Public, Educational and Government Access Television (PEG-TV), founded in 1969, and the Cable-Satellite Public Affairs Network (C-SPAN), which was launched in 1979. The development of Warner Cable's multichannel QUBE system in the late 1970s also owes a direct debt to "Blue Sky," with its interactive elements and commitment to local programming and special interest channels. But the QUBE concept proved unsustainable, and when it finally failed, many of its specialty channels would simply be recast in the 1980s as basic cable channels such as Nickelodeon and MTV. In 1989, Warner Communications and the remnants of QUBE were bought up by HBO's parent to form Time Warner.

The "Blue Sky" hue and cry for better programming, combined with cable's perceived threat to broadcast television, also led to one of the peak periods in American broadcast television. In the early 1970s, the highest-rated programs—*All in the Family*, *M*A*S*H*, *Sanford and Son*, *Good Times*, *Maude* and *The Mary Tyler Moore Show*—featured high-quality writing and acting, and focused on a wide range of serious social issues, from poverty, racism, and sexism to war, abortion, and aging. The history of what we now refer to as "quality" television is often said to begin here. Such a response is typical of a medium in crisis. Two of the peak periods of American cinema, for example, emerge in direct response to dire threats from without. In the 1950s, Hollywood responded to the threat of television with big-budget, Technicolor, widescreen spectaculars and the sort of gritty, censor-flaunting fare one could not find on television; and the 1970s "New Hollywood" phenomenon rose from the ashes of the moribund studio system of the 1960s. Television history presents similar patterns. The next wave of "quality" television in the 1980s, with shows like *Hill Street Blues* and *St Elsewhere*, was a direct response to two crises: the home video revolution, which threatened the advertisement pricing structure of broadcast and basic cable services by allowing viewers to "time shift" (tape and review programs at their leisure) and skip over commercials; and the massive expansion of cable channels, which significantly increased competition for audience. Broadcasters and cable operators met these challenges in a number of ways. The first was through the courts, in a series of highly publicized, but ultimately fruitless copyright cases, including *Sony v. Universal Studios*—a.k.a., "the Betamax Case"—which slogged its way through the courts from 1976 to 1984 before being settled in favor of Sony. The second was to develop programming with "buzz": what came to be known as "appointment TV" or, in the parlance of the famous NBC slogan of the 1990s, "Must-See TV." These shows demanded to be seen at first broadcast, lest the viewer felt left out of a larger cultural conversation. And the last was to direct programming at particular demographic groups using a strategy that, as we will soon see, grew right out of "Blue Sky."

The price of progress

Broadcasters tend to be conservative and defensive rather than proactive in their response to changes in the market because their model is one of increased coverage, range, and domination. They perceive all competition, especially from new technologies, as a threat to their massive infrastructure investments, so their first impulse is to strengthen fortifications. When cable threatened broadcasters, they attacked it in the courts, and in the court of public opinion by rousing public fears about having to pay for television. Then they strengthened ties with carriers and content providers to shut the fledgling cable companies out.

HBO, on the other hand, has always been a remarkably agile enterprise, able to shift with the conditions of the market, to be first in, and to exploit change while others struggle to take its measure. Key to this agility is the fact that HBO has always seen itself as a content provider, rather than a television network in the monolithic sense described above. While broadcasters and MSOs have had to struggle with the hardware of a massive infrastructure, HBO has been able to concentrate its attention on the programming. Though Chuck Dolan should be credited for securing the Sterling Manhattan license in the mid-1960s, when the FCC was approving virtually none, the success of HBO has less to do with his considerable talents for developing cable systems (on full display at Cablevision) than with the fact that he perceived it as a service, rather than a system, content rather than cable. In a memo to the Time board written ten months before HBO's initial appearance, he spelled it out plainly:

> In the long run, we may think of ourselves as the Macy's of television, shopping everywhere for programs that some public, large or small, will buy. If we are successful in meeting these "retail" program needs of the region we are attempting to serve... we will later use whatever efficient transmission systems become available, from microwave to satellite, to sell television programs worldwide to any public that signals its specific demands to us.[15]

This "whatever becomes available" mantra would serve HBO well. When the Sterling Manhattan system proved unsuitable for HBO, it simply pivoted to rural Pennsylvania. While small cable operators struggled to compete with broadcasters under the weight of crippling content and carriage restrictions in the 1970s, HBO touted itself as elite, offering content unavailable on broadcast television. When the home video revolution threatened to undermine broadcasters and basic cable companies in the 1980s, it would prove a significant boon to HBO. It actively encouraged subscribers to tape its programming—effectively expanding the customer's perceived value of the service, since they were now able to watch more of it—and jumped into what would eventually prove to be the highly lucrative video distribution business.

Despite this high degree of flexibility, the HBO brand is and has always been built upon the principles of exclusivity and specialization known collectively as "narrowcasting." "Narrowcasting" was yet another contribution to "Blue Sky" rhetoric from Internet pioneer, J. C. R. Licklider, who coined the term in a 1967 paper prepared for the Carnegie Commission Report on Educational Television entitled "Televistas." In the paper, Licklider describes "a multiplicity of television networks aimed at serving the needs of smaller, specialized audiences."[16] His vision of a cable-based system for "interactive" television draws heavily upon his work on computer networking and electronic libraries, and sounds more like contemporary media convergence than what we traditionally think of as television. As such it represents the ultimate "Blue Sky" ideal: television that adapts to the needs and interests of a highly diverse audience. Or, what the Sloan Commission report would later call "particularity."[17] Licklider dubbed this sort of programming "narrowcasting" in direct repudiation of "the constraints imposed by commitment to a monolithic mass-appeal, broadcast approach."[18]

Today, when we use the word "narrowcasting" to describe television, we mean two things, neither especially utopian. First, we mean programming that cannot be had for "free." Narrowcasting requires direct payment, typically to a cable or satellite service. It offers exclusive access only to those willing and able to pay the price of entry. Precisely upon these grounds, advocates of "free" broadcast television have long demonized cable and pay television schemes as disdaining the poor. Second, we mean a marketing strategy by which programming is specifically designed to attract a target audience, typically to draw their attention to particular advertisers. This strategy takes in demographic information about the target audience—age, race, class, geography, income, spending habits—as well as perceived preferences and values. It is also called target marketing or niche programming. This latter definition of narrowcasting would become particularly important in the 1980s and after, when the massive expansion in the number of available cable channels would force providers to carve out a place in an expanding field of competitors. Hence the prevalence of cable news, home improvement, lifestyle, family, sports, and adult networks. But prior to that expansion, both definitions found expression in the first successful pay television venture, HBO. HBO offered a narrowly defined service to a self-selecting clientele who directly expressed their consent through their subscriptions.

If a premium channel devoted to movies and sports seems like a crass corruption of Licklider's idea of narrowcasting, it is also a crass corruption of the original concept of pay television.[19] Subscription-based television was first advocated in 1929 by the Zenith Corporation, which began work on what would become its Phonevision service in 1931. At the time, industry players in the still-infant medium were actively debating how television broadcasts would be financed: directly through subscription or indirectly through advertising. Though ad-driven "free" television won the day, the pay television idea persisted in the minds of many entrepreneurs because it offered so much profit potential and a chance to expand television content. When Phonevision first appeared in the early 1950s, it presented the direct-pay model as an alternative to ad-based television as well as cinema, promising to "bring the box office into your home." But despite enormous investments on Zenith's part and an enthusiastic response from test subscribers, Phonevision and similar services like it Skiatron's Subscriber-Vision and Paramount's

Telemeter never gained traction, due in large part to overly cautious federal regulators and the lobbying power of local theater owners and the major television networks. In fact it, was not until 1969 that the FCC awarded its first commercial system license. Until then, pay television systems were allowed to operate only on an experimental basis. But even a cursory glance at these early experiments reveals a pattern of problems within the systems, themselves.

The first had to do with content. The advocates for pay television in the 1950s and 1960s tended to be white-collar progressive and liberal groups like the National Association of Educational Broadcasters and Americans for Democratic Action, who saw pay television as a competitive alternative to the low-brow, least objectionable programming that made up the bulk of broadcast television. They imagined a menu of high-culture programs that offered an alternative to the banalities of broadcast television, including the highest quality American and foreign films, televised lectures, opera, dance, and Broadway shows.[20] But the statistical data from early pay television experiments hardly supported this vision. The most popular programs by far were the mainstream films and sporting events, and the least popular—viewed by a mere three percent of subscribers—were the cultural and educational programs.[21] When given a choice between haute cuisine and comfort food, the vast majority of the television audience—or at least that faction willing to pay a premium for it—overwhelmingly favored comfort food. These content problems might have been easily fixed, but the advocacy groups were insistent that, given the right regulatory environment and adequate resources, pay television subscribers would warm to, and eventually seek out the cultural programming. In the end, that insistence would have a negative effect on the development of pay television. Its opponents—who included broadcasters, labor unions, senior citizen groups, civil rights leaders, and veterans' organizations—had long insisted that it excluded the poor. They could now add cultural elitism to the charges.

The arguments on both sides were simple. Broadcasting advocates insisted that "free" television was the right of every citizen, and pay television advocates insisted that broadcasters' obligations to advertisers all but guaranteed lowest common denominator programming because they strove for the largest possible audience, and that the only way to improve the quality of television generally was to introduce competition. The former saw television as a public utility, whereas the latter saw it as a matter of consumer choice.[22] But while there was a growing sympathy for the pay television argument at the FCC and in the United States Congress, the majority of the general public was against it. As *Time* magazine reported in a 1964 piece on the growing opposition, many viewers feared that they would "one day find themselves paying to see shows they now see for nothing" and that "pay TV could become just as commercial as contemporary network television."[23] It would be decades before history would prove their predictions right, but the sentiment behind them was having an immediate impact. As a result of increasingly vocal public discontent, Congress convened four public hearings on pay television between 1956 and 1969, and though no bills restricting pay television ever made it out of subcommittee, Congressional attention to the issue made the FCC skittish, and they responded much as they would toward cable during the "Blue Sky" period. Though optimistic about the prospects of pay television, they persisted in issuing only experimental licenses and restricting content, while they considered where subscription services fit in the universe of television.[24] Meaning, of course, broadcast television.

If the FCC content and carriage restrictions would make it difficult for cable systems to grow beyond antenna services, they would eviscerate pay television operations, which relied entirely upon their unique content to attract customers. This was especially true of pay television systems like Phonevision, which broadcast over-the-air, and so were subject to tighter restrictions than cable-based systems like Jerrold Electronics' Telemovies and Paramount's Telemeter. But at a time when the FCC still did not know what to do about cable, none escaped scrutiny. A near-fatal blow came in the form of the FCC's 1968 *Report and Order on Pay TV*, which forbade pay service providers from showing serials, movies between two and ten years old, and sports programs carried on national broadcast networks over the previous ten years. These "anti-siphoning" rules, as they came to be known, protected the interests of the broadcast networks, and would not be successfully challenged until the Washington, DC Circuit Court struck them down in 1977, in a suit filed by HBO while still a fledgling pay television operation.[25] Prior to that ruling, simply filling the schedule was a monumental challenge, and with so little content to choose from, it was no wonder system operators were unable to attract sufficient subscribers to maintain viability. Even the most successful pay television operation of the pre-HBO era—the Phonevision experiment begun in 1962 in Hartford, CT, which operated in the evenings on WHCT (day programming was non-subscription)—eventually collapsed under the weight of these restrictions. Though it ran six and a half years and garnered largely favorable reviews for the quality and delivery of its signal, the churn rate remained exceedingly high, thanks to the frequent repetition of its sparse programming. Built upon the expectation of maintaining a subscription base of at least 10,000, the Hartford experiment never exceeded 7,000, and averaged around 5,000.

Regulatory problems were exacerbated by the lack of orthodoxy and organization among pay television systems. With so many different delivery and payment methods—pay-per-view, monthly subscription, over-the-air, cable, metered boxes, phone codes, punch cards—it was difficult to define exactly what pay television was. And because experimental licenses were so difficult to get and system operators so few and so geographically scattered, they had very little organizational clout in Washington, and even less in the local communities where they were attempting to operate. The National Cable Television Association had been founded in 1952, but no equivalent organization existed for pay television operators because their few systems were still in the experimental stages. Membership in theater owner unions like the Theatre Owners Association (TOA) numbered in the thousands, and broadcast affiliates had the limitless resources of the big three networks behind them, but even a well-established company like Zenith, which poured enormous research, development and marketing resources into Phonevision for more than 25 years, had nowhere near the organizing and lobbying power of these well-established groups.

A classic example of this mismatched opposition is the case of Subscription Television Inc. (STV), a three-channel, cable-based system offering movies, cultural events and sports programming to subscribers in Los Angeles and San Francisco, which launched in July 1964 under the leadership of former NBC president, Pat Weaver. At the start, STV showed enormous promise. It was not only ambitious in design, but had attracted high-dollar private investors from the fields of electronics, banking, sports, and publishing, and raised $16 million from an initial public offering. It landed exclusive contracts to telecast Dodgers and Giants baseball games, as well as first-run Hollywood features, theatrical productions, and a number of educational programs. Advertisements in the *Los Angeles Times* promised, "What you see on STV you just won't see through ordinary channels." And to top it all off, the California legislature had recently enacted a law significantly easing restrictions on subscription television. If initial subscription numbers fell well short of expectations—9,000 subscribers as opposed to the projected 40,000—they had reason to hope that good press and word of mouth would create a surge of interest. For at the time of launch, their press had been anything but good.

It all began in October 1963, when an advertisement appeared in the California edition of the *Wall Street Journal* under the banner headline, "A LAW TO OUTLAW PAY T.V." The advertisement, paid for by the Southern California branch of the TOA, announced a petition for a ballot initiative to outlaw pay television in the state of California. It would be the first stage of a massive lobbying and mass media scare campaign undertaken by the TOA with the help of the Citizen's Committee for Free TV and the California Federation of Women's Clubs, who feared that "pay TV" would put an undue economic burden on working-class families. Television spots and newspaper advertisements warned "THIS COULD BE THE LAST WORLD SERIES ON FREE TV!" and "IF PAY TV TAKES OVER—CBS, NBC AND ABC WARN UNDER OATH BEFORE U.S. CONGRESS THAT THEY WILL BE FORCED TO GO INTO PAY-TV!" STV met the onslaught with an antitrust lawsuit against the theater owners, and launched their own public relations campaign, spearheaded by Pat Weaver himself. But the opposition was stronger than they first imagined, and its misleading rhetoric fed into the anxieties of a viewing public already heavily invested in the expensive technology of television. In 1963, the average television had a 19–inch black and white screen and cost $300, or the equivalent of $2,100 in 2011. It typically received four or five channels. Today, the average 46–inch flat-screen HDTV sells for $1,100 and hundreds of channels are available.

On November 3, 1964, Proposition 15 passed by a margin of 2–to-1, banning pay television in the state of California. Though the law would be overturned less than two years later, STV was dead in the water. Its investors pulled out, its contracts were dissolved, and the most promising and ambitious pay television experiment the country had yet seen became little more than a footnote in media history.

That is the popular version of the story, though it neglects the lasting impact of STV, which intimated that pay television might succeed on a large scale, and could attract big money and high-value content, if only it could overcome the prejudices of public perception. In 1964, both sides agreed that "[i]f California had approved pay television it would have swept the nation."[26] From that historical perspective, it would have been difficult to see that the process had already begun. STV would prove a test case, a harbinger of things to come, the lost battle that would turn out to be a turning point in the war between "free" and pay television (how many people can still brag that they get their television programming for free?). The failure of STV was not due to a lack of vision or ambition, but bad timing, and an unsuccessful public relations campaign. Or as HBO's first president, J. Richard Munro, would put it years later, "The world was not ready for Pat Weaver. It was ready for us."[27]

Conceptually, HBO was not very different from STV or Telemeter, or any of several subscription services that had been tested over the previous two decades. But it did have several factors working in its favor. Though the FCC's 1972 *Cable Report and Order* attempted to force local programming requirements on cable operators, it met with swift and growing opposition, thanks to the expanded resources and collective strength of the cable MSOs like Telemeter, which were actively developing their own pay television services. HBO had the enormous resources of Time Inc. behind it, which offered not only financial security to weather the early storms (HBO did not turn a profit for its first five years), but access to a legal team that would successfully challenge the FCC's anti-siphoning rules, and an expansive production and distribution infrastructure that would eventually allow the parent company to achieve vertical integration: a model that had not been seen in the world of media since the government effectively broke up the Hollywood studio system by forcing the major studios to sell off their theater interests in 1948. Because of Time, HBO was able to remain solvent in those early years, while building a customer base, expanding content, riding out the slow pace of deregulation, and as we will soon see, risking its future on satellite. Perhaps if Pat Weaver and STV had had a corporate sugar daddy like Time, and had been able to hold out until Proposition 15 was overturned, they might have found a world waiting for STV, not HBO.

Dolan, Munro, and the executives at HBO also had the benefit of hindsight, drawing from the strengths of previous pay television experiments, as well as their experiences with Sterling Manhattan Cable. STV, Telemovies, and Telemeter had shown that using existing cable systems could simplify content delivery by cutting out the phone companies and the broadcasters. Phonevision, which won its first commercial license in 1969 but did not begin providing its service until 1976, would surely have beaten HBO to market were it not for the complexity of its delivery system, which included telephone, cable and over-the-air connections.

Dolan and HBO merely needed to line up cable affiliates in existing systems and secure content. And once the cable operators were invested in the service—having purchased microwave receivers or satellite dishes, and advertised the premium service to their customers—the incentive to actively sell it increased exponentially. Though in the early days HBO representatives went door-to-door signing up subscribers, before long they left that responsibility entirely to their affiliates. When one calls today to connect, disconnect, or complain about HBO, one speaks to a cable operator, not an HBO representative. And it falls to those operators to troubleshoot, negotiate rates, and create incentives for viewers to keep the service, such as bundling it with other premium channels (Showtime, Encore, Starz). HBO provides the content, and the cable systems provide the customer service and sales. This is the primary reason that HBO is able to remain such a relatively small operation despite annual revenues in the billions.

As mentioned earlier, HBO also understood from the beginning the need to streamline content, to distinguish itself in the marketplace while exploiting proven successes. Despite Pat Weaver's grand ambitions for STV, there was little evidence to suggest that a substantial audience existed for the kabuki theater and children's ballet that featured so prominently in advertisements for the service. Hollywood films and sports were what pay–per-view subscribers demanded, so that was what HBO would give them. This is one of the reasons Dolan hired Gerald Levin as his assistant: a lawyer with excellent connections in the sports world who, after being named president of HBO following Dolan's exit in 1973, immediately secured deals to telecast dozens of NBA, NHL and New York Yankees games, Wimbledon tennis and boxing.

Then there was the matter of payment. Like nearly all cable systems, Dolan's Sterling Manhattan service operated on a monthly set-fee subscription. It was clearly a model with which Dolan was comfortable, but there was a much better reason than familiarly to adopt it. The pay-per-view models used by the likes of Phonevision and Subscriber-Vision were not only cumbersome—raising clunky request, delivery, and payment issues—but also put service providers in a position where they were forced to offer a high volume of programming, since users were not likely to pay to see the same programs more than once. And the less the pay-per-view subscribers used the service, the less profitable it became. By contrast, monthly subscribers were paying for open access to *all* of the content, and basing their judgment of the service's value on overall satisfaction rather than an accounting of each individual unit of programming. It was the difference between ordering *a la carte* and stepping up to a buffet.

Of course, there are buffets and there are buffets, from opulent feasts to deli steam tables. HBO was careful to balance subscriber perceptions and expectations, presenting popular movies and sporting events, but identifying itself as an exclusive brand. By exclusivity, I mean both exclusive content and exclusive access. HBO understood early on the importance of both: offering something one could not get elsewhere on television, while fostering the perception that one was part of something special. "Different and First," its ad copy read in 1973. HBO marketing constantly asserts its unique content, because content is the primary measure of value in a subscription service. In the early days, FCC restrictions made it hard to come by, so HBO applied the second principle of narrowcasting—specialization—offering programming that appealed to audiences within specific cable systems. For example, at the Wilkes-Barre launch, *Sometimes a Great Notion* and a local hockey game (the New York Rangers were the nearest established franchise to the area) were followed by a polka festival, which was clearly chosen for its appeal to the largely Polish population in the service area. And while those touches of localism would virtually disappear once HBO became a satellite-delivered national service, specialization and exclusivity have remained its highest-held values.

Exclusivity and specialization also have an important economic component. It is a psychological truism that people grant higher value to things that they pay for, and the more they pay, the higher the assumed value. Here is where the waters begin to muddy for HBO. How exactly does its "premium" brand translate in dollars and cents for the consumer? The question is not simply, "What is a 'fair' price?" but "What is the 'right' price?" The most successful companies—Apple and Walmart, for example—know that assigned value not only dictates access, but has a way of turning perceived value into real value. When selling iconic electronic devices with a reputation for quality and shared interfaces, Apple has a tremendous market advantage in setting and holding firm to a relatively high price point. Despite deceptive on-line ads, people cannot buy discounted new iPads or MacBooks, because discounting them calls their perceived value into doubt, so not only cutting into profits, but also undermining the overall value of the brand. The same goes for Walmart. Although the lower prices of its products allows for far broader access, its slogan "Always Low Prices" emphasizes consistency and familiarity over quality. Walmart does not have "sales": it rolls back prices, and keeps them there. It is worth noting that the subscription rate for HBO has only risen a few dollars since the service first appeared in 1972: from $6–$10 per month to $12–$15 per month, depending upon the cable system and region. Of course, this is simply the perceived cost, since HBO and other premium services are sold with basic cable subscriptions that help to offset the real cost (and alienate potential subscribers, who might willingly pay for HBO a la carte, but are unwilling to pay for the supporting cable subscription). The perceived cost is also meant to reflect the perceived, then real value: what the service is "worth," and whether that price is "fair," "a bargain," or "a rip-off." I will revisit this topic in later chapters, but mention it now to indicate how HBO's entry into the marketplace realized the potential for a new way of thinking about the value and uses of television programming.

Of course, there is more than one marketplace, and price is not the only measure of value. When television critics speak of the value of HBO programming, for example, they are not generally thinking in terms of subscription and production costs. Indeed, critical interest in HBO has been almost exclusively concerned with notions of "quality" original programming that not only go beyond economic issues, but often seem to entirely ignore them. Yet the academic discipline we know as "television studies" grew largely from these very issues, beginning roughly at the time HBO had its launch, in a slim volume by cultural critic and scholar, Raymond Williams, called *Television: Technology and Cultural Form*.[28] Williams' book might easily be shelved among the "Blue Sky" documents mentioned above. Loaded with the familiar scorn for broadcast television, which Williams characterizes in erudite flashes of Marxist criticism as a bland tool of corporate interests, its closing chapter, "Alternative Technology Alternative Uses?" imagines a far greater potential for television, and outlines the political means necessary for achieving that potential. By contrast, former advertising executive Jerry Mander would entirely abandon the "Blue Sky" optimism in his popular book, *Four Arguments for the Elimination of Television* a few years later, in which he argues that television cannot be redeemed because it makes us passive and highly susceptible to the will and interests of advertisers and major media organizations.[29]

Despite his polemic tone and deep pessimism, Mander's analysis of the operations of television is similar to what Williams describes in his book as "flow": the notion that television networks sequence their programs and commercials in such a way that viewers see them as interconnected, part of "an evening's viewing" rather than a series of discrete units to be consumed separately. "Flow" is perhaps best understood as the difference between watching a particular program and "watching TV." This habitual viewing invites the sort of passivity Mander describes, our inability to think clearly and critically about the advertising messages and cultural values we are receiving. The existence of "flow" has frequently been contested, especially in the multimedia age, when we are as likely as not interacting with many different information streams at once: checking e-mail, text messaging, flipping channels, and doing essentially anything we can to avoid commercials. But in the 1970s, when channels were scarce, remote controls few, DVD box sets nonexistent, and radio and print the only other media options, audience attention tended in one direction.

The nature of HBO programming has never overtly lent itself to "flow." From the start, HBO saw itself as an occasional-use service, where subscribers would check in on a new movie, a sporting event, or a favorite series. It has always relied upon variety to entice various constituencies. As a "home box office," it has adapted many of the classical forms of movie presentation, from the variety of the multiplex, to the promotional fanfare at the beginning of each program, promising a "feature," "premiere" or "original." Moreover, HBO does not need to block programs the way ad-driven networks do, because its programming hours are not assigned specific values based upon advertising rates. Which is not to say that the timing and sequencing of HBO programming is random. Far from it. HBO programmers clearly showcase the Hollywood blockbusters and high-profile original series in primetime to attract the largest number of viewers. And when introducing a new original series, HBO has always tried to lead in on the back of a more established "hit," such as the cases of *Six Feet Under* and *Deadwood*, which were both launched in the hour following *The Sopranos*. But because HBO is not beholden to advertisers, and because its has the luxury of repeating movies and original series multiple times in a short span of time—so making the content available to audiences with different viewing habits—it has a far greater flexibility in scheduling.

This approach adds value to the HBO brand in two ways. First, it plays into the notion of the "premium." The "basic" or "ordinary" are associated with the routine. But like the top-shelf whiskey or the exclusive restaurant, finding the "good stuff" on HBO requires a bit of planning and an HBO Program Guide. Also, when cleverly managed, the repetition of programming can be used to suggest plentitude. For example, HBO currently multicasts on seven different channels in America, including HBO Family, HBO Comedy, and HBO Latino. Add to these HBO On Demand and HBO Go, and there are effectively nine, to say nothing of the eight channels offered by its sister network, Cinemax. This distribution model, known as "multiplexing," was first introduced in 1980, with the creation of Cinemax. And while several of the channels their own unique programming, most of it is repurposed from its others in the group, increasing the number of subscriber viewing options at any given moment, while costing HBO next to nothing. In place of flow, HBO offers abundance, like opening the *Whole Earth Catalog* to a random page and being drawn in. Or perhaps more precisely, the effect is a perception of abundance, like a Google search that returns 70,000 options, many of which contain the same or similar information, cut and pasted again and again.

Sweet science

Despite "Wired Nation" prognostications, a national high-speed broadband communication system like those endorsed by J. D. R. Licklider and Ralph Lee Smith remained unaccomplished by the mid-1970s. It was a basic problem of infrastructure. The "highway" of coaxial cable was more like a series of town roads linked by regional connectors. This problem was most evident in the medium of television. While over-the-air broadcasters had achieved national coverage through common carriage on AT&T's coaxial system, signal delivery still relied upon the narrowband VHF and UHF spectra. Cable systems were still relatively few, small and scattered, and even large MSOs like Cox Cable and Comcast, who owned systems all over the country, were prevented from connecting them by FCC regulations and the prohibitive cost of leasing space on the AT&T system or building their own comprehensive network of microwave transmitters. But in 1975, all of that would change. And the unlikely engine of that change would be HBO.

At the time, HBO was still a small, regional concern. Though it had grown to 57,000 subscribers in 42 systems ranging across two states, it still had a dangerously high churn rate, and mounting debts. HBO lost $1 million in its first year, $4 million in its second, and $3 million in its third. Economies of scale were difficult to achieve in regional systems, in which the numbers of potential subscribers were low and content and operating costs high. In order to survive, the service had to expand its reach. But expansion meant building more transmitters and securing more content. Having experience in the cable business prior to HBO, Chuck Dolan and his partners at Time understood this problem all too well, and in the early planning for "The Green Channel" considered a number of solutions, including the use of satellite. At the time, no commercial satellites had yet been launched, and though few doubted that the technology would be the wave of the future, it was impossible to predict when that wave would overtake the market. So Time and Dolan stuck it out with the familiar cable/microwave model, and focused on building their subscription base, while keeping an eye to the future.

In spring of 1973, that future seemed almost within reach. HBO's new president, Gerald Levin, had been contacted by the National Cable Television Association to take part in a demonstration of satellite television planned for the group's annual convention in Anaheim, California. HBO was asked to share its live feed of a boxing match between Ernie Shavers and Jimmy Ellis at Madison Square Garden, which would be transmitted via satellite to the convention center. Levin flew to Anaheim to witness the demonstration for himself, and returned to New York a few days later, convinced that the time had come to move onto satellite. The Time board did not take much convincing. They were among the first media companies to show an interest in satellite, recognizing its remarkable economic advantages. Terrestrial cable and microwave transmission became more expensive as the systems expanded (more transmitters, more cable, more signal boosters, etc.), but satellite signals cost the same to transmit regardless of the number of potential receivers. Though the expense of renting transponder space on a satellite was significant, the cost per subscriber shrank as new systems in the range of its signal signed on to a service. The only additional expense was the satellite dish, which every cable system needed to receive the signal. In the early days of satellite, that cost was considerable—roughly $100,000 per dish—but HBO sold a service, not a system, and the responsibility for purchasing these dishes would fall to the cable operators, themselves. All that Levin and HBO needed to do was sell the MSOs on the economy of scale, and the independent cable operators on the improved signal quality and expanded content. It was no mean feat, but they proved up to the task.

In the spirit of the Wilkes-Barre unveiling, HBO inaugurated its satellite service on October 1, 1975 with a couple of movies: a forgettable Canadian independent about a mountain man who raises wolf cubs called *Brother of the Wind* (1973) and Martin Scorsese's *Alice Doesn't Live Here Anymore* (1974), a comedy about a young widow traveling the Southwestern United States with her young son (inspiration for the sitcom, *Alice*). But the big draw that day was the sporting event that followed, one of the most anticipated heavyweight championship boxing matches in the history of the sport, beamed live, not from New York but the Philippines. This third and final bout between long-time rivals Muhammad Ali and Joe Frazier, dubbed the "Thrilla in Manila," would turn HBO's fortunes for good, at once establishing its reputation as an elite source of boxing—the "king of the ring"—and perfectly demonstrating what satellite technology had to offer, by delivering a crystal clear image live from the other side of the world. The broadcast networks would have to wait days for the films of the bout to be flown in and processed.[30] And the fight lived up to the billing: a 14–round brawl that ended Frazier's career and almost ended Ali's life, which still ranks among the greatest in the history of the sport. It was a blood sacrifice to please the gods of commerce. By the end of 1975, subscriptions were up to 200,000, and would approach 1 million by the end of 1976. In 1977, HBO finally turned a profit. The days of scratching and clawing were over.

Satellite-delivered television was hardly a new idea. In fact, the concept had preceded the actual deployment of communication satellites by nearly two decades, and the "Thrilla in Manila" by three. In 1945, science fiction writer and futurist, Arthur C. Clarke, submitted an article on behalf of the British Interplanetary Society to *Wireless World* magazine, outlining plans for a system of three communication satellites in geosynchronous orbit that, at the proper distance from the earth's surface, could be triangulated to "give television and microwave coverage to the entire planet."[31] The satellites could be launched with modified versions of the V2 rocket that the Germans used to bomb England during the Blitz: Clarke's version of beating swords into ploughshares. Ironically, the first man-made satellites would themselves be seen as ideological weapons of the Cold War, beginning with the Soviet Union's Sputnik in 1957. So began the Space Race, which was itself a direct extension of the post-War Arms Race, in which the United States and the Soviet Union jockeyed for ballistic missile superiority by recruiting

FIGURE 2.2 "Thrilla in Manila": Ali vs. Frazier, 1975

German rocket scientists and seizing technology: particularly that of the supersonic V2. But if the Space Race began as an ideological battle, the very satellite communications that Clarke imagined would be its greatest legacy. Although John F. Kennedy would inspire a Cold-War-weary nation to touch the Moon, once that feat was accomplished, public interest in manned space travel quickly dissipated, and after the Apollo program was cancelled in 1972, NASA set its sights on more terrestrial tasks. No longer would their rockets deliver lunar command modules into space for the glory of Democracy. Now they would deliver communications satellites into earth's orbit for the profit of corporations.

The commercial deployment of satellite technology was a logical extension of what Eisenhower termed the "military-industrial complex."[32] The same government agencies and corporations that built the Cold War defense systems—the Advanced Research Projects Agency (ARPA), the Communications Satellite Corporation (COMSAT), Hughes Aircraft, Boeing—were also working on commercial aviation and communication systems. J. C. R. Licklider's early work on the Internet was done under the auspices of the Department of Defense, and Hughes manufactured communications satellites in the 1960s and 1970s, first for military, then commercial use. Considering the enormous costs and expertise associated with the development of satellite technologies, this cooperation of government and industry only made sense. Technologies tend to develop from the top down, even when their success in the marketplace depends upon retail viability. The success of television as a medium, cable as an industry, and the Internet as a means of communication required the introduction of affordable tv sets, coaxial cable and personal computers, but the infrastructure and research initiatives necessary to make these systems work required powerful investors. Satellite is a perfect example. Without NASA, the Pentagon, Northrup Grumman, and Lockheed Martin, our current communications system would not exist, nor could it continue to function. And even when innovation is driven by independent inventors and entrepreneurs—as in the case of early CATV pioneers—the technologies and systems they put into place eventually rely upon powerful, entrenched institutions for their survival. Arthur C. Clarke may have imagined satellite communications in 1945, but he certainly did not have the resources to build and sustain a viable system.

The major television networks themselves saw the potential for satellite early on. In the late 1950s, when the commercial applications for the burgeoning technology were first being explored in earnest, two models of satellite television transmission emerged: broadcast and direct-to-home (DTH). The broadcast model would simply extend the reach of the existing coaxial and over-the-air transmission system of the major networks, while the DTH model foresaw the development of inexpensive residential receiving dishes. Cable systems were few and far between, and the idea of a "Wired Nation" was still a distant drumbeat, despite an impassioned speech given by Teleprompter president, Irving B. Kahn, at the 1960 NCTA Conference, where he predicted a glorious synergy of the two technologies. But just as communication satellites were reaching the point of commercial viability in the mid-1960s, cable was ascending into its "Blue Sky" period, where it would become a symbol of a new age in communications.

In 1965, Hughes Aircraft sent the first commercial geosynchronous satellite into orbit (INTELSAT 1: aka, "Early Bird"). That same year, at Hughes' urging, ABC filed a petition with the FCC to distribute its programming nationwide via satellite, and articles began appearing in trade publications outlining specific plans for a national cable-satellite system. But the FCC took the same "wait-and-see" attitude toward commercial satellite broadcasting that it had to the expansion of cable and pay television services, in hopes that President Johnson's Task Force on Communications Policy would have something conclusive to say about the issues. When the Task Force's report was finally published in 1968, it concluded that broadband cable, rather than narrowband broadcast or the still prohibitively expensive DTH, offered the most immediate promise for satellite television. In the meantime, still more proposals for a national cable system delivered via satellite had begun to emerge from groups as diverse as NASA and the NCTA, and even as the Johnson Administration maintained a hard regulatory line, cable systems operators were becoming more and more convinced of the future economic benefits of this new technology. Meanwhile, broadcasters, who had so long been the favored sons of the FCC, suddenly found that the same regulatory shield that had once protected them from cable and pay television interlopers now blocked their entrance into the satellite age. If over-the-air broadcasters had long been viewed by the FCC as operating in the public interest, by offering "free" programming over public airwaves, their interest in satellite greatly confused the matter. But cable operators were used to this murky territory, and so were better equipped to respond when the American electorate handed them a gift by electing Richard Nixon president of the United States.

Though Nixon may not have created the Internet, he certainly paved the way for cable and satellite television by forming the Office of Telecommunications Policy (OTP) in 1970, under the directorship of former RAND Corporation economist, Clay T. Whitehead. After Charles Dolan and Gerald Levin, Whitehead is probably the most important figure in the history of HBO. As Special Assistant to the President in 1969, Whitehead had been instrumental in drafting the Administration's "Open Skies" domestic satellite policy, which allowed private corporations to launch communications satellites; and as director of OTP, he spearheaded the administration's efforts to deregulate cable. Ironically, these actions meant the death knell for any remaining "Blue Sky" hopes, because the high cost of satellite broadcasting made it virtually inaccessible to all but large, well-established media companies with deep pockets. And because these companies saw the expanding reach of their services only in terms of profit, not utopian dreams of a television Renaissance, they would lapse easily into the bad example of the national broadcasters who came before, cheaply syndicating the same least objectionable programming and selling air time to advertisers at the national and local level. Gone were the "Blue Sky" ideals of particularity, localism, and diversity, soon to be replaced by lifestyle channels on basic cable and endless re-runs of broadcast programs on satellite Superstations like Ted Turner's TBS, the *second* television service to be delivered via satellite.

But *first* there was HBO, which had managed to beat the broadcast networks, as well as the largest MSOs, onto satellite thanks to its natural agility, the resources of Time, and others' ill fortunes. The 1973 satellite demonstration in Anaheim had been organized by Teleprompter, which under the leadership of Irving B. Kahn had become the largest cable MSO in the country, the leading advocate for cable-satellite television, and the clear frontrunner for first-to-satellite. But Teleprompter had fallen on hard times. It was the subject of a Securities and Exchange Commission (SEC) investigation into accounting irregularities that would, in the fall of that year, lead to a halt in public trading of their stock and a major corporate reorganization. And their great leader, Irving B. Kahn, had been forced to resign after his conviction on bribery charges in 1971. While Gerry Levin sat in California watching Ernie Shavers and Jimmy Ellis batter each other in New York, Kahn sat in a New Jersey prison cell, waiting out a four-year prison sentence (he would serve 20 months) and laying plans for a life beyond Teleprompter.

Without Kahn, the hard-fisted master salesman at the helm, his former company was having a difficult time convincing cable operators to take a leap of faith into the satellite age. It was a matter of perspective. For the big MSOs, satellite was about distribution and economies of scale, but for the individual system operators, it was about an increased volume and quality of programming. Since the MSOs had, up to that point, shown virtually no interest in producing or procuring quality content, the individual operators had no reason to believe that a new delivery system adopted for the sole purpose of saving those MSOs' money would prompt them to do so (and considering the recycled content of services like TBS, their doubts proved well founded).

Here a pay television service like HBO had a great advantage. Because it was selling premium content, it added immediate value to a cable system. And because HBO was the only pay service with the enormous corporate resources to make a move into satellite, it got the jump on upstart services like Viacom's Showtime and Gridtronics' The Movie Channel, who had followed HBO's lead into the market but still lagged far behind in terms of subscribers and content. As HBO's numbers grew, so did its reputation, and major cable operators began to see the real advantages to offering the service. One such operator, Robert Rosencrans of UA-Columbia Cablevision Inc., had had so much positive feedback in his New York and New Jersey systems that he wanted to introduce HBO to his Florida subscribers. In April 1975, he and Levin announced an agreement whereby HBO would provide their service to UA-Columbia via satellite. Within days, ATC also signed on, and by summer, so had Teleprompter. In 1976, the FCC revised its guidelines for the size and quality of satellite dishes, effectively bringing the cost down to $25,000 each. And with networks like TBS, the Christian Broadcast Network (CBN), Showtime, the Madison Square Garden channel (MSG) and the Entertainment Sports Programming Network (ESPN) soon offering their content via satellite, that cost became easier and easier to justify.

And the news only got better. In 1977, HBO won its anti-siphoning suit against the FCC, which effectively gave the pay cable industry open access to Hollywood movies, original series, and national sports programming, and significantly increased the value of cable systems. Unfortunately, this also meant further consolidation of the industry, as media companies scrambled to expand their cable portfolios. Over the next two decades of cable deregulation, it would consolidate further, shrinking the pool of media vendors even as the channel capacity of cable systems grew exponentially. HBO's satellite launch essentially harkened the age of vertical integration, the media conglomerate, and the multichannel age.

It also unwittingly left the industry open to piracy. Because satellite signals could be picked up over the air with a dish, they were easily intercepted. Cable providers had made no provision against piracy because they assumed that the high cost of satellite dishes would serve as an adequate disincentive. But they did not count on the do-it-yourselfers. In 1976, a former NASA radio communications specialist turned Stanford professor named H. Taylor Howard succeeded in building a DTH dish in his garage from affordable, readily available materials. Howard was not a pirate, but a hobbyist. In fact, after realizing that he had been receiving HBO's feed for free, he tried to send the company a check for $100. HBO returned it, saying that it could not accept payments directly, and advised him to sign up for the service.

Other hackers operated from less innocuous motives. Although many used satellites in absence of adequate cable service, most were simply looking for free television. Some saw themselves as revolutionaries, along the lines of the anti-pay television activists of decades past. Whatever their reasons, their success, combined with the lack of clear legal boundaries on the matter, encouraged several electronic companies to market DTH dishes and kits. Soon thousands were receiving pay services for free, many of them former subscribers. Panicked, the cable industry lobbied Congress, who in 1984 granted them the right to encrypt, or "scramble" their signals, which could then only be seen by subscribers in possession of a decrypter (typically installed in a set-top box). HBO was first to do so. Satellite owners protested, arguing that for most it was the only way they could receive the service. HBO responded by offering a separate DTH signal, at twice the price of the cable service. They were met with more outrage.

All of which came to a head at 12:32am on April 27, 1986, when HBO's signal was interrupted for four and a half minutes by a message reading,

"GOOD EVENING HBO FROM CAPTAIN MIDNIGHT. $12.95/
MONTH? NO WAY! [SHOWTIME/MOVIE CHANNEL BEWARE!]"

Captain Midnight turned out to be John R. MacDougall, the 25–year-old owner of a satellite television company in Florida, whose business was about to go under, thanks to signal encryption. MacDougall would later claim that he sent the message as a lark, but in the days that followed, all hell broke lose. Fearing a security breach to the satellite carrying the HBO signal, its owner, Hughes Communications, threatened to change the satellite's course or to shut down the HBO signal altogether. Meanwhile, panicked executives at HBO painted the hacker as a domestic terrorist; and the FCC, which had launched its own investigation through the U.S. Attorney's office, made proclamations about threats to national security.

When MacDougall was finally caught a week later, tempers and rhetoric had calmed significantly. Faced with a bright, soft-spoken, squeaky-clean young man rather than a chest-thumping rabble-rouser, the FCC and HBO saw an opportunity to turn the crisis to their advantage. MacDougall was presented with two scenarios: go to trial and risk $100,000 fine and jail time, or plead guilty, confess to every detail of what he had done, and receive a much lighter fine and probation. He was offered the latter option not because the FCC and HBO feared losing in court, but because they wanted to know how he had done it. In particular, HBO wanted to be sure that no one would ever be able to hurt the company in that way again.

*****

The Captain Midnight incident would turn out to be a tempest in a teapot. It neither brought HBO and the cable-satellite industry to its knees, nor did it spawn a political martyr for the satellite age. MacDougall would finally plead guilty and receive a $5,000 fine and probation, and satellite signal encryption would become the norm. But as embarrassing as the episode might have been to HBO, it also reveals something of its true nature: a combination of bold risk-taking and jealous self-protection. One often hears HBO referred to as a "closed" culture, in which corporate strategy is as closely guarded as the distribution rights to its high-value programming. As a vendor of premium, exclusive content— as opposed to a network in the traditional sense—HBO must be willing to adapt, and to safeguard its only asset, which is the programming itself. But HBO has had the fortune to nurture this unique and highly successful model as a protected entity. Risk is easier managed when—to paraphrase Ira Gershwin—your daddy is rich and your spreadsheet is good looking. After all, the same Gerald Levin who rolled the dice on the satellite deal and earned himself the nickname, "the man who saved cable," also single-handedly burst the dot-com bubble in 2002 when, as CEO of Time Warner, he merged his company with AOL and nearly brought his company and the entire media sector down. But Time Warner's pockets were deep enough to survive even Levin's second big gamble, thanks in no small part to his first, HBO, which at the time was already bringing in multi-billion dollar profits and establishing its reputation as the destination for exclusive, high-quality programming with shows like *Sex and the City*, *The Sopranos*, *Six Feet Under*, *Band of Brothers*, and *The Wire*.

HBO is a unique entity, not because it was born of a new idea, but because it has succeeded so mightily by exploiting the best features of so many entrepreneurs and enterprises that came before. Though it would not fulfill the grand visions of techno-utopians, nor supplant broadcast television as the pioneers of pay television had hoped, nor create a global communications system as Arthur C. Clarke had dreamed, by success-fully bringing pay cable-satellite television to market, HBO irrevocably changed the history of television, and the history of media in general. No more would we think of television in the monolithic way we had only a decade before. We were entering the age of media convergence, the age of the Internet, the age of "Not TV." HBO would help to pave the way for that age, and then become one of its key players. But before it could do that, it would have to change television again.

3 THE CATERPILLAR

It isn't fair: the caterpillar does all the work, and the butterfly gets all the glory.

The late 1970s and early 1980s were good times for HBO and cable television in general. The satellite launch broke the oligopoly of the three major broadcast networks as cable systems multiplied and entrepreneurs like Ted Turner (Turner Broadcasting System) and Bill and Scott Rasmussen (ESPN) were able to elbow their way into the national marketplace. HBO thrived in this boom time, growing from 600,000 subscribers in 1977 to 11 million in 1983. Though its premium service competitors—Showtime and The Movie Channel—were also making gains, HBO stayed in front by moving from strength to strength. When the cable stations found that many premium subscribers were willing to pay for more than one service, HBO created the lower-priced Cinemax in 1980: a 24–hour movies-only service similar to The Movie Channel. HBO's high subscription numbers allowed the company to leverage much lower cost-per-subscriber deals with Hollywood studios, to buy films in lots rather than individually, and to lock down exclusive television rights by supplying production money to cash-strapped studios. HBO also got into the movie business, first by partnering with CBS and Columbia Pictures in 1982 and Disney in 1983 to form, respectively, Tri-Star Pictures and Silver Screen Partners, and then by creating their own production company, HBO Pictures (later HBO Films), which released its first made-for-HBO feature, *The Terry Fox Story*, in 1983. In short order, HBO had become one of the most valuable properties in television.

But this explosive growth could not last forever. In 1984, the service added only 300,000 new customers, and even fewer the following year.

Though the Cable Communications Act (1984) would lead to unprecedented deregulation of the cable business, investors were taking a "wait-and-see" approach, so few new cable systems were being built. Deregulation also led to a massive expansion in the number of basic cable channels, and a rapid rise in rates. Premium services were now not only competing with the broadcast networks, but with MTV, ESPN, Bravo, and AMC. At the same time, the falling prices of video cassette recorders (VCRs) and satellite dishes were putting them within reach of mainstream consumers. In 1984, VCRs were in 20 percent of American homes, and by the end of the decade that number rose to 75 percent. Meanwhile dish owners—many of whom lived outside the range of cable systems—were grabbing HBO's unprotected signal for free. HBO met each of these challenges aggressively. They launched a series of innovative marketing campaigns, scrambled their signal, got into the home video business, and even tested the basic cable market with The Comedy Channel (which later merged with Viacom's Ha! network to form Comedy Central). But technological tweaks and new markets aside, the key to the long-term survival of a content service is unique content. And the most cost-effective way for HBO to provide it was to create its own.

In the network's early days, original programming amounted to one thing: sports. From 1973 to 1975, the service averaged over 200 sporting events a year. Because FCC "anti-siphoning" regulations made it virtually impossible to acquire major franchise licenses, the offerings were scatter-shot, ranging from the occasional basketball and hockey game to figure skating and surfing.[1] But even after the restrictions were lifted following the 1977 *HBO v. FCC* decision, the company lacked the resources to invest in the most popular sports on a regular basis, and so began concentrating their attention on neglected areas. They picked up the rights to Wimbledon tennis because no one else wanted them, and because tennis appealed to a key HBO demographic: the white and well heeled. Likewise, they were able to become "the home of boxing" because boxing had no home. The most frequently televised sport of the 1950s struggled to compete with televised baseball, basketball, and football in the 1960s and 1970s. Since Joe Frazier's heavyweight loss to George Foreman in 1973, HBO has been the source of record for many of the most remarkable bouts in modern boxing history: Holmes–Cooney in 1982, Hagler–Hearns in 1985, and the classic Mike Tyson fights from the late 1980s that 20 percent of subscribers identified as the primary reason they subscribed to the service. Though critics complain that the network has destroyed the sport by acting as a promoter rather than a presenter—featuring only fighters under contract and ignoring the rest of the field—for good or ill, HBO has become synonymous with boxing.

HBO would also define itself as a major force in television documentary from the 1980s onward, producing hundreds of titles by some of the best-known filmmakers working in the genre—Albert Maysles (*LaLee's Kin*; *The Gates*), D.A. Pennebaker (*Elaine Stritch: At Liberty*), Spike Lee (*4 Little Girls*; *When the Levees Broke*)—while launching the careers of several major talents, including Joe Berlinger (*Paradise Lost: The Child Murders at Robin Hood Hills*), Richard Kuklinski (*The Iceman Tapes*), and James Marsh (*Wisconsin Death Trip*; *Man on Wire*). Under the leadership of Sheila Nevins, HBO has championed a new form of television documentary that draws heavily upon the narrative elements of film, literature and theater to tell up-close-and-personal stories of ordinary people in extraordinary circumstances, from the segregated South to the sex industry. While documentary has exploited the structures of fictional storytelling since at least as far back as Robert Flaherty's *Nanook of the North* (1922), HBO eschews clinical objectivity for the empathy and identification of conventional drama, while avoiding the iconoclasm and irony of Michael Moore and Errol Morris. The formula has earned the network dozens of Emmys, Oscars, and Peabody Awards and, as the most prolific producer of documentaries in America (with over 300 titles since the division launched in 1979), earned them—and Nevins in particular—a reputation as the major patron of the art.

While stand-alone docs and sporting events continue to be valuable assets for HBO, and Hollywood films still comprise the majority of its schedule, the real key to the network's enduring success has been series programming, which encourages viewers to return to the service week after week, month after month. But in order to prompt viewer loyalty, the content must always distinguish itself. This is one way television programming differs qualitatively from theatrical films. The quality of Hollywood product may wax and wane, but "going to the movies" has managed to maintain a relatively steady—if steadily declining— social value, and audience expectations adjust to the available options. Movie audiences have evolved over time, due to such cultural forces as television, suburbanization, and the gradual decrease of leisure time among adults. The proliferation of big-budget summer action and fantasy movies geared to tweens and teens is a direct result: they have the highest percentage of disposable income and time, and the strongest inclination to build social bonds through popular entertainment. But with television, where program options multiply and compete for audience attention with other media (home video, gaming, the Internet), networks must now offer distinct, consistent programming in order to survive.

The most straightforward way to achieve this goal is through genre production. The conventions of genre guide viewer expectations, and allow networks to extrapolate from movie success and network series popularity in order to predict audience demographics and production budgets, and plan marketing campaigns. In other words, genre makes telling and selling more efficient, while simultaneously offering the creators of the programs an opportunity to expand the boundaries of the particular form. True, very few avail themselves of the opportunity. Broadcast networks tend to hew very closely to previous successful examples of medical and legal dramas, sitcoms and reality shows in an effort to attract and keep advertisers looking for predictable returns. But HBO is not bound to advertisers, and its primary imperative is and has always been to offer unique content. So it should come as little surprise that, while developing even its earliest series programming, HBO significantly expanded the bounds of content and form.

Nowhere is this experimentation more apparent than in comedy. Though we tend to associate HBO with high-profile dramas like *The Sopranos*, *The Wire* and *True Blood*, the network has produced more comic programming over a longer period of time than any other genre, using the form to showcase what HBO can do that broadcast and basic cable networks traditionally could not: push content boundaries with profanity, nudity, and controversial subject matter; and formal boundaries by offering new takes on such tired forms as the sketch comedy (with the surreal *Mr Show with Bob and Dave*), the talk show (with the issue oriented, politically engaged *Dennis Miller Live* and *Real Time with Bill Maher*) and the sitcom (with postmodern satires like *The Larry Sanders Show* and *Curb Your Enthusiasm*). Comedy has been the caterpillar to HBO's butterfly, helping the network to transform itself from a movie and sports service into the gold standard of original programming. Though easily derided as cheap, mindless amusement, comedy has often served as a potent vehicle for and response to changing cultural values, from Aristophanes to *South Park*. At HBO, comedy would help to change the way we think about television.

A hard ticket

Though scripted HBO comedies would not appear until the early 1980s, the network got into the comedy business at the time of the satellite launch. On New Years Eve 1975, they aired the first installment of a monthly stand-up series called *On Location*, featuring a one-hour performance by Robert Klein. If the "Thrilla in Manila" advertised the potential of satellite technology by beaming live images from halfway around the world, stand-up offered HBO an opportunity to demonstrate the sort of provocative, uncensored programming only they could offer. Before long HBO would become a new home for stand-up comedy, eventually replacing late-night television as the launch pad for comic careers. As with boxing, HBO got into the business of stand-up comedy because it was available and relatively cheap. And, like boxing matches, stand-up shows had what Gerry Levin called "hard-ticket value": "Both, in a not-so-subtle way, reinforced to the consumer that they were getting box-office value from something even though it was coming through their TV set."[2]

Stand-up also reflected the sensibilities of the programmers at HBO, many of whom had strong ties to the business. Michael Fuchs had been hired in 1976 directly from a career at the William Morris Agency, where he had served as legal representative to several comedians who would eventually make appearances on the network (including Robert Klein). As head of original programming at HBO, he booked such well-known comedians as Phyllis Diller and Eddie Murphy. In 1984, he was elevated to Chairman and CEO of HBO, and tasked with pulling the company out of its mid-decade funk by developing international, theatrical, and home video markets, and investing in original programming. Along with award-winning documentaries (*Common Threads: Stories from the AIDS Quilt*), educational programs (*Braingames*), and children's shows (*Fraggle Rock*), Fuchs green-lighted HBO's first scripted comedies, including *Not Necessarily the News* and *The Kids in the Hall*. But the most important thing Fuchs did to cement HBO's reputation as the home of quality comedy was to hire Chris Albrecht in 1985.

Albrecht began his career as part of a stand-up duo with Bob Zmuda (best known as comedian Andy Kaufmann's co-writer), but finding no success he moved into management. He co-owned a comedy club in New York, then became a talent agent at International Creative

Management (ICM), where he represented, among others, such rising talents as Whoopi Goldberg, Billy Crystal, Jim Carrey, and Keenan Ivory Wayans. It was at ICM that he first drew the attention of HBO, which looked to expand its comic programming and cutting edge credentials. Albrecht immediately wowed them when, in 1986, with the help of his old stand-up partner, Bob Zmuda, he launched *Comic Relief*: a charity telecast and stand-up showcase meant to raise money and awareness to combat homelessness in America. Zmuda got the idea—and the name— from a similar charity launched in Great Britain the previous year, and dedicated the show to the memory of Andy Kaufmann, who died in 1984.

Despite its good intentions, HBO's *Comic Relief* might have easily gone unnoticed—a casualty of charity fatigue in the age of Band Aid (1984), Farm Aid (1985), Live Aid (1985), "Do They Know It's Christmas?" (1984), and "We Are the World" (1985)—but for two factors. First, HBO decided to broadcast it for free, in the spirit of a traditional telethon, allowing millions of non-subscribers to get a glance at the fresh perspective HBO was bringing to American comedy. Second, the show avoided the usual cavalcade of B-level ex-stars for a carefully selected blend of high-value comic talents past and present, from George Carlin and Jon Lovitz to Sid Caesar and Dick Gregory. Hosting the show were three friends and former clients of Albrecht, who also happened to be among the hottest comics of the time: Robin Williams, Whoopi Goldberg, and Billy Crystal. Thanks in large part to their easy chemistry and the charitable spirit of the proceedings, the show was an enormous success, demonstrating to the viewing public and the front office folks their potential for high quality, important television: a mantra that would define HBO for decades to come.

Albrecht would go on to produce seven other iterations of *Comic Relief*, introduce three new stand-up programs to the network—*One Night Stand*, *Def Comedy Jam*, and the annual *Young Comedians* show —and headline the best working comedians around in their coveted one-hour specials. Under the Chairmanship of Michael Fuchs' predecessor, Jeffrey Bewkes, who would invest hundreds of millions of dollars into the development of original programming and so pave the way for HBO's "Golden Age" in the 2000s, Albrecht would ascend to the position of President of HBO Original Programming, where he would shepherd several of HBO's best comedy series (*The Larry Sanders Show*; *Sex and the City*; *Curb Your Enthusiasm*), as well as many others for broadcast and basic cable networks through HBO Independent Productions (*Roc*; *Martin*; *Everybody Loves Raymond*). Albrecht would replace Bewkes as Chairman and CEO of HBO in 2002, and lead the company through that Golden Age, right up to his forced resignation in 2007, following an arrest for assault. And though many credit this ascension to his development of such acclaimed dramas as *Oz*, *The Sopranos*, and *Six Feet Under*, like Fuchs before him, he would build the network's reputation on the foundation of comedy laid in HBO's earliest days.

The 1970s had been a challenging decade for stand-up comedy on American television. The vaudeville-style variety shows that dominated primetime in the 1950s—Milton Berle's *Texaco Star Theater*, Sid Caesar's *Your Show of Shows*—had been reduced to a series of recycled routines delivered by the vanilla personalities of *The Sonny and Cher Comedy Hour* and *Donnie and Marie*. Following in the tradition of *The Honeymooners* and *I Love Lucy*, sitcoms still offered a venue for stand-up comedians such as Bob Newhart (*The Bob Newhart Show*), Redd Foxx (*Sanford and Son*), and Jimmie Walker (*Good Times*), but while their shows often scored high in the ratings, their comic performances were reduced to the easy one-liners, catch phrases and camera mugging that had defined the genre from its earliest days. But comedy—especially stand-up—had changed. Since the late 1950s, the vaudevillian style had been giving way to the long-form routines of Jonathan Winters and Nichols and May, the improvisation of Chicago's Second City troupe, and the topical "sit-down" humor of Shelley Berman and Mort Sahl. This new breed of comedians riffed, ranted, and challenged their audiences to think faster, more deeply, and very often beyond their comfort zone. And no one did it with more zeal and determination than Lenny Bruce, the comedian with the most immediate influence on stand-up in the years following his untimely death in 1966.

Though his career was cut short by legal persecutions, bankruptcy, and drugs, Bruce had taken on the sacred cows of American society, from racism and sexual mores to religion, homophobia, patriotism, and our anxieties surrounding "dirty words." He honed the cutting edge for future generations of comedians, and offered them an alternative to the canned routines and one-liners of the Copacabana and the Jack Parr Show: an open, improvisational style driven by personal observation, confession, and social critique that cut through the thick veneer of burlesque to expose something raw and vulnerable. His short career and sudden death in 1966, just as the countercultural revolution was shifting into high gear, inspired a handful of young comedians who would leave their own indelible mark on American stand-up. Richard Pryor had a life-changing revelation that comedy "wasn't about telling jokes" but "telling the truth" while listening to a Bruce record in the late 1960s. Robert Klein was inspired by Bruce's example to display, rather than hide his intelligence. And George Carlin, who once shared a paddy wagon with Bruce after being arrested at one of the elder comedian's performances in 1964, borrowed liberally from Bruce's stage material: including his infamous "Seven Words You Can Never Say on Television" bit, which was inspired by an earlier Bruce routine outlining the nine words that could get you arrested for obscenity.

Also emerging from the 1960s was an alternative comic venue, the "showcase" club. Unlike the traditional nightclub, which might offer a program of one or two opening acts and a headliner, the showcase club offered variety and volume, featuring dozens of comic performers over a given week, and sometimes a single night, doing short sets. It was a place for young talent to find an audience, and for established comedians to work out new material: a sort of comic cooperative, where the performers worked for free but learned invaluable lessons about their craft. The first of these clubs was opened in 1963 by an unsuccessful Broadway producer named Budd Friedman, in midtown Manhattan. The Improvisation, or "Improv" as it came to be known, was originally meant to be an after-hours spot for Broadway performers, but soon young comics started showing up, looking for a stage and a friendly audience. Word spread, the talent pool widened, and by the early 1970s, similar clubs had begun springing up all over the country: The Comic Strip, Dangerfield's, The Comedy Connection, Catch a Rising Star, The Comedy Store. In 1975, Friedman opened a second Improv on the West Coast and left the New York operation in the hands of his business partner, Chris Albrecht. Over time, the clubs had become magnets for *Tonight Show* booking agents and television producers looking for writers and performers around whom they might build sitcoms.

Some comedians, like Gabe Kaplan (*Welcome Back, Kotter*) and Robin Williams (*Mork and Mindy*), found that their material and comic personae easily adapted to network television, but many of the acts were simply too improvisational, too political, and in many cases too "dirty" to make that transition. Although an entire generation of comedians had come up after Lenny Bruce in the shadow of Woodstock, Kent State and Watergate, and even Hollywood had acknowledged a broadening of audience sensibilities by awarding its 1969 "Best Picture" Oscar to an X-rated movie (*Midnight Cowboy*), broadcast television comedy remained stuck in a time warp, in which the most popular performers— e.g. Bill Cosby and Carol Burnett—offered nostalgic alternatives to the social upheavals of their times. Even a relatively tame outlet like *The Smothers Brothers Comedy Hour* (1967–9) would prove too controversial for network television because it took a critical view of the war in Vietnam and made jokes about religion. *Saturday Night Live*, which premiered a few months before HBO's *On Location* series in 1975, sought to fill the void by offering edgier performers a slot on late-night television, when the content restrictions were somewhat more relaxed. Like HBO, they would help to launch the careers of dozens of performers and writers, from Andy Kaufmann to Tina Fey.

But HBO was still the only place on television where a comic could work without the formal restrictions of the standard 6–minute talk show "spot" or the content restrictions of the FCC. As with sports, HBO cast its comic net wide in the early days, featuring old-school Las Vegas acts (Pat Cooper, Norm Crosby), along with comedians in their prime (Bette Midler, David Brenner) and a few newcomers (Steve Martin, Billy Crystal). But with Albrecht's arrival, the one-hour special would become the *sine qua non* of contemporary comedy, with seminal stand-up performances such as *Whoopi Goldberg: Direct from Broadway* (1985), *Robin Williams: Live at the Met* (1986), and *The Roseanne Barr Show* (1987). And HBO showcase series like *Young Comedians* and *One Night Stand* would constitute an informal apprenticeship network for promising young talents, from Bill Hicks to Louis CK.

On New Year's Eve 1975, however, there was only Robert Klein.

Klein might seem an odd choice to launch what would become HBO's stand-up empire. While Lenny Bruce's other progeny—Pryor and Carlin—went on to superstardom, Klein never achieved the same level of popular or critical acclaim. But in 1975 he may have been the most influential comic working. While Pryor and Carlin pushed the limits of content and created unique stage personae—one a profane raconteur, the other a rubber faced wiseass—Klein developed the style most other young comedians would adopt: pop literate, clever and polished, but lacking any obvious affectation or bombast. He was a "slicker, soft-rock alternative to Carlin and Pryor" who "made stand-up comedy hip and relevant and accessible for that vast group of younger comics who weren't ready to storm the barricades like Carlin and who didn't have

FIGURE 3.1 *On location: An evening with Robert Klein, HBO*

the autobiographical raw material of Pryor."[3] Klein was relatable, offering a clever play on a familiar reference or a winking aside framed as an everyday observation, amounting to subtle assurance to his audience that he was one of them. Though his material was often intellectually challenging, his manner was more that of a graduate student than a revolutionary. And in the early days—while the FCC was still debating how much jurisdiction it should have over cable and pay television—HBO was very careful to frame their comic performances as socially and intellectually liberating, rather than merely profane. They were about freedom of expression. "This is mature," Klein opened his first HBO performance. "We're grown up. We can say anything." Then after a brief pause: "Shit! How do you like that?"

On Location would follow up the Klein performance with Freddie Prinze, fresh from the success of *Chico and the Man*, and Redd Foxx, who brought his "dirty" nightclub act to an audience who knew him primarily as the gravel-voiced junk dealer on *Sanford and Son*, clearly hoping to trade off of their celebrity. But they would not find their true comic voice until 1977, when *On Location* featured a performer who had spent the better part of the decade recording gold records, selling out arenas and college tours, and publicly battling obscenity charges surrounding the "Seven Words You Can Never Say on Television" routine first recorded on his 1972 album, *Class Clown*. And though he would play host to the inaugural episode of NBC's *Saturday Night Live*, make 27 episodes of a low-rated sitcom for Fox, and eventually lend his talents to PBS' *Shining Time Station* and *Thomas the Tank Engine and Friends*, his true television home was and would always be HBO.

Dirty words

George Carlin's associations with HBO were many. His first HBO special aired on March 5, 1977, two months shy of his fortieth birthday, and his fourteenth was aired on March 1, 2008, just three months before his death. His third, *Carlin at Carnegie* (1982), would mark a triumphant return to the stage following a five-year hiatus due to cocaine addiction and a pair of heart attacks. Beginning with his fourth, *Carlin on Campus* (1984), all of his comedy records would be drawn directly from his HBO specials. In 1985, he attempted to develop one of HBO's earliest sitcoms, *Apt. 2C*: a proto-*Seinfeld*, where Carlin played himself interacting with neighbors and friends in a New York City apartment building. But after a decade and a half as a solo act, he found it difficult to work with a group of writers, and the project never got past the pilot stage. He stole the show at HBO's first *Comic Relief* broadcast in 1986, performing his legendary "A Place for My Stuff" routine. He breathed new life into political stand-up in such HBO specials as *What Am I Doing in New Jersey?* (188) and *Doin' it Again* (1990), and earned a CableACE Award for *Jammin' in New York* (1992). In 1995, Carlin was chosen to host the retrospective, *20 Years of Comedy at HBO*, in which he applauded the network for championing freedom of expression, describing HBO as the "Comedians' Bill of Rights." Upon his death in 2008, HBO released a statement acknowledging, "No performer was more important to helping our network define itself in its early years," and put that legacy on display in a two-day marathon of Carlin's HBO specials.

To understand the significance of George Carlin to the history of HBO comedy, it is worth comparing him more closely to his idol Lenny Bruce, and his contemporary Richard Pryor. Each had had early success with traditional stand-up—impressions, characters, one-liners—but around age 30 recast themselves as provocateurs, challenging audience attitudes about what constitutes comedy. Controversy was accompanied by fame, legal persecutions, and spiraling drug problems, but while

Pryor and Carlin managed to survive each—thanks in large part to Bruce's example—Bruce's legal troubles would eventually bankrupt him, and he would be discovered dead of an overdose of morphine on the bathroom floor of his Hollywood home at age 40. At 40, Pryor would set himself on fire during a freebasing binge, but survive even that and go on make *Live on Sunset Strip*, *Here and Now*, and a dozen films. And at 40, Carlin would tape his first HBO special, beginning a new phase of a career that would last another 30 years.

It is tempting to say that, had HBO launched a decade earlier or Bruce held on a decade longer, he might have found a home there, since his material inspired so much of Carlin's. But the similarities between the two comedians obscure important differences. Lenny Bruce made a career critiquing what he called "The Lie": the system of political, religious, racial, economic, sexual, and moral hypocrisies upon which our society is built. In routines like "Religions, Inc.," "Tits and Ass," "To Is a Preposition, Come is a Verb," "Would Your Sister Marry One of *Them*," and "Wear a Blue Suit to Court," he took those hypocrisies on, often at great personal and professional expense. Bookings were harder to come by with each new obscenity charge, and audiences became increasingly alienated by Bruce's uncompromising critique. As Bruce himself said, "When I pulled the covers off, the great crime I committed, I didn't have anything to replace it."[4] Revealing "The Lie" without offering an alternative or palliative exposed him not only to litigation but the distain of an audience looking to be amused. According to Freud, humor traditionally serves to contain the things that make us uncomfortable, not rub our noses in them. But to tell a joke—or do "a bit," as Bruce scornfully described the polished comic routine—for nothing more than a cathartic laugh seemed disingenuous to him. "I'm not a comedian," he was fond of saying. "I'm Lenny Bruce."

Carlin was just as acerbic, incisive and erudite as Bruce, but unlike his crusading mentor, he trafficked in the sort of winking irony that one could easily mistake for genial goodwill. Bruce was scandalized by all of the hypocrisy he saw, and said so directly. He was an angry satirist in the vein of Jonathan Swift. Bruce's 1959 recording, *I am Not a Nut, Elect Me!*, features a cover image of the comedian standing between an Asian woman and a black woman, holding up a sign reading "Togetherness." Behind them is a row of cloaked and hooded Klansmen, wielding canes and bowler hats. Behind them is a statue of Abraham Lincoln

But Carlin was more like the scamp curmudgeon, Mark Twain, wrapping what he called his "disappointed idealism" in the sharp agnostic

FIGURE 3.2 Lenny Bruce, *I Am Not a Nut, Elect Me!*, Fantasy, 1959. (Reprinted with permission.)

wit of a Catholic schoolboy in disgrace. The cover of Carlin's 1972 *Class Clown* album pictures Carlin seated in punishment before a schoolroom chalkboard: hair grown below his shoulders, denim shirt defiantly open, middle finger stuffed comically up his nose.

Carlin shared Twain's conviction that the "funniest things are the forbidden,"[5] but like Twain, he addressed those forbidden things to our inner child, with its natural love of fart jokes and talent for spotting bullshit. As Jerry Seinfeld put it on the occasion of Carlin's death, "His performing voice, even laced with profanity, always sounded as if he were trying to amuse a child. It was like the naughtiest, most fun grown-up

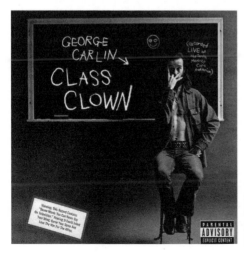

FIGURE 3.3 George Carlin, *Class Clown*, Little David/Atlantic, 1972. (Reprinted with permission.)

you ever met was reading you a bedtime story."[6] Bruce simply challenged us to grow the hell up.

Richard Pryor's comedy, on the other hand, addresses his own inner child: the damaged by-product of neglect, abuse, and segregation, who was raised in his grandmother's brothel by a brutal father and grew into a man who would battle his own violent impulses, cruel addictions, and crippling self-doubt in the company of junkies and opportunists.[7] Carlin used humor as a form of rebellion, but Pryor made people laugh in order to protect himself: ironically, by laying bare the sometimes tragic and often unflattering facts of his own life. And it paid off. In the 1970s, there was no more popular comedian than Richard Pryor. Despite, or maybe because of- the racial charge of his humor, he had enormous crossover appeal, especially among young white males. He had become a minor movie star in feature films like *Silver Streak* (1976) and *Greased Lightning* (1977), and even landed a primetime variety show on NBC (though *The Richard Pryor Show* aired only four episodes in 1977, before Pryor quit over censorship disputes). But other than frequent airings of his popular stand-up films from the early 1980s (*Live on Sunset Strip*; *Here and Now*), HBO made little use of Pryor. Perhaps he did not need them as much as Carlin, who made only one film in the 1970s (*Car Wash*, which also featured Pryor) and had only one regular television gig: a recurring guest spot on *Tony Orlando and Dawn*. And in 1977, HBO might not have known what to do with Pryor, anyway.

Critics have long noted HBO's tendency to segregate black and Hispanic comedians through showcase venues like Russell Simmons' *Def Comedy Jam* and P. Diddy's *Bad Boys of Comedy*, which target audiences versed in race humor and hip hop culture. But in the 1970s, HBO was still young, their subscribers were overwhelming white, middle-aged, and middle class, and given the racial tensions of the time, the network might have been skittish about spotlighting a performer whose discography includes titles like *That Nigger's Crazy* (1974) and *Bicentennial Nigger* (1976). Lenny Bruce had played on racial anxieties in routines like "Are There Any Niggers Here Tonight?" and "How to Relax Colored Friends at a Party," arguing that the only way to rob words like "nigger" of their sting was to overuse them to the point where they became as familiar as "good night." But Pryor goes significantly further, offering a sophisticated and controversial critique of the word's cultural meanings that goes beyond skin color to a pervading sense of loss, failure, and marginalization, as well as a paradoxically empowering attitude that comes of being excluded from the mainstream. However derogatory (and Pryor did find "nigger" derogatory, eventually swearing it off after a trip to Africa in 1979), he finds unexpected richness in it. To be a "nigger" is to walk with swagger one moment, then run in fear the next; to know want and need, and to be frustrated in the satisfaction of both; to love and hate, often with a brutal passion; to struggle equally with desire and despair, often mistaking one for the other.

In his well-known routine, "Jewish and Goyish," Lenny Bruce makes a similar point by distinguishing two ways of perceiving and engaging with the world: one authentic, the other cultivated; one fertile, the other sterile; one street wise, the other book learned; one funny and sarcastic, the other humorous and ironic; one Jewish, the other goyish. In Bruce's scheme, Eddie Cantor and Al Jolson are goyish, but Count Basie, Eugene O'Neill, Dylan Thomas and Ray Charles are Jewish. Anyone from New York is Jewish, but anyone from Butte, Montana is goyish. White bread, Kool-Aid, instant potatoes, and lime Jello are goyish; but pumpernickel, black cherry soda, and fruit salad are Jewish. "Titties are Jewish. Mouths are Jewish. All Italians are Jewish."[8] And by Bruce's standard, Richard Pryor's comedy is undeniably "Jewish," reflecting a messy view of life as filled with highs and lows, kindnesses and cruelties, virtues and vices, offering precious few, though jealously guarded, glimpses at the profound.

Carlin dealt with decidedly tidier material: observational humor, social commentary, and the peculiarities of the English language. Though he identified with the counterculture of the 1960s, his occasional hip references were more than balanced by his scorn for its failed ideals. In the 1960s, he cultivated a television audience by parodying that counter-culture in the form of an innocuous, vaguely stoned character known as "Al Sleet, the Hippie-Dippie Weatherman," and though the bulk of his stage material would take a more biting and satirical turn from the 1970s onward, he never aligned himself with any particular group or ideology. Carlin may not have been "goyish," but he certainly wasn't a "nigger." If anything, he was culturally amorphous. He made a point of separating himself from the mainstream *and* the margins by avoiding direct identification with either. Carlin laughed at, rather than critiquing, the status quo and the counterculture. While Pryor and Bruce made their comedy personal and particular, Carlin favored irony and imper-sonal observation, grimacing and exaggerating with precisely the same expression and tone, whether talking about jumbo shrimp or genocide.

And as it turned out, that ironic, unallied posture was a perfect fit for HBO: profane but literate, serious but funny, radical but nonpartisan. He stirred the pot, but never let it boil over.

Carlin's approach was decidedly postmodern. He applied the principles of deconstruction—in which concepts are analyzed to identify the sources of their power—and de-legitimization—in which that power is undercut by the simple act of revealing its flimsy pretext. This process was most clear in his deconstruction of the English language, from euphemisms and seemingly innocent phrases like "Have a nice day" and "One thing leads to another" to "dirty" words like "tits" ("sounds like a snack cracker") or "prick" ("which is only sometimes dirty...Yes, you can prick your finger, but don't finger your prick"). "By and large," he said, "language is a tool for concealing truth,"[9] and he saw it as his job, not to reveal the truth so much as to undermine the value of the language that conceals it. He applied the same principle to seemingly innocuous human behavior (driving, sports) and to "heavy shit" like religion and death. His humor could at times seem downright silly ("Cats and Dogs"; "Little Things We Share"), but it was always pointed and analytical, getting the laugh not for saying, "Hey, everybody farts, and that's okay," but asking, "Why does the sound of word 'fart' make us laugh?"

Bruce's and Pryor's comedy was meant to produce catharsis—an emotional release to ameliorate some of the suffering it exposed—while Carlin played a game of wits, revealing the absurd lapses in human behavior and expression. But the game had a serious intent. If Bruce revealed "The Lie" then left nothing in its place, Carlin turned "The Lie" on its head by undermining its basic premise. "There are no bad words," he said. "Bad thoughts, bad intentions, and wooooords."[10] The value of those words—just like the value of common objects and ideas—is contingent upon a variety of factors, some internal and some external. But all of them can be undone with enough wit and force of will, and a venue like HBO, where they could be discussed without having to be euphemistic or solemn. Though Carlin's comedy never aspired to justice or empathy (as Bruce's and Pryor's did), and though it never tried to change the world, it certainly affected the way we look at that world and the strange beings that occupy it. For all of its detachment, it is remarkably self-reflexive.

Carlin's postmodern approach to comedy would serve as a template for countless other comedians, from the droll ironies of Steven Wright, Jerry Seinfeld, and Mitch Hedberg, to the cutting socio-political commentary of Bill Hicks, Bill Maher, and Jon Stewart, to the profane erudition of Sam Kinison, Chris Rock, and Louis CK. If Bruce had freed comedians to improvise and Pryor to access their vulnerability, Carlin taught them the importance of disciplined writing. Like Bruce and Pryor, he showed them that no subject was off-limits, but he also showed them that comedy could be both a profession and a discipline. One of the reasons Carlin had so much success at HBO was because he wrote an entirely new hour of material for each year's special. And in preparation for that special, he toured, constantly shaping and polishing. This regime not only made for a greater variety of material, but also forced him to constantly explore new territory.

Carlin's approach held great appeal for HBO, especially in the 1980s, when they were struggling to distinguish themselves in the expanding market. Whereas A&E might have been producing a higher volume of stand-up programming hours with *An Evening at the Improv* and *Caroline's Comedy Hour*, and Showtime was having some success featuring physical comics like Gallagher and Super Dave Osborne, HBO would aspire to quality and consistency. George Carlin offered both. While introducing his first HBO special in 1977, journalist and television personality, Shana Alexander, commended Carlin's commitment to free speech in the FCC obscenity case, compared his work to that of Aristophanes, Chaucer and Shakespeare, and declared him "one of this generation's philosophers of comedy, defining, reflecting and refining the way we see our times."[11] A dozen years later, while launching The Comedy Channel, HBO Chairman and CEO Michael Fuchs would declare, "Comedy is a sacred trust at HBO."[12] If so, Carlin was the network's patron saint. In his work, even the silly seemed profound and important because it was so well crafted, and because it sounded like wisdom, rather than anger, pain, or desperation.

Though "Seven Dirty Words" made Carlin famous, his most popular routine is the one he performed at the first *Comic Relief* show: "A Place for My Stuff," a seemingly innocuous bit about how we define ourselves by the things we accrue over the course of our lives. Not objects of value or sentiment *per se*, but ordinary things: "keys, comb, wallet, lighter, hanky, pen, smokes, rubbers and change."[13] Without them, we feel unmoored, unprotected. The routine offers us Carlin at his most cheerful and animated, though also his most critical. On the surface, it seems no more than a fairly innocuous swipe at conspicuous consumption, but it actually looks at a far deeper issue: our need to be affirmed, validated in a world that seems indifferent or hostile. In the piece, our "stuff" takes the form of baggage carried on a vacation trip, but it can also be taken for any other sort—emotional or otherwise—that we use to give ourselves substance, and to make our existence seem real, if not meaningful. Like so much of Carlin's best work ("The Planet is Fine"; "Cars and Driving"; "Modern Man"), "A Place for My Stuff" uses humor to mirror our insecurities and narcissism. But the mirror also allows us a level of dissociation that the highly personal comedy of Pryor and Bruce does not. He is more interested in *what* we see in that mirror than *how* we see ourselves. Like hearing our own voice on an answering machine or seeing photos taken of us unawares, Carlin's comedy feels at once familiar and alien. This is, in fact, what makes it funny: we laugh to signal recognition *and* to cover our discomfort. But it also allows us a level of insight into the ways our reality is constructed that the more cathartic comedy of Bruce and Pryor does not. Where they are satisfied to make us *feel*—anger, pathos, pleasure—Carlin demands that we take a step back from those feelings and look at how they are constructed. And this, as we will see, is his ultimate contribution to HBO's comic legacy.

The reality taboo

After the success of *Comic Relief* in 1986, HBO began casting about for projects that would further identify the network with quality comedy. They stumbled first upon *It's Garry Shandling's Show* (1986–90): a radical deconstruction of that most popular television genre, the sitcom, for which HBO made an unsuccessful bid. Traditional sitcoms feature unchangeable characters stuck in unchanging situations, who have 22 minutes to solve a fabricated crisis, all while trying to get a laugh. Usually, the crisis is quickly resolved and everything returns to normal, but in the hall-of-mirrors world of *Shandling*, "normal" means recognizing that the situation is itself an artifice. In the series, comedian Garry Shandling plays a version of himself, interacting with fictional friends in fictional situations, all the while aware that the story takes place on a sound stage where—despite Garry's frequent efforts to go "off script" by directly addressing the camera and the studio audience—no truly meaningful stories with genuine obstacles and transformations of character are possible. Episodes of *Shandling* do not end so much as fall apart, having nowhere to go.

Seinfeld would follow *Shandling*'s lead, purporting to be "a show about nothing," but the point of the earlier show is that *all* sitcoms are finally "about nothing." Characters and situations cannot and will not undergo change because, by doing so, they would drastically alter the fictional world of the program. In *Seinfeld* George, Elaine, Jerry, and Kramer will never sustain long-term relationships outside their group; and in *Everybody Loves Raymond* everybody will continue to love Raymond, despite the mounting examples of his shortcomings as a husband, a father, and a son. That familiar regularity is what attracts us to sitcoms in the first place. In place of jeopardy and revelation they give us one-liners and sight gags. But *Shandling* comically reintroduces jeopardy and revelation by turning the show into an exercise in navel-gazing. It drops the fourth wall, and the "real" world floods into the obvious fakery of the sitcom.

Like all traditional fictions, the sitcom is built upon a reality taboo: an unspoken assurance that the narrative will maintain the continuity of the fictional "real" of the story. Like the Freudian joke, this taboo contains our anxieties about the chaos of meaninglessness that may lie beyond the boundaries of the fiction. When the reality taboo is breached in *Shandling*, it creates the same sort of humor and crisis one experiences in the postmodern comedy of George Carlin, raising, but not attempting to answer a series questions: Where does one world end and the other begin?; Does the fakery mean that *nothing* about the show is genuine?; And if not, why do we bother to watch?

Though HBO lost out to Showtime in the bidding for *It's Garry Shandling's Show*, the series whetted the network's appetite for another projects that played with form and drew attention to the reality taboo. This one would be a mock-documentary collaboration between *Doonesbury* cartoonist Gary Trudeau and *Nashville* director Robert Altman, called *Tanner '88* (1988). Produced on-the-fly during the 1988 presidential primary race, *Tanner '88* is a searing critique of empty political rhetoric and media-made politicians that uses the very same media to fabricate a dark horse candidate who, in a series of scenes that blur the line between reality and fiction, interacts with real-life primary contenders (Bruce Babbitt, Gary Hart, Jesse Jackson). Jack Tanner, played by Michael Murphy, is a young, eminently likeable left-of-center Congressman, who begins his campaign without much to say and less to show. Over the course of the series, we watch as Tanner develops both his political persona and platform, while the cameras roll. With little more than a campaign slogan, "For *Real*," Tanner—and the episodes themselves—were largely made up as the series went along. Trudeau worked out plot points during shooting in order to follow as precisely as possible the actual primary race, and episodes were edited and aired within days of shooting. Clips would even occasionally appear in actual news coverage of primary events, further obscuring the line between the two media versions of the primary campaign. And in Trudeau and Altman's fiction, Tanner comes close to securing the Democratic nomination by calling for the legalization of drugs, by condemning scandal mongers, and by naming a cabinet that would include Robert Redford, Gloria Steinem, Studs Terkel, and Ralph Nader.

Tanner '88 demonstrated HBO's commitment to making truly unique television. Produced by two outspoken American artists, it did not shy away from ideology or direct satire of politics and media. It also demonstrated several features of the mock-documentary form that HBO would adapt and exploit in future programs. Documentary production techniques like fly-on-the-wall camera work, staged interviews, and stentorian narration constantly remind us that we are observing recorded events, rather than slipping into the alternative reality of fiction. The effect is to create a clinical distance between the viewer and the subject that, despite empathy or identification with that subject, cannot be bridged. Fictional characters stand in for us, but the real-life subjects of documentary are their own agents. Mock-documentary further exaggerates this distance by introducing irony, while the earnest narrator, objective camera, and probing interviews amplify the hilarious insignificance of the subject, be it an aging rock band (*This is Spinal Tap*), a Kazakhstani journalist (*Borat*), a middle manager at a second-tier paper company (*The Office*), or a fictional presidential candidate adrift in a sea of real-life phonies (*Tanner '88*). It explodes the reality taboo by compelling us to take an arch view of the real, at least as the traditional documentary constructs it.

HBO was messing with the comedic line between fiction and reality even before *Tanner '88*. Its award-winning first foray into series comedy, *Not Necessarily the News* (1984–90), was a television news parody adapted from the British *Not the Nine O'Clock News* (1979–82), but owed an equal debt to *Monty Python's Flying Circus* (1969–74) and the "Weekend Update" segment of *Saturday Night Live*. HBO's earliest sitcom, *1st & Ten* (1984–90), built its sophomoric locker-room-sex-comedy hi-jinx around real-life football players. And while *Tanner '88* raised the bar significantly and achieved some real flashes of brilliance, many early critics and subscribers complained that the real/fake conceit was too self-conscious and gimmicky. In order to be successful, it would have to evolve beyond a fourth wall gag and seamlessly integrate into the mode of storytelling. This is where HBO's first great scripted series, *The Larry Sanders Show* (1992–8), would truly stand out.

Though HBO failed to secure *It's Garry Shandling's Show* in 1986, when that series ended in 1990, the network let Shandling know that it was still eager to work with him. At the time, the late-night television wars were heating up, with Jay Leno and David Letterman vying to replace the retiring Johnny Carson at *The Tonight Show*, and the other networks scrambling to make a play for Carson's audience. Shandling, who had been a frequent guest host for Carson, was approached at the time about doing his own late-night show, but he put the idea aside for another: a sitcom where he *plays* a late-night talk show host whose program is losing out to Leno and Letterman, and whose insecurities are slowly overtaking him.

The Larry Sanders Show is really two intertwined narratives: the "public" one seen through the lens of a fictional late-night talk show called "The Larry Sanders Show," and the "private," backstage petit drama surrounding the struggling production and its self-centered host, referred to here as "The Larry Sanders Meltdown." In *Sanders*, style is a direct extension of substance, moving well beyond the rhetorical restrictions of the mock documentary, while still blurring the line between reality and fiction. The series draws specific aesthetic distinctions between "The Larry Sanders Show" and "The Larry Sanders Meltdown" that are meant to reveal different levels of reality. The late-night talk show itself is recorded in vivid color, "live on tape," using three stationary cameras, applause prompts, and studio lighting and sound. It looks, in effect, like a real late-night talk show. The "Meltdown" scenes, however, are recorded using a single roving camera and grainy film stock that produces muted colors from the ambient, mostly fluorescent light of the production office sets. But unlike the probing, voyeuristic eye of the behind-the-scenes documentary camera, it is a casual observer in Larry's offices, or tracking Larry and his producer, Artie, in hallway dialogues that might be prototypes for Aaron Sorkin's famous "walk-and-talk" shots in *Sports Night* and *The West Wing*.

The facsimile of a late-night talk show, "The Larry Sanders Show," offers the polished, carefully-orchestrated "public" Larry that America presumably loves: a version of himself that the "private" Larry insists on watching each night in bed, often with a willing sexual partner by his side to sublimate his autoerotic fixation. Of course, the "public" Larry is nothing but an empty suit, reading lame jokes off cue cards, flattering movie stars, and generally braying like an ass. In him, Shandling has reduced the late-night host archetype to a mere shell, lacking Carson's wit, Letterman's goofiness, or Leno's blue-collar charm. But the "private" Larry may be just as hollow: a composite of relentless ego and neuroses, who obsesses about his falling ratings and his fat ass, and seems constitutionally incapable of sustaining any meaningful relationship outside the workplace. At commercial breaks, he pours paranoid rants into his producer's patient ear and takes cheap shots at his moronic sidekick Hank. Yet he still manages to seduce the occasional female guest with an amalgam of self-deprecating humor, impish charm, and his own celebrity cache. Like his marriages, these flings never last, because the women soon discover that behind the humor, the innuendo and the double-breasted suits lies a quivering mass of insecurities, and that one hour a night, five nights a week is probably all that anyone can stand of either Larry. The "private" Larry seems to know this. And despite his narcissism, one cannot help but be moved by his descent, because it is presented without the gloss or practiced rhythms of his "public" narrative. He is just a man falling apart.

Sanders was both a critical and popular success, winning four Peabodys, five CableACE Awards, and three Emmys, and scoring a total of 56 Emmy nominations, including best comedy series all six years of its run (losing out each time to the ratings juggernaut, *Frasier*). It also became HBO's first "water cooler" program. Though the network had had an earlier hit with the divorced dad sitcom, *Dream On* (1990–96), *Sanders* developed a fiercely loyal following, especially among people working in show business, who made sure to watch on Wednesday nights. In *Sanders*, Shandling turned self-referentiality not just on the form (the sitcom) and character (a talk show host caught between the world of his show and the messier "real" one that surrounds it), but Hollywood, with its Darwinian social structure and cult of personality.

At one level, it is a conventional show business workplace sitcom, like *The Mary Tyler Moore Show* or *Murphy Brown*. But where those programs presented the workplace as a series of challenges that the characters had to meet, *Sanders* and many of the shows it would directly influence—*Newsradio*, *The Office*, *Parks and Recreation*—use the workplace to supplant the inner lives of characters. While Mary Richards and Murphy Brown are independent women attempting to balance professional fulfillment with meaningful relationships outside the office, Lisa Miller *(Newsradio)* and Leslie Knope (*Parks and Recreation*) have invested their entire identity in their jobs, and any relationships they may have are built upon the social hierarchy of the workplace, where the distinctions between boss, friend, lover, and family member are not only difficult to find, but over time largely irrelevant. Their jobs define their lives, and themselves.

The Larry Sanders Show asks probing questions about celebrity, many of which brush up against the reality taboo. For example, at what point do celebrities' personae begin and their "true selves" end? And does such a self exist in a world where ones image is so thoroughly mediated? For a show focused upon a character who shares so many traits in common with the comedian who plays him, it can also be surprisingly self-critical. By all accounts, Larry Sanders' faults and fears are merely Garry Shandling's writ large. But like Carlin's comic musings on language and social custom, *Sanders* is less interested in revealing some "Lie" concealed by celebrity culture (for example, "They're all a bunch of conceited assholes!") than in understanding our fascination with people who pretend to be something they are not—in life and on television and movie screens—especially when the pretense may undermine the possibility of their ever truly being known or knowing themselves. We all realize that the culture produced by Hollywood—in the form of movies, television shows, and celebrities—is fake. When Larry's producer, Artie, says that he speaks "fluent bullshit" in the pilot episode, he is only confirming what we already know. But *Sanders* asks us to consider why we find the fakery so amusing, comforting, perhaps even more satisfying than our real lives, particularly when faced with the ugly, behind-the-scenes reality we seem bent on discovering in the tabloid pages. We laugh when Artie says this, and like him better for it.

By asking these questions, *The Larry Sanders Show* invests the sitcom with an importance it had rarely, if ever known before. Not the earnest self-importance of 1970s programs like *All in the Family* and *M*A*S*H*, with their strident liberal commentaries concerning racism and war and late season attempts to create real dramatic character and story transformations, despite the prohibitions of the genre (as each of those series progresses, it becomes more maudlin and less funny). *Sanders*, on the other hand, is about the banalities of Hollywood, late-night television, and the sitcom form itself. Though peppered with references to the news stories of the day—O.J. Simpson, Monica Lewinsky, John and Lorena Bobbitt—it is largely apolitical. Contemporary references are meant to comment upon how talk show culture has made tepid jokes of murder and scandal, widening the gap between reality and our image of it. The result is a not-so-startling revelation about what holds the show business community together: mutual investment in its own artifice. Beyond the facile theme of "Hollywood phonies," Shandling's winking fiction is driven by real, deeply flawed and only slightly exaggerated people revealing their manias, insecurities, and existential crises. And despite their almost universally repellent qualities, they evince a good deal of sympathy for doing so. In Shandling's capable hands, both Hollywood and the sitcom cease to be entirely banal because he focuses so much critical attention on the sources of that banality, best exemplified by Larry himself: the never-ending conflict between ego and insecurity.

To better understand the television legacy of *The Larry Sanders Show*, a comparison between two contemporary programs about show business offers a valuable point of reference. Aaron Sorkin's short-lived drama-comedy, *Studio 60 on the Sunset Strip* and Tina Fey's critically beloved sitcom, *30 Rock* both offer perspectives on the backstage culture of *Saturday Night Live*. Sorkin adopts the liberal tradition of 1970s producers like Norman Lear (*All in the Family*) and Larry Gelbart (*M*A*S*H*), turning what might have been a serviceable workplace sitcom into an earnest essay on gender inequality, free speech, and the place of religion in public discourse. With a pedigreed cast (include *Friends'* star Matthew Perry, and *West Wing* alum Bradley Whitford) and Sorkin's famously brilliant dialogue, the show has much to offer. Yet it failed utterly with audiences and critics, for at least two reasons. First, it is difficult to invest in the jeopardy of the show, built as it is upon the stale axiom, "The show must go on." Even old Hollywood musicals never took that plot point very seriously. And second, it is so earnest in its desire to engage "serious" issues that it is very difficult to find funny.

By comparison, *30 Rock* makes a running joke of this narrative crisis. In that series, the show-within-the show that must go on—*TGS with Tracy Jordan*—goes on. But it does so despite the backstage chaos and the antics of its preening stars: not because the show's creator, Liz Lemon (played by Fey herself), and her ragtag crew of writers and producers are courageous or brilliant, but because that is just what happens in a sitcom about producing a television show. Like *Sanders*—which Tina Fey cites as the central inspiration for *30 Rock*—it is both a meta-sitcom and a broad parody of a media culture that has become increasingly familiar to us. In the world of *30 Rock*, we think nothing of Al Gore and Brian Williams rambling eccentrically to Jerry Seinfeld and Kenneth the page in the NBC hallways.

Though moderately successful in its time, *The Larry Sanders Show* is far less known today than the many series it helped to inspire. This is perhaps due to its spotty history of syndication, its late arrival on home video, or its dated pop cultural references. But the impact of the series has been enormous. Ricky Gervais and Stephen Merchant (*The Office; Extras*) cite it as a primary influence on their work (Gervais has described *Sanders* as "Probably the most important sitcom of a generation"), as have Ken Finkelman (*The Newsroom*[14]; *Good Dog*), Steve Coogan (*I'm Alan Partridge; Knowing Me, Knowing You*), Sasha Baron Cohen (*Ali G. Show; Borat*), Armando Iannucci (*The Thick of It; Veep*) and Mitchell Hurwitz (*Arrested Development; Sit Down Shut Up*). Their work reflects *Sanders'* penchant for biting satire and reality taboo breaking. As does the later work of many *Sanders* alumni, such as John Riggi (*The Comeback; 30 Rock*), Paul Simms (*Newsradio; Flight of the Conchords*), Tom Saunders (*Just Shoot Me!; Arrested Development*), and Ken Kwapis (*The Bernie Mac Show; The Office*). For some, *The Larry Sanders Show* would serve as both a proving ground and an incubator for their talents. Judd Apatow (*Freaks and Geeks; 40–Year-Old Virgin*) and Drake Sather (*NewsRadio; Zoolander*) found their comic voices in the *Sanders* writing room. For others, like broadcast veterans Chris Thompson (*Laverne and Shirley; Bosom Buddies*), Peter Tolan (*Home Improvement; Murphy Brown*) and *Sanders* co-creator Dennis Klein (*The Odd Couple; All in the Family; Buffalo Bill*), it would be a creative haven, away from the censors and corporate sponsors: a place to rediscover or reinvent their voices.

Above all else, *The Larry Sanders Show* proved that HBO could make unique shows that were *also* exceptional. When Michael Fuchs left HBO to run the Warner Music Group in 1995, his replacement, Jeffrey Bewkes (who has since risen to the ranks of CEO and President of Time Warner), invested unprecedented resources into original programming, effectively kick-starting the network's Golden Age. HBO's first successful dramatic series, *Oz*, would follow shortly after, then *The Sopranos*. But mostly HBO made comedies built upon the central *Sanders* themes: celebrity culture and the thin line between reality and artifice. Programs like *Arli$$*, *Tenacious D*, and *Entourage* poke fun at the very notion of celebrity by breaching the "real" world of the sports, music, and movie businesses, while sketch programs such as *Mr Show with Bob and Dave* and *Tracey Takes On...* make sport of the neurotic, self-centered personae of their hosts. Even HBO talk shows—*Dennis Miller Live, The Chris Rock Show, Real Time with Bill Maher*—delight in exploding the conventions of the form, with monologues that devolve into obsessive rants, and guests who say what is on their mind rather than playing nice to plug a movie or book. While there certainly were HBO comedy programs that drew little or no inspiration from *Sanders'* example—*Sex and the City, The Mind of a Married Man*—they veer in the direction of drama (or "dramedy"), favoring weighty plot lines and character arcs over experiments in form.

But the true legacy of *Sanders*—and the most direct through-line to many of the programs named above—is HBO's longest-running comedy series: Larry David's *Curb Your Enthusiasm*, which began in 2000 and continues to date. In *Curb*, the *Seinfeld* co-creator plays a dyspeptic version of himself, resting on the laurels of his television success in Los Angeles. With too much time and unlimited resources, Larry spends his days doing precisely what we would expect of the man upon whom *Seinfeld*'s George Costanza is based: pissing off family, friends, and half of the celebrities in Hollywood by pointing out their failings, while refusing to do anything about his own. Shot with hand-held cameras and only partially scripted, the series has a lively docu-realistic feel: not surprising, given the fact that Robert B. Weide, who has produced and/or directed every episode of the series, got his start making documentaries for HBO. Weide and David use the immediacy of documentary to amplify uncomfortable silences and discordant lines in the largely improvised dialogue, resulting in what may be the ultimate American "cringe comedy": a form that has been popular on British television since at least as far back as *Monty Python's Flying Circus*, but that has only gained popularity in the U.S. over the past decade or so.

Curb is an excellent example of the sort of American comedy that could only have been at HBO in 2000, not just because it is frequently profane and potentially offensive to just about any minority group you care to name, but because David refused to make it anywhere else. After *Seinfeld*, the broadcast networks had nothing left to offer him. He was worth hundreds of millions of dollars, his show was roundly considered one of the greatest television comedies ever produced, and every one of his former cohorts was suffering from "the *Seinfeld* curse," unable to launch a successful project on its own merits. No amount of money could have induced him to take that chance. But HBO offered David something far more valuable than money: nearly unlimited freedom. And he knew just what to do with it.

Worlds collide

Before teaming up with Jerry Seinfeld in 1989, Larry David was ten years into a career as a stand-up comedian, actor and television writer. His first big break came in 1980, when he joined the cast and writers' room at ABC's answer to *Saturday Night Live*, *Fridays*, which ran from 1980 to 1982. When that show was cancelled, he found a place at *SNL*, but after a year and only one skit aired, he quit, and earned a living driving a taxi. In 1987, he landed a job at *It's Garry Shandling's Show*, where he got to know several future *Seinfeld* writers, learned the craft of the sitcom script, and found inspiration in Shandling's new vision for television comedy. *Seinfeld* owes much of its "show about nothing" soul to *Shandling*, even taking a meta-sitcom turn in its fourth season, when Jerry and George pitch NBC a sitcom similar to *Seinfeld*. And though *Seinfeld* had been on the air three years before *The Larry Sanders Show*, the friendship and shared comic sensibilities of the shows' creators created some natural synergy. Jerry and Jason Alexander (who plays George) even appeared on *Sanders* a number of times, beginning with a late Season 2 episode that aired around the time *Seinfeld* moved to its coveted Thursday night "Must-See T.V." slot. In the episode, Jerry guest hosts "The Larry Sanders Show." Moments before taping begins, Larry's sidekick, Hank, walks off the set, peeved about some perceived slight, and is eventually discovered on the "Jerry's Apartment" set of *Seinfeld*, by Jerry himself. Hank is sprawled out on "Jerry's" iconic blue couch, in a self-pitying funk reminiscent of George.

Hank's migration makes geographical sense, since the sound stages for *Seinfeld* and *The Larry Sanders Show* were actually on the same Studio City lot, but it also makes sense from a purely symbolic point of view. Like so much of *Sanders*, Hank's escape into the alternate reality of the popular sitcom highlights both the artifice and comforting familiarity of television. It is a place to escape the pressures and humiliations of "real" life. In the final season of *Sanders*, Jerry returns to say his on-air goodbye to the retiring Larry. During a commercial break, he comments that he'll look forward to watching Larry in syndication, but when Larry responds that his show will not be syndicated, Jerry quips, "Oh that's right, that's me." This winking acknowledgment of fortune's favor—that *Sanders* would never approach the popular success of *Seinfeld*—is also a brilliant, self-deprecating display of pathos and profundity that the relatively sterile *Seinfeld* would never achieve. By placing the insecurity and egotism of the show's creator/central character at the very center of the satire—so pushing against the reality taboo—*Sanders* is able to generate genuine sympathy for its otherwise unlikeable host.

If *Seinfeld* exists in symbiotic relationship with *Sanders* (they even went off the air only eight days apart), *Curb* steals directly from its playbook by peeking behind the Hollywood curtain at the "real" lives of celebrities. Only *Curb* cuts much closer to the bone by stripping away the "public" version of Larry David as George Costanza, for a "private" version of Larry David who actually bears his face and name (as opposed to Garry Shandling's sound-alike "Larry Sanders"), but who is able to say and do things that the "real" Larry David would never have the courage to say and do. The distinction between George and the "private" version of Larry is most stark when we see the worlds of *Seinfeld* and *Curb* collide. In Season 2, Larry tries to convince first Jason Alexander (George Costanza), then Julia Louis-Dreyfus (Elaine Benes) to develop a new show based on their post-*Seinfeld* careers. But their efforts or inevitably undone by the pettiness and paranoia of Larry's inner George. When Jason characterizes George as an "asshole," Larry (not without justification) takes the remark for a personal attack and refuses to work with Jason. Julia is more diplomatic, and she and Larry have a much easier time working together. But before they are able to finalize a deal for a new show with HBO, Larry accuses one of the network's executives of stealing his take-out food, and they shut him out. Though one might imagine similar plots playing out in *Seinfeld*, the tenor and tone would be very different. Jason Alexander, who plays "George" as self-pitying and exasperated—somewhere between Woody Allen and Lou Costello—is a far cry from Larry's self-assured pedant.

In Season 7, Larry attempts to win back his aspiring actress ex-wife, Cheryl, by arranging for a reunion episode of *Seinfeld*, and writing a role for her. Like all of Larry's schemes, it is bound to fail because he does not think it through. Jerry wants to cast someone else in the role. But even after Larry secures her the part, his inner "George" takes over again. He becomes convinced that Cheryl is having a fling with Jason, and quits the show when Jerry refuses to let Larry fire him. The refusal scene is a classic collision of the *Seinfeld* and *Curb* universes. As Larry struggles to convince Jerry that he is the best person to play a character based on himself, Jerry is forced to confront him with a hard truth: that "George" is no longer simply a version of Larry, but a separate entity, defined less in relation to Larry than to Jason. "Do you understand what this is?" he asks an incredulous Larry. "This is iconic television here." He points around the room: to the set, and to each of the principal actors, ticking each off with the word "Icon!" He then points to Larry: "No-con!"

The redress is delivered in the perfectly timed, shrill—indeed, iconic— voice of a comic legend, but it is more than a banal bit of observational humor. The "joke" is that Jerry and Larry's iconic sitcom bears only one of their names and faces, despite the fact that it is largely inspired by Larry's own personal experiences and dark comic worldview.

All successful sitcoms achieve some level of icon status because the static characters and situations eventually come to "stand" for something. In absence of change, they become symbols or ideals. But in *Curb Your Enthusiasm*, *The Larry Sanders Show* and the many comedy programs they have inspired, the iconic characters and situations are deconstructed, exposing and de-legitimizing the sources of their power. Whether satirizing the pretenses of celebrity (*Extras*; *Eastbound and Down*), revealing the banalities of the workplace (*The Office*; *Party Down*), or tweaking traditional values like family (*Arrested Development*; *Modern Family*), friendship (*Peep Show*; *It's Always Sunny*

FIGURE 3.4 "Icon!" *Curb Your Enthusiasm*, HBO

in Philadelphia), education (*Freaks and Geeks*; *Community*), or civics (*Parks and Recreation*; *Reno 911*), these shows breathe life into stale forms, imbuing them with a new sort of authenticity. Each of them is populated by deeply flawed, and in some cases despicable characters, whom we like nonetheless because their lousy behavior gives the lie to the false ideals they were meant to embody. We don't need Gob Bluth (*Arrested*), Frank Reynolds (*Sunny*) or Ron Swanson (*Parks*) to be heroes: only to be honest, even when that honesty reveals something dark and ugly. Like Carlin's comedy, they are both familiar and alien, compelling us to laugh out of recognition and discomfort.

Some might argue that *Seinfeld* does precisely the same thing, with its irredeemable characters. But we like them for the same reason we like the sniping petulance of the characters on *Friends*: because they are hermetically sealed within a fake version of Manhattan filled with wacky eccentrics, making clever jokes and double entendres that have little bearing on anything but their tiny lives. *Curb*'s version of a *Seinfeld* reunion episode features a running gag about a bankrupt George trying to get back with his ex-wife after having been wiped out by Bernie Madoff's Ponzi scheme: broad comedy with little or no interest in the subtext because, in the world of *Seinfeld*, even global financial crises cannot intrude upon the safety of a booth at Monk's Cafe. The Hollywood environs of *Curb* may be "fake" in the sense that no one except Larry seems entirely genuine, but it is hardly sealed, hardly safe. Like any society, it is bound by unwritten rules of conduct and prescribed values that fall roughly under the heading of "political correctness": Embrace diversity and fair trade. Practice tolerance and charity. Protect children, the poor, the elderly, and infirm. And under no circumstances should you use the handicapped toilet if you do not have a disability. *Curb* is full of jokes about race, religion, sexual orientation, incest, and just about any taboo you care to name, but like Carlin's humor, the jokes are less *about* these subjects than about the social discomfort surrounding them. Taboos are created to contain and control our anxieties, like a dam holding back a river. But once the dam is breached, those anxieties pour out with a chaotic force, causing panic.

That panic is the source of *Curb*'s humor. A typical episode of *Curb* begins with Larry questioning a taboo, and peaks with his inadvertently breaking it, while otherwise sane people turn into hysterical moralists and brand him as a pariah. Though not its immediate target, Hollywood is the arena of *Curb*'s satire because, when rules or values are challenged there, people have the resources to make their displeasure felt. Whether an indignant friend (Marty Funkhauser, Richard Lewis) or a slighted celebrity (Ben Stiller, Christian Slater), everyone has the power to bring Larry's deeds to light. Despite the fact that his causes amount to little more than a rich guy complaining about social conventions, we are meant to identify with the comic anti-hero Larry because he plays the petulant rebel who, like Lenny Bruce before him, insists on exposing hypocrisies and inconsistences—"The Lie"—in our social taboos. The show has little interest in exploring "The Lie" itself. It only means to draw humor from the anxieties surrounding those taboos. Larry, who seems genetically predisposed to challenge them despite the inevitable wrath it will bring, is simply the catalyst for unleashing those anxieties.

David Gilotta argues that Larry is a classic *schlemiel*, or bungler, whose inevitable failure at the end of each episode "serves as a direct challenge to the status quo and encourages viewers to question the myriad unwritten rules that we follow in our everyday lives."[15] But Gilotta seems to miss the point. *Curb* does not question whether or not we should be sensitive to people with disabilities or incest survivors: it merely tweaks that sensitivity, forcing us to laugh in spite of ourselves. And despite Larry's miscalculations and petty impulses, it is hard to see failure in a character that, no matter what mess he leaves in his wake, remains the most clear-eyed and least perturbed among his peers and persecutors. He merely shrugs off others' scorn, like the comic horns at the start of *Curb*'s opening and closing theme, Michelini's "Frolic": it's all just a joke, a game, a silly antic to pass the time.

As Richard Butsch points out,[16] American sitcoms are filled with bunglers, Joe Lunch Pail dreamers and schemers like Ralph Cramden (*The Honeymooners*) and Homer Simpson (*The Simpsons*) looking for the American Dream. Only where the Dream once embraced the nineteenth-century values of self-reliance and rugged individualism, in the post-War world of the corporate economy and middle-class suburbanization, those notions gave way to the twin ideals of comfort and security: career advancement and the white picket fence. Traditional sitcoms make characters like Ralph and Homer the butt of every joke because they lack the wherewithal to achieve these ends, because they are failures. But we also identify with their aspirations and frustrations, which are only exaggerated versions of our own. In their very striving they display values and vulnerabilities that humanize them. They may be losers, but they are lovable losers. In the **über**-rich Larry, however, we see a more grotesque manifestation of the post-War Dream, where comfort and security breed self-centered pettiness. Larry doesn't challenge conventional values because they are oppressive or dangerous, but because they inconvenience or annoy him. "Why shouldn't I use the handicapped stall if no one else is in there?" It is a reasonable, but utterly insignificant question. Against what is Larry taking a stand? And who among the millions who *have* used the vacant handicapped stall would be willing to stand with him? Yet we like Larry too, not for any hidden virtue or humanizing vulnerability, but because he exercises the ultimate prerogative of the wealth and security: he refuses to take shit from anyone. And in the comedic universe of the HBO series, where principles like justice and truth are just more logs in the dam of the reality taboo, that is as close to greatness—let alone goodness—as anyone is likely to get.

"I Took a Risk"

Season 2 of the FX Network's cult comedy, *Louie*, opens with a scene where the show's creator and star, comedian and divorced dad Louis CK, lovingly brushes his five-year-old daughter's teeth while she innocently informs him that she loves her mother more than him.

For a show that continually demonstrates the theme that all illusions collapse of their own weight (love, faith, even innocence), the scene is

FIGURE 3.5 Father and child. *Louie*, FX

amusing but not surprising. Nor is Louie's reaction: after a brief pause, he continues brushing, then sends her off to bed, giving his beloved daughter the middle finger behind her back.

Louie is a perfect example of HBO's comic legacy: the brainchild of a comedian who got his first national exposure on HBO's various stand-up showcases, and later created a profane take on the blue-collar sitcom for the network (*Lucky Louie*). When that show was cancelled after a single season, he simply adapted the reality taboo shattering model of *Curb Your Enthusiasm*—a portrait of the artist as a series of cringe-worthy comic vignettes—to his own brand of confessional humor and DIY production methods, and came up with *Louie*. Some critics have compared *Louie* to *Seinfeld*, because it threads together fictionalized versions of real-life incidents with CK's stand-up performances, but where *Seinfeld* was a show about nothing, *Louie* systematically dismantles the traditional sitcom themes—fatherhood, dating, aging, education—with mercilessly dark humor and honesty, finding comedy in the pain and unwanted wisdom that comes from those collapsing illusions. It is a show that reflects just how much content boundaries have expanded, with gags about pedophilia, the Crucifixion, homosexuality, and mutual mastur-bation peppered through stories of escalating humiliation and cruelty. It is also deconstructive comedy.

In a scene from early in the first season, Louie sits at a poker table making "faggot" jokes with a group of friends, one of whom is gay. Not condemning, but only in the spirit of clarity, the gay friend explains the horrific origins of the word: in medieval times, homosexuals were used as kindling when burning witches at the stake. The conversation stops dead in its tracks. But only for a moment. Seconds later, one of the group retorts, "All right, enough of this, faggot," and the room explodes into cathartic laughter. Like his mentor, George Carlin, Louis CK skillfully combines an explanation and a diffusion of the word's power, not by demanding sensitivity or reform, but by reducing it to a mere word.

Over the past half-decade, FX has carved out a niche for itself producing cult comedies about chronically self-obsessed anti-heroes—*It's Always Sunny in Philadelphia*; *The League*; *Archer*—that serve as a measure of HBO's influence on contemporary comedy. But that influence can be found across the channel spectrum. Thanks in part to HBO, virtually no subject is off limits to television comedy, even the dirtiest of Carlin's "Seven Dirty Words." The third season of NBC's *30 Rock* featured a long-running gag about an NBC *Survivor*-like reality show called *MILF Island* (MILF being an anagram for "Mom I'd Like to Fuck") that promises "25 super hot moms, 50 sweaty eighth grade boys, and no rules!" And in a Season 3 episode of the popular ABC mock-documentary sitcom, *Modern Family*, the two-and-a-half year old adopted Vietnamese child, Lily—whose parents are a well-adjusted gay couple—blurts out the word "fuck" at a friend's wedding.

Comedy has also become far more deconstructive, foregoing the easy pathos and identification of the traditional sitcom for a more critical look at what amuses us and why. Many contemporary sitcoms push the boundaries of funny to the point of discomfort (something British comedy has been doing for decades), often resulting in more authentic moments of pathos and identification. Take, for example, the painfully funny moments when Michael Scott's misplaced loyalty to his bosses collides with their contempt in NBC's *The Office*; or in Starz' *Party Down*, the simmering humiliation of the aspiring actors and shell-shocked has-beens in catering uniforms who press hors d'oeuvres and head shots into the indifferent hands of Hollywood power brokers.

Popular mock-documentary series (NBC's *Parks and Recreation*; BBC's *The Thick of It*), fake news programs (Comedy Central's *The Daily Show with John Stewart* and *The Colbert Report*) and any other programs that blur the line between reality and fiction owe some debt to the network that shattered the reality taboo, not merely as an ontological gag (as in Woody Allen's *Take the Money and Run* and *Zelig*, and Christopher Guest's *Best in Show* and *A Mighty Wind*), but to undercut every conventional narrative platitude. In NBC's *Community*, the "nerd" character, Abed, recognizes that he is stuck inside a sitcom and tries to rewrite the script because, in the current version, the "cool guy," Jeff, has too little in common with the "cool girl," Britta, to get past a one-night-stand. In Mike Clattenberg's Canadian mock-documentary, *Trailer Park Boys*, perennial felons in a Nova Scotia trailer park hatch absurd money making schemes like smuggling hashish across the U.S. border using a model train stolen from Patrick Swayze, not to get rich and move out of the park, but to make just enough money to get drunk and high with their friends. Maybe even move out of their car and into an actual trailer.

It is a testament to HBO that the network was able to attract comic talents like George Carlin, Garry Shandling, and Larry David, but even more so that it allowed these artists the freedom to articulate a new comic vision: a model HBO would adopt for all of its original productions. Unfettered by advertisers or censors, HBO has challenged just about everything we know about television comedy for more than three decades, from stand-up to the sitcom and beyond. Though its many imitators have made it more difficult to launch a successful comic series in recent years (only a few of HBO's recent comedies have lasted more than a season or two), they continue to press against the boundaries of the form, with a deglamorized 20-something revision of *Sex and the City* (*Girls*), an animated podcast of unscripted conversations (*The Ricky Gervais Show*), a white trash parable of baseball glory (*Eastbound and Down*), and a scathing political mock-documentary about the powerlessness of the powerful (*Veep*). The work of proven talents—some of whom have long-standing relationships with HBO (Judd Apatow, Ricky Gervais, Stephen Merchant)—they nonetheless chart new territory in American television.

****

But that has been the key to HBO's success, in comedy and in all other areas of original programming. In the words of *Curb*'s Larry David, when asked by his annoyed wife, Cheryl, why he thought it would be okay to joke with a young boy about the size of the child's penis: "I took a risk." And given the success HBO has had with comic programming over the years, clearly that risk has paid off.

4 EVERYTHING. EVERYONE. EVERYWHERE. ENDS.

Life is pain. Get used to it.

LISA KIMMEL FISHER, *SIX FEET UNDER*

It was worth it. Wasn't it?

DET. JIMMIE MCNULTY, *THE WIRE*

On July 10, 2007, HBO terminated the eight-year run of its most popular and critically acclaimed series, *The Sopranos*, with a scene that has been dissected and debated as much as any in the history of television. In it, beleaguered mob boss Tony Soprano sits alone in a diner booth, scanning the room full of strangers, then the tabletop jukebox for a song to suit the occasion. He stops on several: "Who Will You Run To?" and "Magic Man" by Heart; "Don't Stop Believin'" and "Anyway You Want It," by Journey; and "I Gotta Be Me" and "In a Lonely Place" by Tony Bennett. If Tony were a typical Hollywood gangster, we would expect him to choose Bennett, whose songs might serve as bathetic metaphors of damned nobility for men who choose to live outside the law. But in a nod to his own musical past and his anxious frame of mind, Tony chooses "Don't Stop Believin'." As the piano introduction begins, his wife Carmela enters, and a look somewhere between relief and contentment rushes over Tony's face. She slides into the seat across from him, her own expression distant, and his becoming uneasy as they punctuate the silence with occasional utterances about when their children are due to arrive, a business associate who will be testifying against Tony, and what looks good on the menu. Tony continues to scan the customers, and the audience counts them off with a growing sense of dread: one in an adjacent booth with the brim of his hat pulled down, two by the pastry case, and one who looks vaguely familiar coming through the door just ahead of their son A.J., who slouches into the booth next to his mother.

The three Sopranos trade talk about A.J.'s job with a familiar mix of hostility and wounded sincerity. Meanwhile the stranger who came in with A.J. has taken a seat at the counter, where he glances over now and then before disappearing into the bathroom. At this point, the scene shifts to outside the restaurant, where daughter Meadow struggles to parallel park her mother's Lexus. A moment later, we see her crossing the busy street, and heading for the diner door. Inside, a basket of onion rings arrives: "for the table," Tony explains, glancing up from the menu to the door, his searching face in close-up as Journey singer, Steve Perry, is cut off mid-chorus:

Don't stop—

The scene cuts to black, and the only sound we hear is the tinkling of the diner's doorbell as the door is pushed open. A full ten seconds of silence pass before the end credits appear.

Like the shirt button conversation that opens and closes *Seinfeld*, this diner scene has the feel of an absurd and elaborate joke. The build-up of tension is extraordinary. We expect either brutal violence or some sort of a cathartic breakthrough, but are given neither. After eight years of rich storylines and complex characters the likes of which television had not

FIGURE 4.1 Family dinner. *The Sopranos*, HBO

seen before, *The Sopranos* ended with a shrug rather than a bang. Public debate raged over the days and weeks that followed. Was it a tease to a long-rumored feature film, a cruel hoax, or a sincere affirmation of the notion that, despite our efforts to make meaningful stories, life simply continues, whether on a path to tragedy, comedy, or some other ultimate state? The wide variety of responses should come as little surprise since *The Sopranos* audience was actually two overlapping audiences: those who watched for the sex and violence, and those who marveled at the thoughtful deconstruction of the postmodern gangster. For the first group, the ending surely felt like a sharp stick in the eye, or at very least a cheat. But for the latter, it might have seemed a fairly consistent, if not entirely satisfying way to conclude their relationship with the world of the story. After all, the show had been confounding viewer expectations from the start: undercutting character sympathy with deliberate acts of cruelty; killing off beloved characters; rarely tying up loose ends; and generally treating its moral compass like the spinner in a game of Twister.

HBO is famous for its controversial endings, which frustrate familiar expectations of satisfying closure. Viewers of *Sex and the City* were equally divided (sometimes within themselves) about whether to celebrate Carrie's reunion with Mr Big in the series finale, or to condemn her for making the all-too-common mistake of settling for a man unworthy of her. *The Wire* bowed out after five seasons of painting the richest, most complex picture of American society ever attempted on television, with a morally simplistic montage of the victors and victims in post-industrial Baltimore, which is clearly meant to underscore the theme that the powerful get stronger on the backs of the weak. The Mormon polygamist drama, *Big Love*, ended with a seemingly naive affirmation of the faith and the choices of its main characters—Bill, Barb, Nicolette, and Margene Hendrickson—after years of subjecting that faith to every soap opera convention one could imagine. The psychotherapy sessions that gave structure to *In Treatment* ended when therapist Paul Weston's doubts about the efficacy of therapy compelled him to quit the profession, so forcing the viewer to ask whether the three seasons of "work" (as Weston calls therapy) have been a waste of time. And David Milch went still further with the frontier saga, *Deadwood*, and "surf noir" drama, *John from Cincinnati*, abruptly pulling the plug on the former to make room for the latter, only to have it die an early, and to the few who watched, perhaps inscrutable death. Meanwhile, the creators of such series as the Depression-are horror-fantasy, *Carnivale*, and historical drama, *Rome*, were forced to compress plotlines and abandon loose ends following premature cancellation.

Millennia of stories have taught us to mistake endings for meaningful conclusions, rather than mere stopping points. The assumption being that the accrued significance of a story can only be fully realized in its resolution. Hence our mixture of surprise and self-satisfaction when the detective reveals the answer to the mystery we imagine our part in calculating, and our joy and/or grief when any hero with whom we identify either achieves or falls short of an ultimate goal. Endings offer assurances that meaningful continuity is possible, in fiction if not in life, and that our intellectual and emotional investments will pay off. True love endures, faith is tangibly rewarded, and if justice is not always served, it is always to be striven for. While it is true that literature and film are filled with examples of stories that end with a head scratch or a shrug, from *Waiting for Godot* to *The Graduate*, television drama has been far more conservative, because it has traditionally used mounting suspense and satisfying resolutions to hold audience attention and reward viewer loyalty. Of course, there have been exceptions, especially in the realms of fantasy and supernatural mystery. American series such as *Twin Peaks*, *The X-Files* and *Buffy the Vampire Slayer*—to say nothing of the rich British dramas of Dennis Potter (*Pennies from Heaven*; *The Singing Detective*)—were trading in narrative traps and loose ends long before the lights went out on the Soprano family. But unlike the HBO series and despite a few abandoned storylines, each of these other series *did* eventually satisfy audience hopes for wisdom, for knowledge, and for resolution.

HBO series rarely reward such hopes. With few exceptions, they are grounded in an all-too-familiar reality, where characters are frequently confronted with the certain truth underlying that reality: that "real" life, even in the telling, is filled with loose ends. Lives intersect, characters come and go, and plans fail far more frequently than they bear fruit. A headshot Russian mobster disappears into the snowy woods in a third season episode of *The Sopranos* ("Pine Barrens," 3:11), and we never forget that he may one day reappear to make trouble for Tony. But we also know that he will not appear riding an alien spacecraft or wielding Thor's hammer. He is just another man, just another problem among many that Tony faces, neither inconsequential nor inconceivable.

Sometimes, supernatural elements *do* emerge in HBO series, such as *True Blood*'s vampires, or *Game of Thrones*' dragons. But even then, they reflect the socio-political commentary of the story. In *True Blood*, vampires are meant to evoke fear of the exotic and alien (the show has been used as a metaphor for racism, homophobia, and nativism); in *Game of the Thrones*, the dragons stand for the forces that challenge human will and ambition (climate change and other forces of nature, for example). They are not objects of fantasy, escapist alternatives to our own world of dangers and conflicts, but more and bigger problems requiring, and typically confounding, old solutions. The message is plain: simply slaying vampires and dragons does not end these dangers and conflicts. We must learn to adapt to the changing conditions of our world.

Even when we see ourselves as agents of that change. At the end of the fourth season of *Big Love*, polygamist Bill Hendrickson is elected to the Utah state Senate, and in the series finale he successfully introduces a bill to decriminalize polygamy. This personal triumph is followed by an even greater one, when Bill receives a prophetic vision during Easter Sunday services at his recently founded Church of the New Pioneers. But upon returning home, and immediately after scribbling this vision onto the pages of a yellow legal pad, he is shot to death by a desperate neighbor jealous of Bill's success.

It is a fittingly realistic debasement of the martyrdom of the Church of Latter Day Saints' founder Joseph Smith, who we are reminded earlier received the teachings of the Church on golden tablets inscribed by the angel Moroni, and who died at the hands of an angry mob that saw his

FIGURE 4.2 The prophet? *Big Love*, HBO

1844 candidacy for President of the United States as a conspiracy to transform the nation into a polygamous theocracy.

Not all ambitions are quite as lofty as Joseph Smith's and Bill Hendrickson's, but all are met with violence. In Smith's case, that violence only elevated his religious status. But what about vengeance-seeking drug dealer Omar Little, from HBO's *The Wire*, who rose to the position of mythic hero by robbing and gunning down rival dealers, only to be shot in the back of the head by a kid while buying cigarettes at a corner store? Like so many agents and victims of gangland violence, he did not see the bullet coming, and his death—though deeply grieved by fans of the show—changed nothing. In the end he is just another dead black man from West Baltimore, whose murder does not even warrant mention in the local papers. But that's the way it is for characters caught in the harsh realities of the HBO dramatic series. As Omar himself would say, "All in the game, yo."

Everybody's waiting

HBO's best series are built on a sort of narrative entropy. Tony Soprano enters therapy in the pilot episode of *The Sopranos* claiming that he has "come in at the end" of the long and storied history of the American mafia, and the series traces the inevitable unraveling of the New Jersey mob; *The Wire* tracks the decay of an American city at every level; the 1930s rural American setting of *Carnivale* is presented in its opening monologue as the fearsome end of the age of magic; *Deadwood* offers a bloody elegy to the closing of the American frontier; *Oz* slams the barred gate on the reformation of the American penal system; and even seemingly jingo-istic miniseries like *Band of Brothers* and *John Adams* are finally about America's lost innocence, and the heavy personal costs of liberty. Phrases like "triumph of the human spirit" rarely come to mind while watching HBO dramas, or the many shows the network has influenced: such as *The Shield*, which maps the inevitable consequences of police corruption, and ends with its main character being stripped of all human comfort, morality, or purpose; or *Mad Men*, which contrasts Don Draper's successes in the advertising business with an existential identity crisis that makes him increasingly erratic and distant; or *Rescue Me*, which observes the emotional decline of a New York City fireman haunted by ghosts of 9/11.

Nowhere is this fatalism more apparent than in Alan Ball's acclaimed HBO funeral home drama, *Six Feet Under*. The tagline from its fifth and final season, "Everything. Everyone. Everywhere. Ends." might serve as a summary statement for the program itself, and for HBO dramatic programming in general. The pilot episode begins with the death of the Fisher family patriarch, Nathaniel Sr, and all but the series finale dramatize the death of a soon-to-be client of the Fisher funeral home. Over the course of the series—particularly in that final episode—we also bear witness to the deaths of every one of the main characters. If the over-arching theme of *Six Feet Under* is that "everything ends," what sustains it for five seasons is the principle that meaning (or what makes meaning impossible or inscrutable) is tied up in irresolvable, or unending conflicts. As with most stories, the characters in the series attempt to grow and change while the world and their obligations to it shift beneath their feet. And in the course of doing so, they come to learn important things about themselves, particularly about their propensities for self-destructive behaviors. What binds the surviving Fishers—the children Claire, David, Nate, and their mother Ruth—is the recognition that each is engaged in a very specific struggle to produce some form of meaningful resolution from this knowledge.

As the show's centerpiece, Nate Jr exemplifies the struggle. Nate's conflicts are laid out in his first scene in the pilot episode: an airport flirtation with then-stranger Brenda Chenowith. Part confession, part seduction, Nate's banter reveals his fear of commitment, his need to be loved, and his nascent spirituality. Over the course of the series, we will see the way that each of these elements plays out in relationships with a half-dozen women (two of whom he marries, but none of whom he loves), his family, and the family business (both of which he sees as confining and defining). Indeed, Nate's efforts to transcend the banality of middle age, where the rebellion of his youth has only led him to a dead-end job and an active but empty sex life, comprise the central narrative of the series. From the start, he is marked as the hero of the tale, whose choices in the face of adversity will lead to a meaningful transformation. But by the time Nate dies, two episodes short of the series finale, any notion that he has resolved his existential and spiritual issues is merely the delusion of those he has left behind. Lying in his hospital bed, recovering from a seizure, Nate tells his pregnant second wife, the very same Brenda, that they do not belong together, just moments before an undetected aneurysm kills him. Though the turn of events is shocking, his revelation is hardly profound, as it echoes precisely what he told her the first time they met and had sex in the airport bathroom.

Nate is one of many HBO characters embarking on a mid-life crisis of sorts in shows like *The Sopranos, Big Love, In Treatment,* and *Hung,* who strive to make meaning in their lives by reconciling their earlier failures with a nagging sense of their own diminution and mortality. This crisis is the reason for Tony Soprano's panic attacks, Bill Hendrickson's political ambitions, Paul Weston's blinding passion for a young patient, and Ray Drecker's decision to become a male prostitute. In a media environment that has become increasingly youth-oriented, where untold resources are invested in *Transformers* and *Twilight* franchises and movies geared to an adult audience often struggle to find distribution, HBO has, until recently, been one of the few places on television where the subject of aging has not been reduced to a series of one-liners in a sitcom, or the eccentric grumblings of a lovably-gruff detective, doctor, or lawyer in a primetime drama. Though historically the number of television characters in the 35–44 age group is exceeded only by those in the 20–34 group,[1] they have traditionally been rendered as stereotypes: the socially and emotionally stable spouses, parents, and professionals that anchor stories, rather than the engines of their own dramas. That is, until the recent spate of characters like Walter White (*Breaking Bad*), Hank Moody (*Californication*), Don Draper (*Mad Men*), Adam Braverman (*Parenthood*), and Terry Elliot (*Men of a Certain Age*): all of whom meet the harbingers of age and mortality—illness, despair, economic crisis, emotional detachment—with increasingly bold and perverse choices, as though aging itself were merely the by-product of a failure to act. And it isn't just the men. Since *Sex and the City* first spoke to the problems of sexually liberated urban women in their 30s and 40s, television has been offering far more complex and dramatically volatile female characters whose ages exceed those traditionally associated with marriage and child rearing: women like Patty Hewes (*Damages*), Brenda Johnson (*The Closer*), Nancy Botwin (*Weeds*), and Alicia Florrick (*The Good Wife*), who are driven not only by personal and professional ambition, but a profound sense of loss: of youth, opportunity, promise, and ideals.

In *Six Feet Under*, Nate Jr and Brenda's bond is predicated upon a more acute sense of loss. Nate Sr's death brings them together, and fresh tragedies—including the deaths of Brenda's father and Nate Jr's first wife, Lisa—sustain that relationship. From the beginning, their lives—indeed, the lives of all of the show's characters—are held together not by love or custom, but by grief: the engine of countless stories, dating at least as far back as *The Epic of Gilgamesh*. But if grief has inspired innumerable acts of literary heroism—from Achilles' revenge to Harry Potter's rebirth—in *Six Feet Under* it is merely the condition under which characters operate, and arguably the only condition that resolves itself over the course of the series. We are accustomed to seeing television characters grieve. In many cases, grief is simply a shorthand way of creating empathy, as in the countless saccharine deaths of *Touched by an Angel*, or Izzie Stevens' overwrought response to Denny Duquette's passing in *Grey's Anatomy*. In other cases, it can serve as a moment of profound meditation on the fragility of life, such as the grief that follows the deaths of Lt. Col. Henry Blake in *M*A*S*H* and Buffy's mother in *Buffy the Vampire Slayer*. In these examples, the grief is sudden, and short-lived, and it strengthens the bonds between survivors. But *Six Feet Under* grieves for five seasons, and grief is often the only thing its characters share in common. It is the sort of psychosocial bond that cannot last, like the loyalty of the corrupt cop conspirators in *The Shield* or the trust of Walter and Skyler White in *Breaking Bad*. As the object of grief/loyalty/trust recedes, so does the need for connection.

If *Six Feet Under* begins with the sudden death of Nate Sr.—a death that throws all of the characters into a state of crisis—it climaxes with Nate Jr's. This fresh grief brings the now-chronic existential crises of David, Brenda, Ruth, and Claire into hard focus, and they respond in precisely the way we expect fictional characters to react: they move on, which is another way of saying that they attempt to learn from the past by eradicating it. David and his lover, Keith, turn the antiquated funeral parlor into a postmodern dwelling; Ruth drops her patrician *façade* and reinvents herself as a quasi-hippie dog-walker; her schizophrenic husband George is improbably restored to mental health; Brenda forgives Nate his many failings; and Claire wrecks the old green hearse left her by her father, buys a new Toyota Prius with trust fund money (also left her by her father), and leaves Los Angeles for New York.

In the penultimate scene of the final episode, titled "Everybody's Waiting" (5:12), all concerned parties gather around a strange dinner table in David and Keith's strange new home to toast Nate Jr, thus officially ending the period of mourning his death. It is a tender, if sentimentalized moment of half-shared memories and small gestures of reconciliation between clan members, which might serve as the resolution to countless domestic melodramas. Yet the moment seems oddly out of place in a series where the deaths of other primary characters have had such cataclysmic effects. Though it took five seasons to mourn Nate Jr's father and one and a half to make some sense of the loss of his first wife, Lisa, the terrible feelings stirred up in others by his tragic passing appear entirely resolved within two episodes.

Whatever the impact of the dinner table scene, it is nothing compared to what follows. In the series' final sequence, Claire travels the highways of America in her Prius, while a fetishistic montage of, again touching, but no less clichéd tableaux of union and death unfolds, perhaps in Claire's own mind's eye. In each the characters' deaths are dramatized and dated, beginning with Ruth's 20 years into the future, and ending with Claire's own 60 years later, at age 97. This closing montage is an extraordinary reversal of the "you know not the hour" theme under-lying all other deaths in the series, which many critics and fans of the show read as an affirmation of memory and the preciousness of life. As the life force leaves them, Ruth and David are reunited with their lost loves—Ruth's two Nates and David's Keith—who appear in the forms of idealized memory images. And as Claire lies on her deathbed, she stares through cataracts at her own photos of the great loves of her life.

One cannot help but be moved by the tender longing in Ruth's, David's, and Claire's clouded eyes. Yet by effectively wiping the Fisher clan off of the face of the earth, the sequence appears to undermine every one of the series' presumed lessons about character, human nature, faith, love, destiny—you name it—by resolving all conflict, all character, all

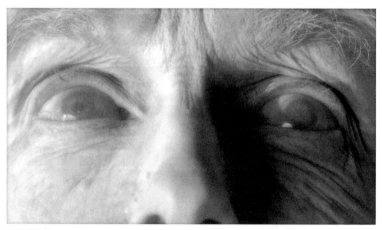

FIGURE 4.3 Claire Fisher's dying gaze. *Six Feet Under*, HBO

meaning in an act of narrative entropy. Like many narratives, the drama of *Six Feet Under* is circumscribed by a movement toward death. Most stories use death as a source of meaning: death as entry into eternal life, as sacrifice for the greater good, as a welcome release or a dirty trick. But for the Fishers, whose profession teaches them to mask all death in significance, it is finally revealed to be nothing more than a fading from view. As the fiction ends, they cease to exist anywhere but in the mind's eye of the audience.

In traditional narrative, "endings" are not about the cessation of being, but the end of being-as-one-was: once in a relationship, now single; once in turmoil, now at peace; once young and foolish, now older and wiser, etc. The preceding story is about a hero facing obstacles, which force him to make choices that transform his sense of the world and himself. What we call the "climactic action"—the final irreversible choice that necessarily leads to the resolution or "ending" of the story—is really a beginning, a coming-into-being or self-actualization. For even when the hero sacrifices himself, he does so to enact the destiny of his "true" self and to effect change upon the world he leaves behind. In *Casablanca*, Rick chooses to send Ilsa off with Lazlo, and to fight the Nazis, so bringing 'closure' to their love affair in Paris, bolstering the anti-fascist cause, and effectively leading America into the war (the events of the story occur in the days before the attack on Pearl Harbor). The ending is the beginning of a global engagement and "a beautiful friendship" between Rick and the former Prefect of Police, who stand for America and France: the two nations responsible for bringing democracy to the modern world.

A grand commencement, indeed, but nothing compared to *Six Feet Under*'s narrative ambitions. The genius of the show is that its setting demands characters contemplate profound metaphysical and ontological questions, particularly those having to do with death: what it means, why characters fear it, how it transforms and transcends each character's idea of him- or herself. Though television narrative frequently uses death—by natural causes, disease, violent crime, etc.—as a plot device, only recently has it become the subject of philosophical speculation. Comedies like *Reaper* and *Dead Like Me* intersperse gallows humor with moments of genuine mortal angst. The hero mythology of *Lost*, with its stories of self-sacrifice and romantic longing, treats death as a subjective space for confronting our personal truths, successes, and failures. The island itself is a sort of death. *The Walking Dead* uses the conventions of the zombie narrative to speculate on the limits of human society. *Dexter*'s psychopathic serial killer—played by Michael C. Hall, the actor who brought David Fisher to life—reflects on the tragic absence of an emotional life between ritual acts of murder, weaving together threads of horror and elegy from memories of his mother's and wife's brutal murders, and the ghostly memory of his father/mentor. Though there are still plenty of television programs that use death as little more than a puzzle piece—police procedurals, hospital dramas, forensics shows—even these genres are not immune to morbid speculation, and most spotlight at least one character haunted by ghosts of the past, or openly grieving a lost loved one: Dr Cameron in *House*, Stan and Mitch Larsen in *The Killing*, Adrian Monk in *Monk*. For these characters, death is both a call to action and the backdrop against which their perceptions are shaped.

The ghost of Nate Sr, who to some extent "haunts" all members of the Fisher family, is the through-line of his family's grief. He not only represents the past that none is yet ready to leave behind, but serves as an avatar of each character's unspoken fears: for Ruth, fear of loneliness; for Nate, fear of meaninglessness; for David, fear of exposure; for Claire, fear that she may not have the talent she presumes. Nate Sr, or the version that each constructs from memory, has passed beyond the point of biological inevitability and returned to share a few pearls of wisdom about life being wasted on the living, and the need to embrace life's "infinite possibilities," rather than whining about lost opportunities. None is more drawn to this ethic than Nate Jr, a directionless bon-vivant-wannabe forced to acknowledge his failed ambitions while still clinging to the possibility of discovering a better self. Each morning he jogs: an act of self-discipline, meditation, and stress release that allows him to recover his balance and optimism. NBC's *Parenthood* makes an ironic allusion to this ritual in its pilot episode, when Peter Krause—the actor who plays Adam Braverman in that series and Nate Jr in *Six Feet Under*—is seen attempting a morning run in a facsimile of Nate's workout clothes. But he is older now, father of two children and emotional anchor for a sprawling, extended family attempting to dig themselves out from under their own failings. After barely making it a block, he turns back. But rather than returning home to the simmering quiet of the Fisher funeral home, his own house in *Parenthood* is in a state of chaos, with a teenaged daughter rebelling against parental authority, an autistic son climbing the walls, and a high-strung wife demanding emotional support. It is precisely the sort of scene that would send Nate Jr heading for the hills.

Not that Nate is an unsympathetic character. On the contrary, he manages to turn failures into pithy life lessons by imbuing them with a sense of grand purpose and hope. When a funeral home patron asks him why people have to die, he responds, "To make life important. None of us know how long we've got. Which is why we have to make each day matter." But like his father, Nate Jr has a hard time practicing what he preaches. When his wife, Lisa, dies in Season Three he all but abandons their daughter, Maya, to what he sees more and more as a chaotic, if not malign, universe. At his lowest moments, Nate Jr seems to share Senior's sentiment that life is little more than a cruel joke. While staring at his father's corpse in the pilot episode, Nate Jr has his first encounter with the old man's ghost. Nate Sr mocks him, calling him the "prodigal":

> This is what you've been running away from your whole life, buddy boy. Scared the crap out of you when you were growing up, didn't it? And you thought you'd escape. Well guess what? Nobody escapes. (1:01)

Indeed, even television characters must face their inevitable obsolescence, the time when their dramas come to an end, and their choices cease to create meaning. Where goeth Chandler and Joey (*Friends*)? Who will take over Norm's barstool (*Cheers*)? What will George and Jerry do once they are released from jail (*Seinfeld*)? When will Carrie and Mr Big call it quits (*Sex and the City*)? Who will shoot the guy who shot the guy who shot J.R. (*Dallas*)? These are insignificant questions in the grand scheme of things, because we have seen the characters make far more meaningful choices. Series end—with quips, with tears, with pithy sentiments—and invite the viewer to imagine better lives ahead for the characters they have grown to care about. But if we are honest, we finally have to agree with *Six Feet Under's* Brenda that, at least where fictional characters are concerned, "the future is just a fucking concept we use to avoid living today."

A tradition of quality

An entire school of popular criticism has grown up around the notion of "grieving" the loss of fictional characters like Harry Potter and Sherlock

Holmes, to deal with the terrible fact that, despite any meaning we may draw from their lives and actions, their stories do finally come to an end. This sense of loss is felt particularly strongly with characters from literary serials because our commitment of time and attention only increases our strong bonds of identification. They seem to have fully lived in our imaginations, and whether or not they actually die in their own stories, the termination of those stories is cause for grief.

Until recently, television has largely stood outside of such a consideration. To understand why, we must first delve into how television tells stories. Television series fall into two broad, though frequently overlapping categories: episodic and serial. An episodic program is built upon a set of recurring characters and narrative situations, though the events from one episode have no essential bearing on or connection to the next. Take, for example, *Law & Order* or *CSI*. Though characters come and go, and all but the central setting (the lab, the police precinct) may change from one episode to the next, no backstory is necessary to jump in at virtually any time, and episodes can easily "stand alone." Serial narratives, on the other hand, extend their stories over multiple episodes, sometimes multiple seasons and entire series. Though they typically offer single-episode storylines for viewers' immediate gratification, they require regular viewing in order to reveal their larger meanings or resolve any ongoing problems or mysteries. Imagine, for example, trying to decode the closing scenes of *Lost* without having seen the rest of the series.

Television networks have traditionally shied away from serials because of their potential to alienate viewers unwilling or unable to stay current with a program's story. From the 1950s to the 1980s, soap operas were the primary vehicle for long-form television narrative, with stories that might stretch across decades, even generations (the longest-running drama in history, *Guiding Light*, ran continuously for 72 years: the first 15 on radio). But while soaps might follow the same characters or storylines for many years, they are essentially episodic and open-ended, offering variations on the same plot points, and shunning resolution for passing intrigues. Serials, on the other hand, are largely defined by change and the promise of long-term resolution.

There is another reason networks so long shied away from serials: given the unpredictable nature of television—the unexpected hits and cancellations—one has to adapt imagined complications and resolutions to ratings realities. A story intended for, say, 50 one-hour episodes might be cancelled after only five, or become so popular as to require 150. Though premium subscription networks like HBO and Showtime might have more latitude in this area (since they sell a service, not individual programs), broadcasters historically saw little reason to take the risk.

That attitude began changing in the 1970s, when networks started the practice of compiling viewer numbers based not only on audience size, but socio-economic demographics. Recognizing that they could attract higher-value advertisers to programs that appealed to the most desirable group—affluent, educated 18–49 year olds—they began to offer more sophisticated programming, primarily in the form of socially conscious sitcoms like *The Mary Tyler Moore Show* and *All in the Family*. But the so-called "quality demographic" would become particularly prized following the cable/satellite explosion of the late 1970s and early 1980s, since the available audience was now being spread across a much broader channel spectrum, which included broadcast networks, basic cable channels, and premium services. To attract the "quality demographic"—for which advertisers were willing to pay as much as four times the standard rate—networks started thinking big. The enormous ratings successes of miniseries like *Rich Man, Poor Man* (1977), *Roots* (1977), *Holocaust* (1978), *Shogun* (1980), and *The Winds of War* (1983) reflected a growing appetite for long-form television narrative (the production of these miniseries was due in large part to the popularity of earlier British ones, such as *The Six Wives of Henry VIII* [1970] and *I, Claudius* [1976], which aired in America on PBS). So beginning with *Hill Street Blues* in 1981, networks made significant investments in serial narratives that played off of conventional television genres such as the police procedural (*Cagney and Lacey*), the medical drama (*St Elsewhere*), and legal drama (*L.A. Law*), with programs that offered topical themes (corruption, gender identity, AIDS), morally ambivalent characters (*Blues'* Lt. Frank Furillo; *Law's* attorney Arnie Becker), and overlapping storylines woven together with a complex but evolving coherence that stood in stark contrast to the sensationalistic plots of the other popular serials of the time: primetime soap operas such as *Dallas* and *Dynasty*.

Though the shows did not always do well in the overall ratings (*Hill Street Blues* fared particularly poorly in its first season), they not only attracted the attention of the "quality demographic," but piqued the interest of critics, who fell over themselves to praise many of these new series, and avid fans, who sometimes became vocal advocates for beloved programs in danger of cancellation. The most visible of these advocacy groups was Viewers for Quality Television (VQT), founded in 1984 by Dorothy Swanson, with the sole purpose of saving *Cagney and Lacey* from cancellation. After resurrecting that series, VQT went on to advocate for several other programs, including *St Elsewhere*, *Designing Women* and *Sports Night*. At its peak, VQT would have 5,000 national members.[2] As the cultural capital of these series increased, many became "appointment television" for a rapidly expanding community of discerning viewers. Critics came to refer to this particular strain of programming as "quality" television for its rich story worlds, unique visual styles, and strong writing. *Hill Street Blues*, for example, drew praise for its "multiple centers of audience identification; complicated personal lives; overlapping dialogue; hand-held camera shots; [and] busy, crowded *mise-en-scènes*."[3]

By the 1990s, "quality" television had become both a branding strategy and a remarkable creative opportunity for saavy networks and writer/producers like Steven Bochco (*Hill Street Blues*, *L.A. Law*, *Murder One*, *NYPD Blue*), James L. Brooks (*Taxi*, *Lou Grant*, *The Simpsons*), and Joshua Brand and John Falsey (*St Elsewhere*, *I'll Fly Away*, *Northern Exposure*). Popular shows such as *ER*, *Chicago Hope* and *The Practice* picked up where *St Elsewhere* and *L.A. Law* left off, and *NYPD Blue* and *Homicide: Life on the Street* took the gritty realism of *Hill Street Blues* to a new level of explicit brutality, while sharpening the storytelling skills of two future HBO masters, David Milch, and David Simon (both of whom wrote for the series). With *Twin Peaks*, ABC allowed filmmaker David Lynch and *Hill Street Blues* alum Mark Frost an opportunity to mash up the conventions of the detective story, horror, melodrama, thriller, exploitation, and screwball comedy into a remarkably rich, at times convoluted analysis of the nature of evil. FOX Network took on the paranormal with the *The X-Files*. And the WB Network deconstructed the vampire myth with *Buffy the Vampire Slayer* and race, religion, and politics with the sci-fi space opera, *Babylon 5*. From top-ten Nielsen ratings to cult fandom, each of these shows garnered devoted audiences drawn to their rich story worlds, well-developed characters, and increasingly complex plots.

Beginning in the late 1990s, HBO would extend these trends with a string of programs that would push the boundaries of genre, turning the high drama and moral platitudes of the gangster narrative on end (*The Sopranos*), recasting the domestic melodrama in a dysfunctional funeral home (*Six Feet Under*), using the Western frontier myth as a metaphor for unchecked capitalism (*Deadwood*), pulling on every loose thread of the social problem drama (*Oz*, *The Wire*), and turning the monsters of horror into fanged politicians, hustlers and dead-end losers stuck in eternal lives of quiet desperation (*True Blood*). To achieve these ends, they would draw on talent with a pedigree in "quality" television. Their breakthrough series, *Oz*, was the brainchild of highly successful director/producer Barry Levinson (*Diner*, *The Natural*, *Rain Man*) and writer Tom Fontana (*St Elsewhere*), who had worked together on *Homicide: Life on the Street*. David Chase had helmed *I'll Fly Away* and two seasons of *Northern Exposure* before bringing *The Sopranos* to HBO. Alan Ball had produced *Cybill* and won multiple awards for his *American Beauty* screenplay prior to developing *Six Feet Under*. Robert Colesbury interrupted a Hollywood producing career that included films like *The King of Comedy* and *Mississippi Burning* to join former *Baltimore Sun* writer and best-selling *Homicide* author, David Simon, to make *The Corner* and *The Wire* for HBO. And prior to *Deadwood*, David Milch had honed his craft on *Hill St Blues* and *NYPD Blue*.

As a premium service, HBO took creative advantage of its lack of content restrictions, injecting liberal doses of profanity, sex, and violence into these series. Though obscenity standards had begun shifting in American television long before *Oz*'s first prison rape scene aired in 1997, HBO transformed the way we think about the uses of "graphic" content. Take, for example, the language of *Deadwood*. No one outside of the series has ever spoken in precisely the same manner as its characters. But Milch has long claimed that the series' singular style of dialogue is only meant to mimic the *effect* of frontier speech on the nineteenth-century ear, by mixing profanities with the highly mannered syntax of the "civilizing" forces pressing in on the town (represented expressly in the well-spoken widow, Alma Garrett). Critics often refer to *Deadwood*'s dialogue as "Shakespearean," which sounds like shorthand for "archaic" and "poetic." But while Shakespeare wrote one form of dialogue for nobles (poetry) and one for commoners (prose), Milch employs contrived dialogue to reflect the class distinctions on the frontier. Similarly, in *The Sopranos* mobsters mix obscenities with malapropisms ("She's an albacore around my neck"; "the Reverend Rodney King Jr.") in a way that makes them seem at once ridiculous, banal and truly horrifying. This is especially true when—as in so many cases—the characters' inability to express themselves verbally leads them to act in violent, anti-social ways. In any case, obscenities are used to enrich our sense of characters like Al Swearengen and Tony Soprano, while also making them true to life.

HBO series deal similarly with sex. In Al's and Tony's worlds, women are sexually objectified and brutalized by a grinding patriarchy. But rather than dwelling upon platitudes about dead-eyed victims of serial abuse or hookers with hearts of gold, *Deadwood* and *The Sopranos* present their female characters as fierce in their vulnerability, demanding to their peril, and capable of great enterprise. And when it comes to violence, HBO series have shown a particular talent for force-feeding an audience's bloodlust. Given our taste for gladiatorial entertainments like professional wrestling and mixed martial arts, it should come as little surprise that one of the highest rated episodes of *Deadwood* ("The Two-Headed Beast," 3:5) features a five minute bare-fisted, head-bashing, ear-biting, puddle-drowning, hair-pulling, eye-gouging single combat. Or that the scene of Tony beating Ralph Cifaretto to death with a hot frying pan and a cold tile floor ("Whoever Did This," 4:9) remains one of the most talked-about in the history of *The Sopranos*. But these scenes are completely devoid of spectacle: no long speeches, no swelling music, no chanting from onlookers, only mounting agony and exhaustion as a battle of wills quickly devolves into a animalistic grasping for life.

"Bold," "uncompromising," and "provocative" are words one often hears in HBO's advertising copy, as well as critical assessments of their programming. "Authentic" is another, connoting an attention to details of setting, character and story meant to create a sense of familiarity. We see it in the mud and blood of *Deadwood*'s Main Street, the tacky McMansions of *The Sopranos'* suburban New Jersey, the abandoned

FIGURE 4.4 A battle of wills. *Deadwood*, HBO

furniture and clotheslines in the courtyards of the Baltimore housing projects of *The Wire*, and the frostbitten faces of the Men of the Night Watch who guard Westeros' Wall in *Game of Thrones*. And we see it in the powerful sense of place these details help to evoke: towns, cities, civilizations with their own unique character and culture. Whether real or imagined spaces, they are places we find not only on a map, but in the nuances of "insider" knowledge that make it easy for viewers to confuse the real with the fictional worlds. Though few would ever want to live in the Western District row houses of *The Wire* or the Grand Central Hotel of *Deadwood*, we feel as though we have visited these places, just as we do the South Central Los Angeles of FX's *The Shield*, the Albuquerque of AMC's *Breaking Bad*, and the South Central Los Angeles of NBC's/TNT's *Southland*.

Beyond mere setting, "authenticity" is captured through HBO's series characters. With a mix of sympathy and disgust, we recognize the outlines of Tony Soprano's existential dread in his ruthlessness, or the orphan's trauma at the core of Al Swearengen's unconscionable avarice. Neither of the two are villains (whose intentions are entirely evil) nor are they anti-heroes (who are self-serving, but end up benefiting the greater good). They become "ordinary," and so more familiar men, like the Vic Mackeys (*The Shield*), Don Drapers (*Mad Men*), Walter Whites (*Breaking Bad*), and Christian Troys (*Nip/Tuck*) that would follow.

"Authenticity" also expresses itself in labyrinthine, often unresolved plots. Stories don't just "happen": as in life, they are set in motion by the untidy, sometimes unpredictable, often sprawling consequences of characters' actions. And those consequences nearly always have larger real-world implications. What does our history tell us about our national character? What do we want from our police force and prison system? Where does the criminal end and the legitimate begin? In an oft-noted example from the first season of *The Sopranos*, Tony points out that the nefarious and un-prosecuted deeds of chemical companies who dump "all this shit into the rivers" make mob activities seem small by comparison ("Down Neck," 1:7). Even HBO fantasy series eschew the escapism that defines the genre to focus upon real-world issues. *True Blood* and *Thrones* emphasize the political and personal over the mythical and eternal. Though magical powers exist in both *True Blood* and *Game of Thrones*, they are merely elements of a violent, cruel battle between the brutal, the depraved, and the hopelessly lost. They become part of a larger critique of human nature. Mythical beings and magical powers serve to amplify that critique, where in typical fantasy they offer an escapist alternative to "the way we live now."

A long story

That last phrase comes from the 1875 novel of the same name by Anthony Trollope, perhaps his harshest satire on the avarice of so-called "civilized men." I mention him here to offer a bridge to another concept often associated with "quality" television in general, and HBO programming specifically: its "literary" attributes. Critics of *The Sopranos* often refer to it reverently as having the characteristics of a novel (its length and complexity, its combination of epic and intimate scale, its focus upon character development), and as a matter of course, reviews of *The Wire* make off-handed comparisons between its grand deconstruction of the modern American city and Honore de Balzac's efforts to paint a complete picture of nineteenth-century French society in his massive *Comedie Humaine* (the show's creator, David Simon, was among the first to refer to *The Wire* as a "visual novel"). Calling a television program "literary" is problematic in much the same way as assigning the term "cinematic" to a work of literature. These expressions are almost always meant as praise, yet their underlying meanings remain elusive.

At one level, "literary" simply suggests that the narrative is easily adapted from one medium to another. Many of the popular and critically acclaimed broadcast miniseries of the 1970s and 1980s (*Roots, Shogun, The Winds of War, The Thorn Birds*) drew from works of literature, as had so many memorable installments of the celebrated anthology series from television's first Golden Age in the 1950s (*The Philco Television Playhouse*; *Kraft Television Theatre*; *Playhouse 90*), not to mention countless works for radio and film before them. The literary associations lent television legitimacy, first by demonstrating it's capacity to adapt itself to "high" culture, and second by inviting literary scholars to impose their critical perspectives on the programming. The programmers certainly understood the power of this association. For example, when NBC television bought the rights to the first two *Godfather* movies in 1977, they broadcast them as a miniseries, re-arranging the events of the two films into chronological order and re-titling the work, *The Godfather: A Novel for Television*. It was an enormous ratings hit.

Serial television owes a great debt to literary serials: in particular the Victorian novels of Trollope, William Thackeray, George Elliot, and most importantly Charles Dickens, who published nearly all of his novels (*David Copperfield, Oliver Twist, A Tale of Two Cities*) in bi-weekly and monthly magazine installments. Only later were they republished in book form. Of course, serial narrative is much older than Dickens, going back at least as far as the Homeric epics. But thanks to two important factors, Dickens was most responsible for transforming it into mass-market popular entertainment. The first was the invention of the steam press in the early nineteenth century, which made cheap printing possible. At the time, single- and multi-volume novels were prohibitively expensive, due to the cost of labor and materials associated with bookbinding. The steam press made low quality, mass-produced newspapers and magazines available to all. Before long, book publishers were exploiting these new media by bowdlerizing popular novels and licensing them to high-circulation magazines to be printed in installments. But while they were simply trying to leverage more profit from their back catalog, Dickens, who worked in the magazine trade, saw an opportunity to significantly expand his readership by developing narrative strategies uniquely suited to the periodical form. While still working in the scale of the novel, he wrote each installment as a distinct episode, with its own rising and falling action and resolution, punctuated by cliffhangers meant to entice readers back. His stories dealt with poverty, crime, and injustice, offering sympathetic characters and compelling dramatic turns that instantly appealed to readers.

Television serials have generally adopted the Dickensian model, combining episodic with serial narratives, creating imperfect but ultimately sympathetic characters, and evoking story worlds that offer complexity, continuity, and closure. This is particularly true of the "quality" network series of the 1980s and 1990s. Despite the multi-layered crises that might arise in the precinct houses, the hospitals, courtrooms, and bedrooms of these series, order would prevail, the damaged-but-ultimately-good would be rewarded, and the audience would be given their satisfaction in the end. Dickens might have easily adapted himself to the writers' rooms of *NYPD Blue* or *St Elsewhere*, finding humanity among the blood and violence, guiding our way through darkness of the world with glimpses of virtue and humor, and when all was said and done, giving us reason to hope for better.

In the early 1990s, then-HBO President and CEO Michael Fuchs made a deliberate attempt to brand the network as "playing the role of Dickens"[4] in American television by making "socially conscious" documentaries, miniseries, and feature films about issues such as AIDS (*Common Threads: Stories from the Quilt*, 1989; *And the Band Played On*, 1993), corporate malfeasance (*Dead Ahead: The Exxon Valdez Disaster*, 1992; *Barbarians at the Gate*, 1993), and "the chronic problems of the underclass" (*I Am a Promise: The Children of Stanton Elementary School*, 1992; *Gang Wars: Bangin' in Little Rock*, 1994). And indeed, several subsequent series feature characters who could broadly be defined as "Dickensian" (in particular, the "corner kids" in *The Wire*, who might have stepped out of a modern-day production of *Oliver Twist*). Still, it would be difficult to image Dickens penning an episode of *Oz*, or *The Sopranos*, or *The Wire*. Though rich in character and story, Dickens' work lacks the moral and narrative ambivalence of these later works. While the scale, duration, and episodic aspects of the Victorian serial allowed Dickens an opportunity to develop plot points and characters to a degree rarely before known in the novel, he took care to link even the smallest anecdote to the broader motifs and themes of his stories, and to link them back to the main narrative, amplifying rather than confusing the overall meaning of the text. Not so these HBO series, which dress themselves in familiar themes (crime, violence, poverty) and generic conventions (prison reformation or escape in *Oz*; the redemption or destruction of the gangster in *The Sopranos*; the righting of society's wrongs in *The Wire*), but ultimately upend them. Perhaps the cynicism of Trollope, or the relentless realism of Balzac would have better suited the HBO writers' room.

Joy DeLyria and Sean Michael Robinson make the contrast between Dickens and HBO particularly clear in their lovingly-constructed work of parody/ scholarship, *Down in the Hole*, which imagines HBO's *The Wire* as a long-lost serialized Victorian novel by Horatio Buxley Ogden (HBO). Richly illustrated by Robinson (under the pseudonym, "Baxter Black"), with pen-and-ink drawings meant to evoke the Victorian etchings of Dickens' collaborators, George Cruikshank and Hablot Knight Browne ("Phiz"), *Down in the Hole* makes this fictional leap into the past, partly to amplify the notion that *The Wire* was ahead of its time, and partly to reflect upon how our sense of story has changed and/or remains the same over time.

Here I want to focus primarily in the changes.

Though DeLyria and Robinson point out that both Dickens and *The Wire*'s fictional author, "Ogden," wrote in a manner "more complex,

FIGURE 4.5 Detectives McNulty and Moreland at work. *The Wire*, HBO

more psychologically and metaphorically contiguous"[5] than other story-tellers of their age, *The Wire* distinguishes itself, not only from Dickens' work but from any serial, by several factors. Primary among them is the grinding effect of its pacing and scale:

> [R]ather than providing the short burst of decisively circumscribed fiction so desired by his readership, his tangled narrative unspooled at a stately, at times seemingly glacial, pace…. Though lauded by a few critics, the general public found the initial installments slow and difficult to penetrate, while later installments required intimate knowledge of all the pieces that had come before.

Here DeLyria and Robinson play off of the commonly held, though increasingly challenged critical notion that complexity is a mark of quality, and that what makes a work of art "great" is often also what makes it "difficult to penetrate." Popular audiences tend to use a more affective standard: was I amused, moved, saddened, distracted? Moreover, unlike more traditional narratives, which lay out their main characters and conflicts at the outset, *The Wire* does not reveal itself all at once. It requires patience, and a willingness to adjust ones perspective:

FIGURE 4.6 The same scene, re-imagined. *Down in the Hole*, Powerhouse Books. (Illustration by Sean Michael Robinson)

To consume this story in small bits doled out over an extended time is to view a pointillist painting by looking at the dots…. [One] might stand back from a pointillist work; whereas the entirety of *The Wire* can only been seen after it has been consumed, a piece at a time.

As Detective Lester Freamon says, "All the pieces matter" ("The Wire," 1.6): not like puzzle pieces, which we assemble in the tacit assumption that a big picture will be revealed, but like the pieces of some enormous lumbering machine, whose movement can only be understood by contemplating each one of its parts. In the age of the DVD box set and On Demand video (two phenomena that HBO was instrumental in popularizing), the ability to see the whole is no longer impeded by a calendar built around single, weekly episodes and long gaps between seasons.[6] But despite being identified as the series that made popular the phenomenon of "binge viewing,"[7] DeLyria and Robinson warn against trying to take the series in all at once:

> To experience the story in its entirety, without breaks between sections, would be exhausting; one would perhaps miss the essence of what makes it great: the slow build of detail, the gradual and yet inevitable churning of the great wheel of the world.[8]

The "great wheel of the world" is *The Wire's* primary subject: what makes it turn, who benefits from its turning, and who is sacrificed to fuel its great engine. Or perhaps it is better to say that that "great wheel" is always in the background, and the *real* subjects of *The Wire* are the ostensible ones that define each of the five seasons of the series: the drug trade, labor unions, education, politics and the news media. *The Wire* is difficult to perceive in its entirety because it is actually a series of televisual novels, as its creator, David Simon describes it. It isn't one story but many, layered on top of each other. It is both "great" and "difficult" for precisely this reason. Truly great works often straddle the perceived line between critical and popular approbation, and the very best eradicate it entirely. Like so many great writers who were also successful (Shakespeare, Twain), Charles Dickens was able to balance the interests of art and entertainment, of profound human expression and commerce. But if Dickens' talent and reputation lay in his ability to bridge popular and literary tastes, the "genius" of Horatio B. Ogden's (and by extension, HBO's) *The Wire* lies in its "sheer size and scope," its "slow layering of complexity," and a "degree of realism and intricacy" to which no work of Dickens could ever compare.[9]

Scale is, of course, a key consideration when appraising the overall legacy of HBO. Though the sprawling narrative ambitions of series like *The Wire* and *Game of Thrones* can easily be mistaken for mere sprawl, HBO series relate stories with remarkable efficiency and rigor. The typical HBO drama runs 12 one-hour episodes per season, yet in that time one is likely to see as many or more plots and subplots played out as in any 22–plus-episode season of a broadcast series. This narrative density is due in large part to the way HBO episodes are structured. For example, the typical 44–minute broadcast drama is broken into four "acts" by commercial breaks, and each act requires a climax, resolution and cliff-hanger to bridge the breaks. So much energy is spent on maximizing dramatic impact around commercials that little is left to deepen the plot. In any given episode of *House, M.D.*, Dr House needs to misdiagnose, nearly kill, and then correctly diagnose a patient, leaving little room to pursue his ongoing personal story beyond predictable patterns of professional malfeasance and personal ruin. *24*'s anti-terrorist Jack Bauer has bombs to defuse and suspects to torture, making it difficult for him to be circumspect about his work or to develop meaningful relationships. But without the commercial intrusions imposing act breaks, HBO episodes allow for a full, unbroken hour to weave narrative threads together into a cohesive whole. Plot is enriched and complicated, rather than merely advanced. This is particularly evident in the early stages of storytelling. The pilot episode of *The Sopranos*, for example, introduces no fewer than 12 plotlines in its first 15 minutes without losing the viewer, thanks in large part to the clever use of Tony's psychotherapy session as an expository device.

Limiting the number of episodes per season also gives HBO the luxury of slowing down production. Though originally only a financial consideration, producers soon realized that shortened seasons offered two significant advantages. First, they could focus more on production values. One of the reasons HBO series like *The Sopranos* and *Game of Thrones* have such a distinctive, "cinematic" look is that directors of photography were given the luxury of time to consider how each scene would be shot, and to develop a unique stylistic grammar for each series. And unlike the typical broadcast series, which begins with an often cheaply-made pilot that, if picked up, serves as a template for what will become a fast-track production, HBO commits resources at the outset, developing and refining the style of each series over long periods of time, before a single episode has aired. This is especially apparent in *Boardwalk Empire*, which is to date the most expensive pilot episode ever shot—estimates range as high as $50m—because so much attention was taken in accurately reproducing the Atlantic City boardwalk of the 1920s. While other networks will occasionally stake enormous resources on an untested series (the *Terra Nova* pilot cost FOX $20m; the *Lost* pilot cost ABC $10m), HBO has made a habit of extravagant investment with series and miniseries like *The Pacific* ($20m per episode), *Band of Brothers* ($12.5m per episode) and *Rome* ($9m per episode).

Second, the shorter span of story time in a single season allows writers to focus more on long-form storytelling. As in British television series, which tend to run only a handful of episodes per season, one could reasonably expect viewers to remember something that happened in the beginning of the season and carry it through to the end. This is particularly important in a program like *The Wire*, which is notorious for inserting a scene or character early in a season, then not making its significance apparent until several episodes down the road. And as Dickens had learned a century and a half ago when readers nearly rioted in New York Harbor while waiting for the latest installment of *Our Mutual Friend*, there are tangible benefits to making audiences wait and leaving them wanting more. Nothing so stimulates the appetite as anticipation.

In recognition of these benefits, other networks now regularly use the short season model for their "prestige" productions, from budget-conscious basic cable networks like FX and AMC (*The Shield*, *Justified*, *Mad Men*, *Breaking Bad*, and *The Walking Dead* average 13 episodes per season) to well-heeled broadcast networks like Fox, ABC, and NBC (Joss Whedon's *Dollhouse* ran two seasons at 13 and 14 episodes, while *Lost* and *Heroes* each began with 24 per season, but soon settled into the mid-teens). Considering the critical—if not always popular—success of these programs, one could certainly make the case that, where quality is concerned, less is more.

A black hole

Of course, there is such a thing as too little. Too little information can make a story impossible to follow; too little conflict can make it dull; and too little of hope can make it a stone cold drag, at least for an audience brought up on happy endings. Which brings us back to DeLyria, Robinson, and *The Wire*. According to *Down in the Hole*, the other key impediment to the program's initial popularity was its "bleak moral outlook." Here they make ironic reference to contemporary values:

> Literature today is no longer concerned with morality the way it was in the nineteenth century. Unrelenting, bleak images of society are celebrated for their realism, as representations of humanity. And yet, we have very few images, representations, or new and challenging canon that captures the essential helplessness, the inevitable corruption, the deep-lying flaws of both society and humanity in the way *The Wire* does.

Here DeLyria and Robinson offer a neat summary of a key deficiency in contemporary social problem drama. We like stories of crime, corruption, serial killings, and so on, but only when they are presented as problems that we may solve, by apprehending the criminal, reforming the system, or scapegoating an individual or institution. In this familiar formula, lack of education, ambition, and stable family structure has transformed the inner city into a breeding ground for crime and addiction. But despite its liberal—even reformist—heart, *The Wire* shows us something significantly darker, more venal, and beyond any platitudes of reform: the failure of social programs like low-income housing projects, "No Child Left Behind," and the War on Drugs.

Perhaps *The Wire* went too far. Perhaps it was simply too dark, too authentic in the picture it paints of a decaying American city. According to David Simon, its primary influence was Humphrey Cobb's 1935 anti-war novel, *Paths of Glory*, and Stanley Kubrick's 1957 film adaptation, the basic themes of which Simon would identify in his "Foreward" to the 2010 Penguin Classic edition of Cobb's novel as "the essential triumph of institutions over individuals" and "the fundamental inhumanity of the 20th century."[10] Elsewhere, Simon compares the worldview of *The Wire* to classical tragedy, where "doomed" protagonists face "postmodern institutions" in place of Olympian gods, as opposed to HBO shows like *The Sopranos* and *Deadwood*, which "focus on the angst and machinations" of Tony Soprano and Al Swearengen.[11]

Considering the prevalence of irony and gallows humor in *The Wire*, perhaps it would be better to compare it to the tragicomedy of Samuel Beckett, who used laughter less to distance the audience from life's horrors than to acknowledge the futility of any other response. In *The Wire*, we laugh at sociopathic defense attorney Maurice Levy's complaint that clients have called him away from his wife's brisket because it so baldly expresses his indifference to his collusion in their crimes; or at cold-blooded stick-up man Omar Little announcing his presence to some soon-to-be victim by whistling "The Farmer and the Dell"/"A-Hunting We Will Go" because the murderous nursery rhyme calls up simultaneous images of Elmer Fudd and Mack the Knife[12]; or corrupt State Senator Clay Davis' trademark refrain, "Shiiiiiit," because we recognize the purr of a cheap hustler. Theirs is a world beyond heroes and villains, where evil is so commonplace that we note it with curiosity rather than shock, and where cold-blooded gangsters like Stringer Bell wear reading glasses, sip tea, and attend business classes at the local community college. When virtue does make its occasional appearance—in the principled stances of Detective Kima Greggs and the conscientious objections of "corner kids" like Wallace and Dukie—it is quickly swallowed up by the surrounding darkness.

Nowhere is this darkness more apparent than in the series' would-be central character, Detective Jimmy McNulty, who seems driven less by a sense of right and wrong than sheer boredom and an excess of cleverness. Some see him as too committed to the job: certainly his ex-wife, who divorces him because he neglects his family for work and other women, and his partner Bunk, who chastises him for "Giving a fuck when it's not your turn" (jumping ahead in the detective rotation by taking cases that would have been assigned to others). Jimmy is a good detective, but a bad cop, and a pretty reprehensible man. He is reckless, fueled by adrenaline, Jameson's Irish whiskey, and a fading charm that is often just enough to draw others into his quixotic projects. But his lack of a traditional hero's objective (to get the girl, save the day, take the bullet, etc.) also makes his actions seem unfocused, and so hard to fathom. This is particularly true in the fifth and final season of the series, when he concocts a phantom serial killer by planting evidence and re-arranging crime scenes in order to foment public fear, so to direct more of the city's dwindling resources into law enforcement. At one point, he even enlists the aid of Detective Freamon, who is willing to look past the moral and legal morass because he can funnel some of those resources into his investigation of Baltimore drug kingpin, Marlo Stanfield. But before long, the hoax is exposed. Faced with a bleak future—McNulty doing marine patrols, Freamon clerking in the evidence room—McNulty insists, "It was worth it." Then, after a pause, "Wasn't it?" ("-30-," 5.10).

Though Freamon responds sensibly that it "depends" upon whether the case against Stanfield will hold, McNulty seems to have already drifted past that point, to thinking about how to get himself out of this particular jam. In the end, he chooses early retirement, the case against Stanfield falls apart, and the balance of power in Baltimore is restored, with the politically powerful advancing, and the junkies and corner boys sinking deeper and deeper into violence, addiction, and oblivion. Despite McNulty's efforts, the machine grinds on, its issue as ugly as it is inevitable.

Though frequently hailed as the greatest program in the history of television, *The Wire* never achieved the popular success of *The Sopranos*, *Six Feet Under*, or *Deadwood*: perhaps because it refuses to do other

FIGURE 4.7 "It was worth it...Wasn't it?" *The Wire* (HBO)

than grind on. First run viewing numbers remained anemic through the series run. Since then, the cult of "Wireheads" has grown significantly, due to home video and international licensing. When the BBC broadcast the series in 2009, ratings were so high that the British press dubbed the phenomenon "*Wire*-mania." The series achieved similar popular and critical success throughout Europe. Of course, one of the reasons so many viewers saw it was that it was offered on broadcast networks, rather than through premium content services like HBO.

But despite a hard-core fan base in America and broader appreciation overseas, *The Wire*, like many other highly lauded works, remains more admired than seen: perpetually knocked to the back of the Netflix queue or video shelf by well-intentioned television mavens, many of whom have watched, and even re-watched the pilot episode but, unable to get caught up in the show's strange rhythms, have yet to succumb to some fan friends' insistence that they "just give it three episodes." And despite being identified as the pinnacle of American television, it has hardly served as a model for subsequent series, on HBO or elsewhere. To date, no series has attempted anything close to its complexity or scale. It has no imitators, as opposed to *Sex and the City*, which gave us the forgettable *Cashmere Mafia* and *Lipstick Jungle* (the later created by Candace

Bushnell, the columnist behind *Sex and the City*), or *The Sopranos*, which spawned the short-lived *Falcone*. If imitation is the highest form of flattery, flattery is the lowest form of praise.

Nor will we find a direct line of descent, as with FX's *Justified*, which transplants Timothy Olyphant's morally conflicted *Deadwood* lawman into modern-day Harlan County, or *Desperate Housewives*, which its creator, Marc Cherry, pitched as a cross between *Sex and the City* and *Six Feet Under*. Mainstream crime dramas have, for the most part, avoided the social realism of *The Wire* in favor of slick whodunit procedurals that pair street-smart cops or federal agents with eccentric social misfits possessing powers of deduction *al a* Sherlock Holmes (*White Collar*, *The Closer*, *Lie to Me*, *Bones*, *The Mentalist*, *Criminal Minds*). And even the few shows that do attempt to emulate the raw "authenticity" of the story world of *The Wire*—*The Shield*, *Southland*, *Detroit 1-8-7*, *The Chicago Code*—are so bound up in the episodic conventions of the police procedural (in which cases are solved and justice sought, if not always served) that they are incapable of achieving anything close to its scope.

There are more comprehensive and complimentary ways in which the HBO effect can be felt in contemporary television drama. Though we often refer to the heyday of HBO programming (typically measured from the launch of *Sex and the City* in 1998 to the sunset of *The Wire* in 2008) as a Golden Age, we might as easily call it a Dark Age, considering the bleak worldview its most acclaimed programming presents. Indeed, this is a large part of its cultural legacy, and appeal. For evidence, one need look no further than the Emmy Award for Best Drama, which is less a measure of quality (after all, *Magnum P.I.* was nominated three times) than of where popular and critical tastes overlap. The 1970s looked to the past with British period dramas (PBS' *Elizabeth R* and *Upstairs, Downstairs*) and nostalgia for the Great Depression (CBS's *The Waltons*), and the 1960s liberalism of the Kennedys (NBC's *The Bold Ones: The Senator*). CBS's timely newsroom drama, *Lou Grant*—which won the Best Drama Emmy in 1979 and 1980—served as a bridge to the "quality" productions that dominated the awards in the 1980s[13]: programs with realistic, ultimately "good" characters who struggle to do the right thing in a morally ambivalent world, like *Hill Street Blues* (4 wins), *Cagney and Lacey* (2 wins), and *L.A. Law* (2 wins). This trend continued through the 1990s, with the addition of "quirky" post-*Twin Peaks* shows like CBS's *Northern Exposure* and *Picket Fences*, and into the new millennium with *Law and Order*, *ER*, and *NYPD Blue* maintaining the standard of "quality," and NBC's *West Wing* dominating the Drama category for the first four years of its run. But though *The Sopranos* was also nominated for Best Drama in 1999, 2000, and 2001, and was receiving more critical and popular attention than any program in the history of cable television, it remained something of a novelty, a brilliant show that seemed to have appeared from nowhere.

Then *Six Feet Under* was launched in 2001, *The Wire* in 2002, *Carnivale* in 2003, and *Deadwood* in 2004, and critics and fans began to see patterns in HBO programming: dark themes, a dearth of sympathetic characters, and stories that replaced resolution with doubt and despair. When *The Sopranos* finally ended the Emmy reign of *The West Wing* in 2004, American viewers had already been introduced to the Fisher family and Stringer Bell, not to mention the fascistic Jack Bauer from *24* and the Las Vegas forensic scientists of the murder porn series, *CSI: Crime Scene Investigation*. To date HBO has received 17 nominations in the Best Drama category, and though it has only won twice (both times for *The Sopranos*), it has profoundly affected the criteria by which we measure critical and popular success in television drama. Since their first win in 2004, the award has gone once each to the apocalyptic *Lost* and *24*, and four times to arguably the bleakest drama on television, *Mad Men* (written by an HBO alum, with the express intention of selling it to HBO). Other nominations have been shared by Showtime's serial killer killer serial *Dexter*, Fox's addict-misanthrope medical show *House*, AMC's chemist-turned-drug-kingpin potboiler *Breaking Bad*, and a pair of trust-no-one legal thrillers, *Damages* and *The Good Wife*, along with HBO's *Six Feet Under*, *Deadwood*, *Big Love*, *True Blood*, and *Game of Thrones*. Though television ratings remain dominated by quirky sitcoms, contest-based reality shows and primetime sporting events, when it comes time to assess the contemporary television programming than "matters"—whether through industry awards, the popular press, or works of scholarship—we find a long line of morally bankrupt characters to rival any in *The Sopranos* or *Deadwood*, the seeping influence of *The Wire*'s "bleak moral outlook," and more and more stories that are unwilling to surrender hard truths about human nature and social institutions to the facile "happy" endings that once dominated award-winning television drama: where questions are answered (*Mission: Impossible*; *Marcus Welby, M.D.*), lessons learned (*The Waltons*; *Cagney and Lacey*), and order restored *Northern Exposure*; *Law and Order*).

****

Near the end of *The Wire*'s third season, David Simon approached then-HBO-president Chris Albrecht about extending its run for two more seasons, despite falling viewer numbers. Though the series had just tied up the Avon Barksdale/Stringer Bell story that for three years served as its through-line, Simon felt there were stories he still needed to tell. After giving the matter some thought, Albrecht responded simply, "Fuck it. Let's do it," reasoning, "If we didn't put it on, who would?"[14] Imagine a broadcast or basic cable network executive making such a statement. Or renewing a series for a second season the day after the pilot episode aired, as HBO would with *Treme, Boardwalk Empire, Game of Thrones,* and *Luck*. In many ways *The Wire* and HBO have set a gold standard for "quality" television that only they can meet. Some have tried to follow HBO's lead, but none has had anything like their success. Showtime and AMC have made concerted—and increasingly successful—efforts to match the quality of HBO original programming. In 2010 for example, both AMC and Showtime exceeded HBO's total number of Emmy nominations for original series, with 24 (AMC), 23 (Showtime), and 20 (HBO). HBO still reigned supreme among all networks, with a total of 101 (including documentaries, miniseries, and sports programs), and the numbers overall are still very strong for HBO, but they do indicate the extent to which they are competing for territory once held exclusively. HBO's one significant advantage over these networks is their deep pockets. Despite several "quality" productions, AMC and FX remain risk-averse, in most cases eschewing HBO's ponderous narratives for more sensationalistic material (FX's *The Walking Dead* and *Sons of Anarchy*, for example). Broadcasters occasionally essay ambitious projects like *Jericho* and *Terra Nova*, but when they do not catch fire, skittish advertisers and bottom-line programmers abandon them. In recent years, Netflix has made it clear that they wish to be the HBO of the post-television age, but despite having its first $1 billion quarter in 2013—which the service ascribes in part to buzz over their recent series, *House of Cards*—original programming has been slow to develop. To date, Netflix has launched only four original series—including a reboot of the FOX comedy, *Arrested Development*.

Whatever the fates of these and other original content providers in the emerging television market, one thing is sure: HBO has effectively reframed our sense of what constitutes "quality" television—in drama as in comedy—by shaking up the conventions of genre, expanding the boundaries of content and form, and injecting an unprecedented sense

5 CHANGING THE CONVERSATION

When I sleep, I dream about a great discussion with experts and ideas and diction and energy and honesty. And when I wake up I think, "I can sell that."

PRESIDENT JOSIAH "JED" BARTLET TO HIS CHIEF OF STAFF,
THE WEST WING

If you don't like what's being said, change the conversation.

AD MAN DON DRAPER TO A POTENTIAL CLIENT, *MAD MEN*

A few days after *The Sopranos* finale in 2007, New York public radio station WNYC aired a segment of *The Brian Lehrer Show* titled "The Politics of *The Sopranos*." Though the discussion covered a range of issues regarding the controversial ending, it focused particular attention on a theory Lehrer conceived while surveying the responses of media critics across the political spectrum: "The more politically conservative you are, the more you hated the ending."[1] In hopes of testing the theory, Lehrer solicited reactions from liberal and conservative listeners, revealing a predictable pattern: most self-described liberals agreed, and most self-described conservatives disagreed. I say predictable because Lehrer's assertion reflects a recent vogue in social psychology linking political orientation to cognitive ability[2] and personality traits,[3] emphasizing that liberals tend to be more intellectually curious, open to experience, and creative, while conservatives tend to be more conventional in their thinking, and supportive of the status quo. In other words, liberals seem to be better able or more willing to process ambiguous, nuanced material, while conservatives tend to want to keep things simple and familiar. And, frankly, who calls into a New York public radio program with the express intent of announcing their distaste for nuance?

Although an anecdotal survey of radio listeners hardly constitutes a serious or conclusive discussion of the issue, the *Brian Lehrer Show* segment does raise two important questions about the relationship between politics and popular culture. First, does television either reflect or transform our ideological beliefs? Consider, for example, the increasingly progressive attitudes of most Americans regarding gay rights. Did television help to engender this shift? Inhibit it? When Vice President Biden came out in support of gay marriage in May 2012, he remarked that the sitcom, *Will & Grace*, did more to transform attitudes about the issue than any law or politician. Yet many in Hollywood also acknowledge that their industry had traditionally been instrumental in marginalizing and stereotyping homosexuals. *Modern Family*, a comedy featuring an openly gay couple with adopted children, is enormously popular among Democrats *and* Republicans. Does this mean that the show has succeeded in "normalizing" attitudes about gay families by suggesting that they face the same problems as straight families? Surely Mitchell's and Cameron's antics seem familiar to any fan of the domestic sitcom, but are we laughing because we identify with their behavior, or because we have grown comfortable with the stereotype of the hypersensitive, obsessively tidy, effeminate gay man?

Second, are our narrative and aesthetic inclinations linked to our ideological convictions? Why, for example, do liberals strongly favor satirical comedy (*The Daily Show with Jon Stewart*; *It's Always Sunny in Philadelphia*) and "cultural" programming (*Masterpiece Theater*; *American Masters*), while conservatives are drawn to work-related reality shows (*This Old House*; *Swamp Loggers*) and collector showcases (*The Barrett-Jackson Car Auction*; *Antiques Roadshow*)?[4] These are by no means casual questions. If the old chestnut is true—that in politics, perception is reality—then we have much to learn from that great engine of perception we call popular culture.

In an attempt to understand the ways HBO programming reflects and effects a shift in how television engages political ideology, this chapter will compare two of the most critically acclaimed, popular television series in recent history, NBC's *The West Wing* (1999–2006) and HBO's *The Sopranos* (1999–2007). *The West Wing* was created by Aaron Sorkin (*A Few Good Men*; *Sports Night*; *The Social Network*; *The Newsroom*) using material left over from his script for Rob Reiner's *The American President* (1995). From the start, critics hailed it as the epitome of "quality" network television, with its serpentine plots, richly-drawn characters, outsized subject matter and opulent production values (the series cost an average of $140 million per season). Nine months prior, HBO had premiered *The Sopranos*, with its decidedly more modest story (no presidents, just a middle-aged mobster stuck in suburban New Jersey), budget (averaging $35 million per season in the early years), and ambitions ("None of us on the show ever thought it would do anything," claimed its creator, David Chase).

These programs share a common history, running concurrently for seven years and often competing for the same Emmy and Peabody Awards, and a common audience drawn from the so-called "quality demographic." But here the similarities end. *The West Wing*, especially in its first three seasons, wears its political heart on its sleeve, imagining an America where the grand ideas of modern liberalism (tolerance, equal rights, empathy for the dispossessed) are given a fighting chance. An early review by conservative John Podhoretz (who, along with several other notable conservatives, would later consult on the series) referred to the program as "political pornography for liberals,"[5] and even some on the left saw it as mere liberal fantasy.[6] While *The Sopranos* avoids direct political commentary, it reflects an America where the fragile dream of upward mobility meets the overwhelming force of bursting economic bubbles and falling towers. Though both series live in a world we recognize as our own, *The West Wing* continues to see in it the seeds of our grandest aspirations, while *The Sopranos* shows us a sober version of what we have become. In that sense, these two series represent the collision of two strains in the history of American television: one marked by a belief that television narrative might serve as an instrument of cultural critique and social change, and the other by a deep cynicism and ambivalence.

Experts and ideas and diction

Scholars and critics have long struggled to understand correlations between politics and cultural production, with mixed results. For example, studies of media bias—whether in news reporting,[7] film,[8] or series television[9]—may challenge our assumptions about what we consume and why, but more often than not they merely reinforce our own convictions by lending them support. This is hardly surprising, since such studies typically rest on the assumption that the producers and consumers of media tend to replicate their own ideology. Hence the frequent charges of anti-capitalism and amorality directed at the products of "liberal Hollywood" by every firebrand conservative from J. Edgar Hoover and Joseph McCarthy to Rush Limbaugh and Sarah Palin. While some of the most powerful figures in the history of the American entertainment industry have been bastions of the Republican party—including Walt Disney, Louis B. Mayer, Arnold Schwarzenegger, and the patron saint of the modern GOP, Ronald Reagan—few would deny that Hollywood is a liberal town. But what makes a movie or television series conservative or liberal? When Fox News commentators and conservative bloggers paint the parody of "vulture capitalism" in *The Muppets* (2011) as "socialist," and the environmentalist forebodings in James Cameron's *Avatar* (2009) as "tree-hugging," they neglect to consider the ways these films also reflect values that conservatives frequently like to claim for themselves, such as entrepreneurialism and spirituality. Indeed, the lion's share of blockbusters trade in such "conservative" ideals as patriotism and self-sacrifice (*300*; *The Dark Knight*; *Captain America*), family values and natural hierarchy (*Toy Story*; *The Incredibles*; *Lord of the Rings*), and the transformative power of faith and love (*Forrest Gump*; *Twilight*; just about any Hollywood film with a happy ending). And what could express a more idealized conservative notion of heriosm than James Cameron's *Titanic*? The captain goes down with his ship, the men tending the boilers give their lives to safeguard those above deck, and a poor young artist allows himself to drown so that his aristocratic lover will have ample room on her raft?

The case made against television has been equally pronounced, with media critics at such right-wing outlets as *Big Hollywood* and *The National Review* finding an especially pernicious strain of leftist "indoctrination" in youth programming, from *Sesame Street* to *Hannah Montana*. But a quick glance across the channel spectrum reveals a richer picture: a celebration of individual talent and free enterprise (*American Idol*; *The Apprentice*); of Second Amendment rights (*Top Shot*; *Chuck*); of moral absolutism (*Buffy the Vampire Slayer*; *24*); of patriotism (*JAG*; *NCIS*), and libertarianism (*South Park*; *The Simpsons*). This is hardly surprising since television, like cinema, has traditionally hewed to a conservative view in order to widen its potential audience. For every Edward R. Murrow attack on Joseph McCarthy in the 1950s, there were a dozen sitcoms idealizing the post-War era with prosperous suburban families led by a strong father figure. While 1960s series like *The Smothers Brothers Comedy Hour* and *That Was the Week That Was* skewered American interventionism and political excess, *I Spy* celebrated American exceptionalism, and *Bonanza* gilded the frontier myth. The so-called "liberal" sitcoms of the 1970s that helped to define "quality" television by addressing issues of social difference (*All in the Family, Mary Tyler Moore, Maude, Sanford and Son*) competed for ratings with more "conservative" programming impelled by nostalgic notions of family (*Happy Days, The Waltons*) and eye candy action heroes (*Charlie's Angels, Six Million Dollar Man*), and would eventually be replaced by comedy content to offer difference without distinction: series like *The Cosby Show* in the 1980s, whose central characters were described by several critics as a white family in blackface; or *Ally McBeal* in the 1990s, which prompted *Time* magazine, among others, to ask the question, "Is Feminism Dead?"[10]

In order to understand the relationship between politics and television, we first need to question two simplistic assumptions: 1) that the politics of any particular series, or the network that produced it are one-dimensional and easily sussed, and 2) that the producers and consumers of media want nothing more than replicate their own ideology. Individual cable networks are often skewed along political lines. Audiences for the Golf Channel, Fox News, Fox Sports Net, and CMT are overwhelmingly republican, and those for MSNBC, Comedy Central, Lifetime and VH1 are largely democrat. This is a natural result of narrowcasting, having less to do with "indoctrinating" viewers than matching audiences to advertisers, from brokerage firms (the Golf Channel) to breweries (Fox Sports Net). But the major broadcast networks—ABC, NBC, CBS, FOX—must aim for a larger target.

And what about a premium network like HBO, which does not need to worry about brokers or brewers and whose audience tends to sprawl across the political spectrum? The New-York-based network is decidedly not part of the Hollywood establishment. In a sense, it is pre-Hollywood, a true independent, harkening back to the days before D. W. Griffith and Mack Sennett abandoned their Manhattan movie studios for the cheap labor and good weather of suburban Los Angeles. But HBO does occupy that *other* metropolis of American liberalism, and it has certainly not shied away from politics and social issues. Quite the contrary. Unbidden by advertisers who balk at the idea of controversy, HBO has distinguished itself by its commitment to politically charged documentaries (*12th and*

Delaware; *Terror in Mumbai*; *4 Little Girls*), feature films (*Barbarians at the Gate*; *And the Band Played On*; *Too Big to Fail*), series (*Tanner '88*; *K Street*; *Veep*), and talk shows (*Dennis Miller Live*; *The Chris Rock Show*; *Real Time with Bill Maher*). Given this penchant—not to mention the liberal bona fides of former network heads like Michael Fuchs and Chris Albrecht—HBO has frequently been accused of harboring a liberal bias.

But what does that mean?

In a storytelling medium like television, the term "bias" should be understood in at least three ways. The most common refers to when a program takes an explicit position on an issue. For example, critics of *Father Knows Best* often brand the series "conservative" for the way it actively endorses paternalistic moral education, even in its winking title. Conversely, *All in the Family* is perceived as "liberal" because it frames Archie Bunker's bigotry as a social problem, comic and foolish, rather than, say, a matter of free speech.

A second meaning of bias typically overlaps the first, but requires a bit more teasing out: the ideological worldview of a program. Some have argued that *Lost*, for example, has a conservative leaning because of its approving representations of faith, gun ownership and personal redemption, while *Downton Abbey* reflects the apparently liberal attitude that social hierarchies are oppressive, even for those at the top.

A third meaning of bias focuses on the ways stories shape the ideological worldview, either by giving it a coherent, and presumably positive presentation, or by revealing its injustices and dramatizing its instability. This brings us back to Brian Lehrer's questionable assumption that liberals favor nuance and complexity, and tend to be suspicious of happy endings (where the problems raised by the story are worked out), while conservatives favor clarity and resolution, and tend to see the narrative as a sort of proof of the values it asserts (where the meaning of the story is either the confirmation or rejection of those values).

By this last standard, most television narrative is inherently conservative, from conventional sitcoms like *Friends* or *Frasier*, with their self-contained, infinitely replicable story structures, to "quality" dramas like *Hill Street Blues* and *Homicide: Life on the Street* which, despite pursuing complex storylines that directly or indirectly critique American law enforcement, labor to resolve key plot points and increase our respect and sympathy for central characters in order to keep audiences engaged. Indeed, shows that might be identified as having a "liberal bias" by the first two criteria often rely upon a conservative narrative structure to promulgate their "message."

The West Wing is one such series. Though it casts a deliberately positive light on issues like the social safety net and education reform, and projects an image of government as nurturing and inherently virtuous rather than a restrictive but necessary evil, its stories are framed by clearly-defined obstacles (scandals, critical decision-making, legislative battles) that challenge its characters and trumpet its core ideological values, resulting in something between a morality tale and a civics lesson. Despite the many failures and failings of the Bartlet administration, the viewer is able to see the whole equation clearly, and to confirm (or reject) the merits of its guiding ideals.

Not all quality TV series have been so structurally conservative. I mentioned *Twin Peaks* in the previous chapter, as an example of a program that offered a considerably more kaleidoscopic narrative model. *Twin Peaks* also endorses an essentially "conservative" worldview, from its small-town values (loyalty, liberty, family, faith) to its clear delineation of good and evil. Other quality TV programs of the 1990s would endorse similarly "conservative" positions: the anti-government sentiments of *The X-Files* and *Firefly*; the good vs. evil morality of *Buffy the Vampire Slayer*; the small-town values of *Northern Exposure*. They would also continue the trend, begun with 1980s dramas like *St Elsewhere* and *L.A. Law*, away from explicit social issues like the sources of crime, racism, and social inequity toward stories of loyalty, hard work, personal choice, and redemption: precisely the sort conservative critics like to claim for their own. But these series also lacked one element that had been essential to the success of earlier series, and one of the primary criteria of the next iteration of quality TV: realism.

Realism is a tricky concept, because it relies on a series of subjective impressions rather than hard-and-fast markers. Still those impressions can be divided into three categories: the sensory (does the world of the story "look right"?), the emotional (do characters' actions and reactions "feel right"?), and the narratively plausible (would the stuff that happens in the story, happen in "real life"?). The first is primarily a matter of style, but good style is always in service to character and story. *Hill Street Blues*, for example, adopts a quasi-documentary style with "quick cuts, a furious pace [and] a nervous camera," which helps to generate "complexity and congestion, a sense of entanglement and continuous crisis that [match] the actual density and convolution of city life."[11] The frenetic hand-held camera and fly-on-the-wall compositions also create a sense of intimacy and continuity, while allowing the viewer to follow multiple overlapping narratives in an integrated, naturalistic setting. The "walk-and-talk" dialogue sequences in *The West Wing* serve a similar function, though like Sorkin's highly polished, witty language, they are meant for theatrical rather than realistic effect.

As I argued in the previous chapter, the dramatic series that would establish HBO as the benchmark in "quality" programming—*The Sopranos, Six Feet Under, The Wire, Deadwood*—all strive for their own brand of authenticity and verisimilitude, even when certain elements (dream and fantasy sequences; over-wrought dialogue) seem to deliberately disrupt the effect. While comedies such as *The Larry Sanders Show, Curb Your Enthusiasm* and *Lucky Louis* play with the lines between the real and the mediated reality, HBO's great dramas attempt to penetrate the reality of the story worlds themselves by focusing on the ways the details of that world seep into the drama. The rough-hewn lumber of frontier construction (*Deadwood*), the drained flesh of human corpses (*Six Feet Under*), the crunch of "tester" vials under addicts' feet (*The Wire*), the tacky emptiness of the suburban McMansion (*The Sopranos*): from these details grow dramas of ordinary lives, often desperate and cruel, with occasional moments of truth, even humor. They seem immediately familiar and "real" to us, not just because they look right and characters act and react in ways we might, but because they are built upon a familiar set of values.

FIGURE 5.1 Politics in motion, *The West Wing*, NBC

Unlike the "liberal" sitcoms and dramas of the 1970s and 1980s—to say nothing of their progeny, *The West Wing*—they reflect the world as we find it, rather than the world to which we might aspire. It is a world in which progressive social ideals have certainly had some impact. For example, we find minority groups and women represented in all social strata. But in this world the only places minority groups have been truly successful "moving on up" (*The Jeffersons*) is in the drug trade (*The Wire*) and prison (*Oz*), and Mary Richards' decision to eschew marriage for career (*Mary Tyler Moore*) has left successful women fearing they have outlived their eligibility for long-term relationships (*Sex and the City*). Although HBO series often begin with some fleeting notion of reform (*Oz* is about a progressive prison unit that emphasizes rehabilitation and socialization, while *Sex and the City* begins by asking the question, "Why can't women have sex like men?"), hope soon gives way to stories of degradation (*Oz*'s "Emerald City" unit only feeds the predatory instincts of its inmates) and acquiescence (Carrie and the girls soon admit that men have enormous social advantages, so retreat into over-idealized notions of love, sex, and conspicuous consumption).

In this sense, HBO series reflect a world steeped in, perhaps trapped by apparently immutable "conservative" ideals like family (*The Sopranos*; *Six Feet Under*), faith (*Carnivale*; *Big Love*), and free enterprise (*The Wire*; *Hung*). Though conservatives might easily characterize these programs as offering cynical, even satirical perspectives, they certainly strike a chord with viewers across the political spectrum. And given the narrative complexity, nuance, and irresolution of these series, it is becoming increasingly difficult to argue that viewers are drawn simply to the sex, violence, and swearing. Perhaps what we are witnessing is the emergence, or at least representation of a new set of normative values in America.

What's being said

The shifting definition of "quality" television mirrors a shifting political reality. On the surface, it seems a simple movement from left to right, from an America driven by the social reforms of FDR's New Deal and LBJ's Great Society to one defined by privatization, outsourcing, unwinnable wars on drugs and terror, and what so-called "liberal" President

Clinton declared the end of "the era of Big Government." Conservative fiscal policy has certainly dominated American politics since the Reagan administration, with supply-side ("trickle-down") economic theory and deregulation having consequences both positive (economic expansion in the 1980s) and negative (a staggering wealth gap). But even as membership in the Republican and Democratic parties has fallen, the number of self-identified liberals has grown at roughly the same rate as conservatives, and the expanding rolls of Independent voters skew right and left in roughly equal numbers.

Given the increased complexities of issue politics—where, for example, America is drifting to the right on gun control and abortion, but left on gay marriage and marijuana legalization—we must also be aware of the ways perceptions of political ideology can be affected by geography, class, religion, gender, race, and sexual orientation. Take the word "conservative" as an example. Historically defined by the values of small government and individual liberty, over recent decades many conservatives have embraced a sort of legal and moral interventionism on the issues of abortion, marriage rights, and stem cell research. And though the GOP has maintained a tenuous balance between fiscal and social conservatives for the past three decades, the interests of groups like the Log Cabin Republicans and Religious Right are often fundamentally in conflict. Then there is the so-called "Overton Window": the notion that general attitudes toward political ideas shift over time. The word "liberal," for example, was once the proud moniker of New Deal and Great Society Democrats, but Republicans since Ronald Reagan have had remarkable success recasting it as antithetical to free enterprise, family values, even patriotism.

The shift in American politics, and political perception is not so much from left to right, as from shared vision to cognitive dissonance. Can a so-called "Reagan Democrat" also identify as a "liberal"? How does a gay man vote for a party whose leadership brands him a deviant? Does the word "socialism" still have any meaning if it can be so recklessly applied to Barack Obama? Is a "neoconservative" really a "conservative"? To illustrate the increasing discordance between and within contemporary political ideas, let us consider the central characters of *The Sopranos* and *The West Wing*, New Jersey mob boss Tony Soprano and U.S. President Josiah "Jed" Bartlet. Although both powerful and accomplished men in their own rights, they could hardly be more different.

The reader may object to my calling Jed Bartlet the "central" character of *The West Wing*, since his story is often not at the center of the narrative. In fact, as the series was originally conceived, the president was not meant to appear at all. But even in physical absence, he remains the ideological core of the series. Bartlet is a New England Blue Blood who came of age in the 1950s and nurtured his liberal values in the ivory towers of Notre Dame, the London School of Economics, and Dartmouth. A Nobel-Prize-winning economist, he holds the Keynesian view that government should actively intervene in the economy through market regulation, the manipulation of interest and tax rates, and public works initiatives: principles that his conservative critics attack as "tax-and-spend" liberalism. A dyed-in-the-wool patriot descended from a Catholic mother and a Founding Father (he bears the name of his great-great-great-great grandfather, who signed the Declaration of Independence), Bartlet embodies the paired virtues of faith and reason espoused by the most esteemed philosophers of Church (Thomas Aquinas) and State (Thomas Jefferson), and believes that the sacred rights of American democracy—public discourse, the making of laws, and most importantly voting—imbue it with a kind of grace. Bartlet reveres the Constitution as a durable and adaptable tool rather than a rigid and absolute boundary. While committed to both the moral and hierarchical principles of law (he makes his initial appearance in the pilot episode while quoting the First Commandment: "I am the Lord your God: Thou shalt worship no other god before Me"), he also believes that law should be even-handed and compassionate (in accordance with Jesus's Commandment, "Do unto others as you would have them do unto you").

Although often caricatured as a "big government" Democrat, Bartlet believes that a democracy "of the people and by the people" can *only* function if the citizens are informed and engaged: an idea directly descended from Jeffersonian republicanism (from the Latin *res publica*, meaning "public thing"). Despite threats to his administration and his physical person, battles lost and never engaged, and occasional lapses of faith in the health of the republic (after watching an episode of *The Jerry Springer Show*, he asks one of his senior staff, "These people don't vote, do they?"("He Shall, From Time to Time...," 1:12), Bartlet remains convinced that progress is simply part of the American character, and that his "once in a generation mind" makes him the right man to inject "ideas and diction and energy and honesty" into public discourse. This confidence is best expressed in his personal mottoes, "Break's over" and "What's next?"

In the final scene of *The West Wing*, Bartlet flies home to retirement after eight years as leader of the free world. When his wife asks what he is thinking about while he stares out the window of Air Force One, he answers simply, "Tomorrow" ("Tomorrow," 7:22).

Compare that wistful coda to the opening scene of *The Sopranos*, where Tony begins his first psychotherapy session by noting that, though it is always good to get in on "the ground floor" of any enterprise, he fears he has "come in at the end" of the glory days of organized crime ("The Sopranos," 1:01).

If Jed Bartlet is the apotheosis of the enlightened leader, Tony Soprano is its cynical opposite. He is only interested in politics when it involves an incumbent on his payroll: a contemptuous example of the maxim, "All politics are local." But then Tony has sworn allegiance to an organization built on precisely that principle: *la cosa nostra* (Italian for "our thing"). Son of a *capo* in the New Jersey mob and a mother who makes Medea look passive-aggressive, he was raised to believe in loyalty and strength. Yet everywhere he looks, these values are undermined. "Made men" turn State's evidence to avoid prison terms. Territorial disputes erupt between and within "families." Old bosses rot in prison, unable to hold onto what is theirs, while men like Tony's father and his childhood friend, Jackie Aprile, are cut down by disease. Then there are Tony's panic attacks, betrayals of body and mind that not only leave him struggling for power (with his treacherous mother, Livia, and uncle, Corrado "Junior" Soprano), but also force him to confront his psychological, if not moral

FIGURE 5.2 "Tomorrow," *The West Wing*, NBC

contradictions. Tony's personal motto is emblazed on the back of his boat: "Stugots," which literally means "balls" (as in "You got some stugots to talk to me that way"), but figuratively expresses disbelief, anger, or disgust (as in "All this work and what do I have to show for it? Stugots").

Tony, a third-generation Italian-American whose father rejected the family trade (stonemasonry) for the gangster's life and eventually brought his son up in it, is smarter than his peers (which is not saying much) and bolder (having made his reputation by holding up a made-man's card game), so seems bound for leadership. But he is driven less by ambition than laziness, choosing his father's path to avoid the difficulty of making another for himself. Born in 1960, Tony came of age in the shadow of a lost war (Vietnam) and lost ideals (Watergate), a time of deep cultural cynicism. Like most Italian-Americans of his generation, Tony was raised Catholic, but for him religion was always more a matter of cultural heritage than faith: something his family had always done. He wears a St Jerome medal around his neck, but doubts the sincerity of those who express faith, including his wife, his sister, and his priest. But if Tony is irreligious, he esteems reason only slightly more, preferring instead a series of rationalizations for his criminal and venal behavior. The gamblers and addicts he preys upon are "degenerates" whom he is helping to hit bottom. His *comari* (mistresses) are "whores" and "gold-diggers" feeding off his success. His murder victims are "rats" and "cowards" who deserve what they get. The only logic that matters to him is the logic of the marketplace, and as he sees it, "This thing of ours is a pyramid: shit runs downhill, money runs up" ("For All Debts Public and Private," 4:01): a succinct description of the "supply-side" or "trickle-down" economic theory.

As Chief Executive of the United States, Jed Bartlet is granted his powers by the Constitution: a document that defines America as a pluralistic republic built upon the principles of inalienable rights and separation of powers. As boss of a New Jersey crime family, Tony Soprano has his authority from the Commission: an alliance of independent "families" (Genovese, Lucchese, Bonnano) that relies upon principles of hierarchy, loyalty and secrecy. While *The West Wing* keeps faith in its Enlightenment ideals, like so many other gangster narratives *The Sopranos* reflects an America that is irrevocably broken. The Great Depression served as the backdrop for such anti-hero films as *Public Enemy* (1931) and *Little Caesar* (1931); the social turmoil of the late 1960s produced nostalgic tragedies like *Bonnie and Clyde* (1967) and *The*

Godfather (1972); and the postmodern disaffection of the 1990s turned nostalgia into pastiche with *Goodfellas* (1990), *Miller's Crossing* (1990), and *Pulp Fiction* (1994).

Although each new cycle reflects a different set of social values (in the 1930s the gangster is a working-class hero, in the 1960s and 1970s a tragic figure, and in the 1990s a pulp icon of cool grace), in every iteration, the gangster is a countercultural figure, preying off American decadence by supplying drugs, illegal gambling, and prostitution, while exposing the venality of the System itself by paying off the Law and operating virtually out in the open. In times of uncertainty, when the cops, the banks, and the politicians cannot be counted on to run things, "organized crime" offers some semblance of order in the form of protection rackets, loan sharks, and a ready supply of high-demand prohibited goods and services. One System simply replaces the other, at least until the next "law and order" politician or bureaucrat either creates new laws to cripple it (the RICO Act) or adopts its model (the deregulation of the financial industry). *The Sopranos* reflects the collapse of both Systems, through mutual collusion (paying off cops and politicians), through disintegrating infrastructure (disloyal mobsters; underfunded federal agencies), and through incompetence. If Jed Bartlet's America can still be inspired by "ideas and diction and energy and honesty," the America of Tony Soprano is driven by simple fear and greed.

The philosophical gap between the two shows also reflects a profound shift in what we have come to identify as the American Dream: an idea that James Truslow Adams, who coined the phrase in his 1931 book, *The Epic of America*, defined as "opportunity for each according to his ability or achievement."[12] The Dream he describes has manifested itself in multiple forms, from the rugged individualism of nineteenth-century frontier myth (homesteaders, prospectors), to the "conspicuous consumption and conspicuous leisure" that has been a measure of social status since at least the Gilded Age.[13] While we continue to identify the American Dream with a sort of spiritual wellbeing, around the middle of the twentieth century new metrics of prosperity began to assert themselves: security and comfort. Where once the Dream expressed a desire to stake one's claim in the wilderness and to pull oneself up by one's bootstraps, frontier, and industry soon gave way to suburban sprawl and corporations; and as the world grew smaller and more competitive, the homestead was reduced to a house surrounded by a fence that seemed to grow taller and more imposing from one decade to the next.

If Bartlet embodies the older ideal, Tony Soprano represents the latter. Tony may admire the "strong, silent," self-determined man embodied by Gary Cooper in Hollywood movies, but he never tries to embody that type. He is driven not by honor or courage, but by greed, pettiness, and fear, which he hides behind a wall of macho bravado, cutting humor, and frequent diatribes directed against those who fail to conform to the mafia code of conduct. In other words, he attempts to buoy himself up by making others just as miserable as he is (this is especially apparent in his relationships with his sister, Janice, and his associate, Paulie Walnuts, who bear a disproportional amount of his cruelty). In some ways, his attitudes and behavior are consistent with his cultural role. According to renowned film and cultural critic, Robert Warshow, the gangster

> appeals to that side of all of us which refuses to believe in the 'normal' possibilities of happiness and achievement; the gangster is the 'no' to the great American 'yes' which is stamped so big over our official culture and yet has so little to do with the way we really feel about our lives… And the story of his career is a nightmare inversion of the values of ambition and opportunity.[14]

Tom Powers (*Public Enemy*) and Henry Hill (*Goodfellas*) thumb their noses at the "suckers" who lead "normal" lives because they know that normal is just another word for struggle and subjugation, and success has little to do with how hard you work. Michael Corleone (*The Godfather*) and Tom Reagan (*Miller's Crossing*) soberly sacrifice happiness for power.

But for Tony Soprano, these movie mobsters are nothing more than pop cultural references. Michael Corleone is reduced to a mocking impersonation by Tony's consigliore, Silvio Dante ("Just when I thought I was out, they pull me back in!"), and Tony's interest in Tom Powers' story has less to do with the mob than with mother issues. And although *The Sopranos* creator David Chase has long acknowledged the stylistic influence of *Goodfellas* on the series, the film barely rates mention among series characters. When Tony's nephew and underling, Christopher Moltisanti, spots Martin Scorsese outside a nightclub in "46 Long" (1:02), he avoids mention of his gangster films, preferring instead to shout tepid praise for the Dalai Lama biopic, *Kundun* (1997). Perhaps Christopher is attempting to impress Scorsese with his knowledge of the director's more obscure work. Or perhaps he neglects *Goodfellas* because the story of Henry Hill's rise and fall is really the story of the degradation of the contemporary mob through broken oaths (Henry is ultimately a "rat"), legal pressure (federal agents use the RICO statutes to bring down his crew), and weakening infrastructure (enterprising mobsters like Henry and Jimmy the Gent find ways to avoid "kicking up" to bosses). By the time we catch up with Christopher and Tony at the turn of the millennium, the mobster is no longer an outlaw rebel or a tragic anti-hero, but a functionary in a failed bureaucracy.

In such men, *The Sopranos* is playing off of Hannah Arendt's idea of the banality of evil,[15] where corruption and culpability are as much the result of passive acquiescence as active choice. Unlike Henry Hill or Tom Powers, Tony Soprano adopts a life of crime not out of ambition, but because he was "too lazy to think for [him]self" ("College, 1:05) Not that we would necessarily judge Tony a bad man for choosing "the life," provided he did it for reasons we found compelling. Michael Corleone, for example, crosses the line into criminal behavior to avenge his murdered brother, Sonny, then to fill the power vacuum left by his deceased father. Indeed, Tony's unresolved existential and psychological crises, which are manifested as panic attacks and force him to expose (and conceal) parts of himself in therapy, beget a natural sympathy in the audience. In the absence of any truly likeable or admirable characters, these crises compel us to relate our fates to his, though we know fully what sort of a man he is, and where his road leads.

Perhaps we recognize our own hypocrisy in his, despite the greater degree, and admire him for occasionally acknowledging it (as opposed to his wife Carmela, who wants the luxury, comfort, and status Tony's crimes supply her, but refuses to be culpable for them). Or maybe we simply wish to live vicariously through him, to experience "the life" from the inside. Perhaps we find his racism, sexism, homophobia, and frequent acts of betrayal and brutality more "real" than the easy virtues of characters like Jed Bartlet. Or maybe his questions are our questions: Whatever happened to the old ways? To a measurable standard of success? To loyalty? To families that stay together? To children we can be proud of? To relatives who would never betray us?

Though not necessarily "conservative" questions, they express longing for an idealized past, when an enterprising man like Tony, and maybe the viewer, could still get in on "the ground floor" of something that mattered. For all of this, Tony quickly becomes someone we can relate to, even like, while Jeb Bartlet is too remote for anything more than admiration: ever obscure behind the mantle of presidential power, and his high-flown rhetoric.

Process stories

Outwardly, the success of *The Sopranos* seems to indicate that we are more interested in the mobster's story than whether he serves as an expression of our values. In real life, we might wish someone like Tony locked up. But like the rogue heroes of literature (Moll Flanders, Huckleberry Finn), he draws us in with his quick wit and ingenuity, especially when dealing with characters we think of as more craven and/ or less interesting than he is, from his spoiled, narcissistic children, and feckless underlings, to the arrogant FBI agents who pursue him. The comparison ultimately makes Tony appear stronger than those around him, better equipped to deal with the crush of reality. At the same time, we are drawn to his flaws and weaknesses—what make him vulnerable, and so richly human—even as we despise (or at least pretend to despise) his actions. But if Tony's insistent sense of dread, and his panic attacks at first appear to be obstacles our hero must overcome (if we can call Tony a hero, at least in the generic sense), they soon reveal themselves to be the traits that define, because they continue to confound him.

In an early review of *The West Wing*, Josh Vasquez argues that the popularity of dramas having to do with people in positions of power owes to viewers' desire "to believe that their leaders, doctors, detectives, and district attorneys suffer the same moral dilemmas as they do and yet are more eloquent, intelligent, and determined enough to, more often than not, make the right decision in the end." He describes this wish fulfillment as "the ultimate fantasy, far more illusionary than any science fiction escapade, and yet an undeniably successful formula in terms of what people agree upon as serious, reality based drama."[16] No doubt, many of the most successful shows on television rely on a sort of moral sympathy to sustain audience interest, even when the objects of that sympathy (Det. Andy Sipowicz in *NYPD Blue*; Dr Gregory House in *House, M.D.*) seem determined to hide their virtues. But over recent years, and thanks in large part to HBO series like *The Sopranos* and *Deadwood*, audiences have developed an increasing appetite for programs that meet these "moral dilemmas" with failure, incoherence and indifference. Do we care if Tony Soprano or Al Swearengen "redeem" themselves? Maybe. But their stories are far more compelling if they do not.

To understand why television has begun to move in this new direction, let us consider a show that seems to have resisted the shift. NBC's *Friday*

Night Lights (2006–11) offers precisely what conservative critics claim dramatic television in the post-*Sopranos* age sorely lacks: inspiring stories about overcoming fear and finding strength through struggle; and morally-centered characters like quarterback Matt Saracen, principal Tammy Taylor, and especially football coach Eric Taylor, whose team motto—"Clear Eyes, Full Heart, Can't Lose"—sounds like the title of a flag-waving contemporary country anthem. Though a perennial Emmy nominee and critical darling for its five-year run, *Friday Night Lights'* season ratings only broke the top 100 once, and its weekly ratings only finished above 50 twice. Like *The West Wing*, it was popular among affluent viewers, perhaps because both shows affirmed the virtues of good character, hard work, and "just" reward by which the wealthy often justify economic inequality. But unlike *The West Wing*, *Friday Night Lights* failed to resonate with the sort of middle-class, Middle Americans toward which it was pitched, who seemed to prefer reality competition shows, feel-good sitcoms, and primetime soaps.

It goes without saying that the majority of viewers will put entertainment above message most of the time. How else would one explain the enormous success of *Home Improvement* (1991–9) or *Baywatch* (1989–2001)? Successful quality TV series such as *The Mary Tyler Moore Show* and *The Sopranos* strike a balance between amusing an audience with Lou Grant one-liners and Bada Bing strippers, and making them think about glass ceilings and sociopathic behaviors. Indeed, this balance is essential to cultivating the richness and complexity of character and

FIGURE 5.3 Faith and football. *Friday Night Lights*, NBC

story that are the hallmarks of quality TV. But while *Friday Night Lights* maintained a high standard of writing and production values, perhaps viewers found Tammy and Eric Taylor lacking in complexity, too generically "good," too predictable. Despite remarkably nuanced performances by the lead actors, perhaps they serve less as characters than as moral reference points. We know from the start that Coach Taylor will always do the right thing, and that he will meet with some sort of success for the effort (he "can't lose," so long as his eyes are clear and his heart is full), though "success" may not turn out to be exactly what he had planned.

With Coach Taylor, as with President Bartlet, it all comes down to a question of character. Their stories remind us that the only true measure of one's character is the willingness to stand up for one's beliefs. The effect is reciprocal: just as the beliefs "prove" the worth of the characters, so the characters "prove" the worth of the beliefs. When the meaning of a narrative is shaped by a specific ideological perspective, characters often "stand for" some quality or other within that ideological frame. The neatest example of this is allegory—in which a character might be named "Charity" or "Hope"—but we find examples even in the most realistic narratives: the stern father and nurturing mother; the angry young man and the wise old sage; the damned and the saved, etc. But thanks to contemporary television programs like *The Sopranos* and *Six Feet Under*, it has becoming increasingly difficult to say what values characters "stand for." If Eric Taylor and Jed Bartlet offer clear moral reference points (the stern but capable and nurturing father; the convergence of optimism, hard work, and talent), Tony and Nate Jr are sprawling psychological templates for men in the chaotic throes of early-onset mid-life crises. We cannot tell what they "stand for" because they do not know themselves.

Of course, many of the best stories focus on the "coming into being" or emergence of character. We observe how characters respond to obstacles in the hope that, by story's end, some "true self" will have emerged. If the hero is the character who most transforms and is transformed by the events of the story, then whatever he "stands for" in the end serves as a sort of apotheosis of that story. At the conclusion of *Lost*, Jack Shepard sacrifices himself for the other inhabitants of the island, finally owning his long-hinted role as a savior figure. And in the final scenes of *Freaks and Geeks* (1999–2000), Lindsay Weir abandons her long-travelled path to academic success to follow the Grateful Dead, proving once and for all that we are what we choose, not what others imagine for us. Though their actions might seem reckless, even maddening to viewers who have invested substantial time and emotion in these characters, each repays the debt by fulfilling the basic premise of the program.

But what about the irresolute narratives and unfulfilled characters HBO has spawned on its own network and the many influenced by its model? What premise does *The Sopranos* fulfill? Certainly not the same one as that *other* story of a mobster (Robert DeNiro) going to a psychiatrist (Billy Crystal) that made its first appearance the same year as *The Sopranos*: *Analyze This* (1999). And what about characters like Walter White from *Breaking Bad*, who is so transformed over the progress of the story as to seem utterly unrecognizable from the honorable, callow loser we saw at the beginning? Is the amoral, murderous drug kingpin he becomes his "true self," or another self entirely: one created, rather than revealed by circumstance? Do Tony and Walter ever "stand for" anything at all, or are they simply fascinating to observe?

These questions become still more pointed when we think in political terms, because of our natural inclination to assign absolute value, to divide people and their principles into distinct categories and factions. But to what end? Political writing—whether the work of journalists, fiction writers, or political scientists—tends to focus on one of two areas: issues and process. What journalists call an "issue story" might look at specific elements of, say, the Affordable Care Act, while a "process story" might look at what sorts of deals were made to get it passed. Though issue stories are essential to keeping people informed about what is going on in government, process stories far outnumber them because most people who follow politics—either in the news, or in the pages of, say, a political thriller—are more interested in the drama and the personalities of the players than the merits of the ideas themselves. Hence the critical and popular success of such Hollywood films as *Mr Smith Goes the Washington* (1939), *The Candidate* (1972), *Dave* (1993), and *The Ides of March* (2011), not to mention HBO's own *Tanner '88* and *Game Change* (2012). The plain truth is that most of us have far less interest in a C-SPAN telecast of a Senate Chamber debate on the merits of tax cuts, than in a Fox News story featuring a Tea Party group standing on the Capitol steps, dressed in Colonial garb, shouting "No Taxation Without Representation."

Process stories adopt the same logic as fictional narrative, in which "ideals" are either explicitly argued or implicitly represented by the story itself. In the example above, the slogans, the costumes, indeed the very name of the Tea Party is meant to invoke the founding principles of our nation. And though these narratives are often built on illogical premises (the Sons of Liberty, who were responsible for the Boston Tea Party, wanted more say in the way government spent its taxes, not less government and fewer taxes), we tend to measure coherence in terms of effect. Look at Jimmy Carter for example. While the narrative of his presidency is marked by a sense of failed ambition and lack of direction, the narrative of his post-presidency reflects the virtues of Christian charity, strength, and faith. Of course, the narrative of Jed Bartlet's presidency is far more compelling than is Carter's because he was the invention of television writers, whose task was to keep the drama interesting, not shape economic and foreign policy. They did so by placing the emphasis on process—the relationships, daily crises, successes, and failures of Bartlet and his senior staff—rather than debating the real merits of his ideological principles.

Even when those principles appear, they resist easy partisan distinction. For example, the Bartlet administration is pro-choice, but as Leo McGarry points out in a conversation with an evangelical leader, Jed Bartlet spent a great deal of his political capital with Democrats during the presidential campaign by "discouraging young women from having abortions" ("Pilot," 1:01). While this revelation is certainly intended to suggest that the abortion issue is far more complicated than the polarizing dogmas of "pro-choice" and "pro-life," its primary purpose is to show Bartlet "playing his role as moral leader," as Leo McGarry puts it. At this point in the series, we haven't even met Bartlet yet, but he already strikes us as wiser, nobler, and more nuanced than any "real life" politician we might name. And though his view of abortion may be more subtle than most ideologues, his values are clear enough.

Of course, some stories are about the negation of values or ideals, unmaking or burying rather than making or discovering. Take, for example, values associated with the monogamous, hetero-normative, two-parent nuclear family. The vast majority of narratives endorse this model, from the lightest of romantic comedies built on the twin principles of eternal love and procreation, to the darkest of domestic dramas about the tragic, traumatic dissolution of families. But what about stories that offer critical alternatives? Take, for example, HBO's *Big Love*, which embraces the notion of eternal love, but rejects the taboo against plural marriage; or *Hung*, in which a divorced dad struggles to restore some semblance of order and financial security to his broken family by becoming a male prostitute; or *Six Feet Under*, where fatherhood is treated as a sort of hereditary curse; or *The Sopranos*, where tidy parallels are drawn between dysfunctional professional and domestic families. Though these series do not idealize the idea of the nuclear family, they certainly do not devalue it. If anything, their characters are far more defined by its dynamic structures than characters in primetime soap operas or sitcoms, who seem bound to siblings, spouses, children, and parents by little more than social custom, economic necessity, and perhaps some lingering affection.

HBO series, and those programs most directly influenced by HBO—*Breaking Bad, The Shield, Mad Men*—do not so much invert the traditional nuclear family as deconstruct those basic structures: the head of household (nearly always the father), the domestic partner (nearly always the mother), and the self-actuating child. In these series, fathers and husbands imagine themselves heroically sacrificing their own wellbeing, and often their sense of right and wrong for the good of their families, while mothers and wives attempt to assert their moral authority and their independence, and children try to find some semblance of order outside the one created by their parents. But what are those sacrifices, where does that moral authority come from, and when might we say that a child has truly stepped out from under the parental shadow?

At first, audiences sympathize with men like Tony Soprano, Walter White, and Vic Mackey because of their disintegrating marriages, troubled (and in Walter and Vic's case, disabled) children, health crises, and professional challenges. But their actions soon reveal a pattern of domination and "tough love" that undermines conventional notions of the benign patriarch. While audiences might initially admire the efforts of Carmela Soprano, Skyler White, and Corrine Mackey to distance themselves from their criminal spouses, their willingness to accept the rewards of crime makes their moralizing sound like grandstanding. And while the children know that their parents are "messed up," they are too immature, too comfortable, too inexperienced, or too anxious to give up the mockery of order they have inherited.

Perhaps these families merely represent the dark side of the nuclear family, one not traditionally seen on American television. Rob, Laura and Richie Petrie (*The Dick Van Dyke Show*) may live in the same New York City suburb and decade as Don, Betty, Sally and Bobby Draper, but their worlds could not be more different. One is defined by warm humor, young love, and the sweet promise of upward mobility; and the other by betrayal, indifference, and a dawning realization that the things that bind them are mere illusions fed by passion, fear, and a sense of obligation. But when the passion and fear give way to hatred and indifference, does obligation die, too? Is "the good of the children" or "respect for parents" reason enough to exercise empty rituals that all but guarantee deceit and resentment? What, finally, connects us beyond biology and social custom?

Challenging conventional notions of the nuclear family is just one of the ways HBO programming and its progeny compels us to look at our values—conservative, liberal, or otherwise—in a more critical light. We might as easily consider views of religion, free enterprise, education or, as we have in the previous chapter, death. The point is, these series are far less interested in taking a position on particular issues than they are with disrupting any easy assumptions we may have about them. Rather than positing ideological or moral absolutes, they force us to ask ourselves what we might do in a circumstance when those absolutes are not so ready to hand, when the values are not embedded in the stories for the express purpose of "proving" them. In the world of these stories, characters are cut adrift from the sorts of easy virtues and ideals that traditionally define people's choices. They are forced to chart new territory. And despite their families, their faith, their enterprise or their education, they chart it alone.

Cut loose

Often what connects people is a sense of disconnection, or alienation. Sometimes this just means finding our place among the freaks and geeks. For examples, see any teen movie comedy, from *Rock and Roll High School* to *Superbad*. But it can also mean recognizing our lack of solidarity, our rootlessness, our miserable turning as a single cog in some enormous, unknowable machine. For examples, see any teen drama, from *Rebel Without a Cause* to *Skins*.

Emile Durkheim, the father of modern sociology, had a term for this latter phenomenon: "anomie." Durkheim's work at the end of the nineteenth century had primarily to do with the ways industrialization and modernity have altered and disrupted our sense of community and of the traditional structures of religion, family, and profession, but it has since been applied to everything from middle-class angst in the 1950s, to the countercultural impulse of the 1960s, punk rock in the 1970s and 1980s, and grunge in the 1990s.

Anomie arises in the absence of social norms, or when those norms become oppressively rigid. Historically it has been associated with periods of social upheaval (for example, immediately following war), of reversals of fortune (for example, economic boon), or at any time when there is an easily perceivable gap between the expressed values of a society and those that can actually be achieved (for example, the "good life" advertising of the 1950s and 1960s). Anomie is also associated with periods of political and cultural conservatism, when a society is most likely to assert a uniform set of norms and "traditional" values. Many who perceive those norms and values as empty will rebel through acts of social deviance. The sexual and social liberation of the Roaring Twenties was in part a reaction to Prohibition and the deportation of 500 suspected radicals following the Palmer Raids,[17] while the Red Scare, the rise of evangelical Christianity, and the restrictive sexual mores of the 1950s helped to spawn the civil rights movement, rock and roll, and an epidemic of juvenile delinquency.

Anomie is a subject of popular, not just scholarly interest. The best-selling modernist novels of the 1920s—such as Sinclair Lewis' *Babbitt* (1922), Theodore Dreiser's *An American Tragedy* (1925), Ernest Hemingway's *The Sun Also Rises* (1926)—depict the shallow values of modern life through the cynical eyes of the Lost Generation. American cinema of the 1950s offers a catalog of Cold War existential crises, from increasingly depraved *films noir* (*Sunset Boulevard*, 1950; *Ace in the Hole*, 1951) and body horror science fiction (*Invasion of the Body Snatchers*, 1956; *The Fly*, 1958), to stories of youth rebellion (*The Wild One*, 1953; *The Blackboard Jungle*, 1955) and bureaucratic anonymity (*The Man in the Grey Flannel Suit*, 1956; *The Apartment*, 1960). Many of these stories are prescriptive, offering their rootless characters platitudes about the transformative power of love, honor, or simply letting go. But many present a much darker view, in which human nature itself seems corrupt, and depraved, and beyond reformation. Characters suffer not because they have failed to see what is important, but because nothing finally is important. They seek meaning because the absence of it is terrifying, but in seeking find only emptiness.

Though anomic characters are richly represented in the history of literature (Oedipus, Hamlet, Raskolnikov) and theatrical film (*L'avventura*, 1960; *Taxi Driver*, 1976; *No Country for Old Men*, 2007), barring a few episodes of *The Twilight Zone* they have been largely absent from television, because networks have long operated on the assumption that the majority of the audience will not return to a series without the tacit promise of a happy ending or meaningful resolution. Even the darker quality TV series of the 1980s and 1990s—police, legal, and medical dramas—offer some relief from the ugliness they present by emphasizing the characters' sense of duty and loyalty, and their stubborn belief that tomorrow things may be different. Each episode of *Hill Street Blues* charts a day in the life of a police precinct, where cops fight battle after futile battle with a city full of criminals, and precinct Captain, Frank Furillo, butts heads with District Attorney Joyce Davenport, who seems bound and determined to weed out police corruption. But each episode ends with Furillo and Davenport returning home to their shared bed, now content to play the roles of lover and spouse. From the chaos and corruption surrounding their public lives, viewers are granted a private promise of order, and a renewed sense of hope for better days ahead.

Not so in the world of HBO dramas. Here Tony Soprano, who feels he has "come in at the end," challenges the efficacy of any authority—moral or otherwise—yet he feels lost, cut adrift, betrayed by everyone and everything, including his own mind and body. Here psychiatrist Paul Weston, from *In Treatment*, doubts that psychotherapy can do his patients or himself any good. Here coach-turned-gigolo Ray Drukker, wonders in the pilot episode of *Hung*, "When did life become something you buy?" And here the insatiable bloodlust of vampires Bill Compton and Eric Northman from *True Blood* leads them to wonder whether being undead isn't the ultimate proof of life's meaninglessness.

Characters like Tony, Paul, Ray, Bill and Eric are often referred to as "damaged," evoking the classical notion of the "tragic flaw": the physical or emotional impediment that they will either overcome or submit to. It is a common enough feature in narrative, including television narrative, and especially "quality" television narrative. Frank Furillo *(Hill Street Blues)* and Andy Sipowicz (*NYPD Blue*) are philandering alcoholics. Fox Mulder (*X-Files*) and Jack Shepard (*Lost*) have unresolved abandonment issues. Dale Cooper (*Twin Peaks*) nurses a broken heart. Jed Bartlet has multiple sclerosis, which proves an increasing physical and psychological impediment over the length of his administration, as well as a moral challenge when it is revealed that he kept the condition a secret through his first presidential campaign. And of course, Tony Soprano has his panic attacks, Paul Weston has his blinding anger, Ray Drukker his jock vanity, and Bill Compton and Eric Northman their fatal weakness for Sookie Stackhouse. But with these latter characters, HBO turns a decisive corner with the idea that heroes or protagonists need be someone who strives to overcome the obstacles that grow from their "flaws" through acts of will and self-determination. The story of Tony Soprano is not about trying to become a "better" man or husband or father or boss or boyfriend, but merely a more functional one. His panic attacks may be brought on by some moral revulsion deep within his psyche, but he shows virtually no patience for teasing it out, rather seeking in therapy a cure for the problem, not a diagnosis of the symptoms behind the symptoms. Like Paul or Ray or Bill or Eric, Tony wants to get better, not be good.

We could say precisely the same of men like Don Draper, Vic Mackey, and Walter White. Their stories begin with a sort of moral crisis, but soon those crises are abandoned for more practical pursuits: how to function more efficiently and effectively, and how to have more control over their lives, and the lives of others. They are interested in power, not salvation, because experience has taught them that virtue is no reward, and that what really matters is strength and security: the new American Dream. If the anomic crises of 1950s film characters like Tom Rath (*The Man in the Gray Flannel Suit*) or C. C. Baxter (*The Apartment*) were brought on by a failure to find personal happiness and fulfillment in an increasingly corporate, consumerist society, they eventually find it in acts of honor, decency, and love. But men like Tony and Don and Vic have come to doubt that happiness ever really existed or whether, as Don says of love, it is just a word "invented by guys like me to sell nylons." For such a man, there can be no happy ending: "You're born alone and you die alone and this world just drops a bunch of rules on top of you to make you forget those facts. But I never forget. I'm living like there's no tomorrow, because there isn't one" ("Smoke Gets in Your Eyes" 1:01).

By now the reader may have noticed that this discussion of anomie has focused almost exclusively on male characters. What about women like Amy Jellicoe (*Enlightened*), Hannah Horvath (*Girls*), Claire Fisher, and Brenda Chenowith (*Six Feet Under*)? Or for that matter, the women of *Sex and the City*, whose conspicuous consumption and relentless pursuit of sex and romance might easily be read as a sort of hedonistic rebellion rather than an embrace of normative values? After all, they insist on being happy (refusing to make the same mistakes as Betty Draper, Carmela Soprano, and Skyler White) despite constant reminders that conventional notions of happiness may no longer be available to them. Several of these characters will be discussed at great length in the next chapter, including the trend in recent HBO programming to distribute narrative authority across genders.

But as Amanda Marcotte points out, the anomic dramas of American television since *The Sopranos* have centered almost entirely on "highly-masculine" environments like the drug trade (*The Wire*, *Breaking Bad*), law enforcement (*The Shield*, *Justified*), athletics (*Friday Night Lights*), *Playboy*-era advertising (*Mad Men*), and of course organized crime. This is hardly new, especially if we look at the history of workplace dramas, which tend to be strongly patriarchal. But Marcotte also points out that, rather than passively reinforcing patriarchal values, these post-*Sopranos* series actively deconstruct them, challenging characters' and viewers' "certainty about the way the world works and what it means to be a man in this world."[18] Though the macho authority and natural charisma of men like Tony, Don, and Vic are clearly born out of the "tradition of gross masculinity," they are also walking anachronisms whose "old boy" networks are under siege by increasingly powerful and independent women (Meadow and Carmela Soprano in *The Sopranos*; Monica Rawling and Claudette Wyms in *The Shield*; Peggy Olsen and just about any of Don's lovers in *Mad Men*). Indeed, Marcotte identifies a sort of feminist strain in much of this work, particularly as women who are defined largely by their domestic roles early in the series take more and more central positions of power as male figures seem to lose their footing. If the traditional male hero embodied the values of his time (Achilles is Greek strength, Odysseus intelligence), Tony, Vic, and Don might have been heroes in earlier days, when men like Tony's father and uncle "ran North Jersey," or good cops were given leeway to bend the rules provided they showed results, or ad men didn't have to contend with the shifting, unpredictable social values and public tastes of the 1960s. But they have arrived too late (Tony has "come in at the end"), gone too far (Vic murders a fellow cop in the pilot episode), or simply lost their edge (Don's story begins with him doubting his until-then natural gift for advertising). Their stories might have been tragic, but tragedy requires the fall of a "great man," and despite their successes nothing they have achieved can be seen as great, let alone good. They merely fall, like the figure of the ad executive tumbling past the skyscraper windows and billboards of Madison Avenue in the opening credits of *Mad Men*.

In "The Summer Man" (4:08), Don Draper allows us a rare glimpse into his thoughts through a diary he keeps following his divorce from

Betty. Among pointed comments about how human beings perceive each other ("People tell you who they are, but we ignore it – because we want them to be who we want them to be") and the cruel wisdom that comes of human desire ("We're flawed because we want so much more; we're ruined because we get these things and wish for what we had"), he makes a "List of Things to Do Before I Die." It contains only two items:

1 Climb Mt. Kilimanjaro, or go anywhere in Africa, for that matter.

2 Gain a modicum of control over how I feel. I don't want to be 'that man.'

A bit abstract for a bucket list, but then desire is only concrete when projected on a concrete object. And it would be hard to imagine a clearer expression of anomic man than Don's list: the desire for something new and exotic, and the desire to feel in control. In some ways, this simple list serves as a sort of Rosetta Stone to Don's psyche, as if Charles Foster Kane (*Citizen Kane*, 1941) had suddenly awakened on his deathbed and explained the meaning of "Rosebud." Only, unlike Kane, Don is not talking about some lost ideal. He knows that we only "wish for what we had" because what we have does not live up to its promise.

Like Tony, Don's past is ugly and full of secrets he has buried deep. So, too, Jed Bartlet, whose father was a petty, cruel, abusive man. Yet while Bartlet shapes those memories into nostalgic reveries about the budding

FIGURE 5.4 The anomic man. *Mad Men*, AMC

friendship with his future secretary, Mrs. Landingham, and his first forays into politics—turning even abuse into a test of mettle ("Two Cathedrals"; 2:22)—Don and Tony are no more nostalgic than the series they occupy. Tony's past is filled with, for him at least, incomprehensible acts of violence and betrayal by his father, which serve as the wellspring of his panic attacks. So, too, Don, a prostitute's son, who is taken in by his embittered biological father following his mother's death, and who later steals a dead man's identity because he so hates his own. Nostalgia, Don explains at a pitch meeting ("The Wheel" 1:13) comes from the Greek, meaning "pain from an old wound" (though this is at best a partial definition of the term). Like Tony he is simply trying to avoid that pain, because he suspects—as Tony does—that "dealing with it" will do nothing to dissipate it.

If nostalgia is a defining quality of the conservative worldview, because it values tradition and established values, it is becoming rarer and rarer in television, thanks in part to the influence of HBO historical dramas like *Deadwood, Rome,* and *Boardwalk Empire,* which supplant the reverie of older programs like *Bonanza, Little House on the Prarie,* and *The Waltons* with a dark, brooding, anomic realism now common even to historical pulp like *Spartacus: Blood and Sand* and *The Tudors.* But the same can be said for an increasing number of dramas set in contemporary times. Despite Jed Bartlet's Blue Blood heritage and Enlightenment message of progress, the notion that the values of the past might somehow redeem the present seems increasingly dubious among television characters like Carrie Mathison (*Homeland*), Jax Teller (*Sons of Anarchy*), Waylon Givens (*Justified*), and Sarah Linden (*The Killing*), who are pressed to navigate their own way through the perils of modern life. Television series and characters no longer pretend to have the answers. When confronted with his flaws and failings, Don does not seek redemption or renewal. He simply shrugs his shoulders and utters the same mantra we have heard a dozen times before: "What do you want me to say?" It isn't as defiant as "Stugots," but it is just as ambivalent. To those who do not descend from the bloodline of a Founding Father, to those who no longer believe that a conversation of ideas and energy and honesty can save the world, to those cut adrift from orthodox values and traditional notions of virtue, there is no continuity, no tradition, no great future, only some money stuffed in a mattress, the odd pleasure where it can be found, and a commitment to live "like there's no tomorrow, because there isn't one."

****

In "Constituency of One" (5:05), Bartlet administration speechwriter Will Bailey (Joshua Malina) decides to leave the West Wing to serve as Chief Strategist to Vice President Robert Russell: a sort of Democratic version of George W. Bush, if one can be imagined, who projects an inoffensive "everyman" quality, and the presumptive party nominee in the next election. When the President's Communications Director Toby Ziegler asks why Will would abandon a president who stands for all of his political ideals for an "empty cowboy suit," Will responds, "I [now] work for a guy who works for a guy who works for the leader of the free world." Will is tired of being a third-stringer. A political junkie, he wants in the game. But Toby is scornful: "This is the NBA. You don't go back to shirts and skins." "Bartlet's never going to finish the job he started," Will responds. "Name an issue, you're still clawing your way back." And though Toby will not admit it to Will, whom he views as a traitor, in private conversation with Leo McGarry, he spells it out plainly:

> Our second term and we're acting like a losing campaign…. FDR built the middle class in 100 days. How many days have we got left?… Where's our Great Society? Where's our New Frontier? Somebody's got to do what we came here to do.

This episode falls at a key moment in the *West Wing* storyline: shortly before Leo breaks with the president over Middle East negotiations (to be replaced as Chief of Staff by Press Secretary, C.J. Craig), and the program launches fully into the campaign of the next Democratic contender, Matthew Santos. The White House is moribund for the last two seasons of the show, trying to make sense of a legacy that is, in effect, no legacy at all. By the end, even Bartlet questions whether he has done anything worthwhile. Although his administration accomplishes several things that would please any contemporary liberal (Social Security reform, job creation, appointing the first Hispanic Supreme Court justice, advancing Middle East peace), his dream of a grand conversation of experts and ideas never quite materializes, despite innumerable rousing speeches. Nor does the Nobel-Prize-winning economist ever successfully balance the budget.

Tony Soprano's failures are more local. As it turns out, the "happy family" he expects to be able to buy with his business success is held together by mere routine and material need, not any strong bonds of affection or mutual concern. His business is on the verge of ruin, thanks in part to internal rivalries, and in part to the case the federal government continues to build against him.

We see these failures come into sharp focus in the stories of Tony's three "sons": A.J. (his actual progeny), Christopher (his nephew, whom he has been grooming to take over the family business), and Jackie Aprile Jr (son of his best friend, who dies of cancer in the first season). All three disappoint Tony because their personal weaknesses make them unsuitable for the gangster life each seeks to embrace. They are undisciplined and suffer from fatal character flaws: A.J.'s panic attacks, Chris's drug addiction, and Jackie Jr's volatile combination of arrogance and stupidity. In the last episode of Season Three, titled "Army of One," we see their stories converge. Jackie Jr is murdered, with Tony's consent, following a botched robbery of a mob card game that leaves one "made" man dead and another badly injured (the robbery is an homage to a similar stunt pulled by Tony as a young man). Christopher is arrested for making book at the cemetery during Jackie's funeral, while the FBI launches a campaign to "turn" his fiancée, Adriana by threatening to charge her with dealing drugs for him. And A.J. is expelled from school for stealing answers to a test. When Tony threatens to send him to military school, A.J. has a painc attack. "It's in his blood," Tony later despairs to his therapist; but similar weakness runs through all of their blood. Each longs to emulate Tony and achieve his success, but none of them have the intelligence, discipline or constitution necessary. If they represent the future of the organization, then the enterprise is surely doomed, and the fear that Tony expresses in the pilot episode, that he has "come in at the end," is entirely justified.

In the first episode of *The Sopranos*' final season ("Members Only" 6:01), Tony revisits the theme of family with A.J., as part of an ongoing campaign to help his son find his way in life. "They're the only ones you can depend on," he tells A.J., as he prepares to visit his now-senile Uncle Junior in a nursing home. It is a remarkably tender moment, given Tony's history with his uncle (in Season One, Junior tried to have Tony killed), and one that another series might have used as a marker of emotional maturity. But not *The Sopranos*. Moments later, the same Uncle Junior, in the throes of dementia, shoots and nearly kills Tony.

What more fitting commencement to the final chapter of a program that has been prodding the "family values" premise from the start? Like all great HBO series, and the many it has influenced, *The Sopranos* compels us to rethink our ideological assumptions: not to make us more "liberal" or "conservative," but merely more honest about our selves, our relationships, and the world we occupy. If these series are any indication, it is a world that, beneath hypocritical rituals and routines, has largely lost faith in traditional ideals like family, community, loyalty, reason, and justice. A world of dissonance, not consonance, driven increasingly by doubt and fear, in which even Jed Bartlet's enlightened republic—built upon Thomas Jefferson's vision of "a more perfect union"—is threatened by a different ideological duality: extremism and apathy.

Is this a "liberal" worldview? Maybe. But only if "liberal" suggests a willingness to concede that perhaps there are no immutable truths, and that values are subjective and changeable (a not uncommon view of liberalism, though usually one espoused by non-liberals). After all, HBO is no more immune to ideological readings than any other media outlet. Scores of books and articles have been written reading *The Sopranos* through the window of psychology,[19] philosophy[20], economics[21] and criminology.[22] It has served as a metaphor for the spiritual bankruptcy[23] and criminalization[24] of American culture, as well as an introduction to Italian-American food and culture.[25]

Perhaps the reason we assign so much cultural value to *The Sopranos* and many of the series it influenced is because, regardless of our politics or cultural point of view, they invite us to be part of a larger conversation concerning the state of our world and our place within it. It is a conversation that has gone on for millennia, but one that has only ever changed direction or tenor when new, often opposed perspectives have been introduced into it. And at least in the insular world of contemporary television, where the conversation has long been defined by rigid dualities—hero/villain, success/failure, conservative/liberal—HBO has been an important instrument of change.

6 SERIOUS NAKED PICTURES

I can't take a serious naked picture of myself. That's just not who I am.

HANNAH HORVATH, *GIRLS*

Television is a woman's medium: so goes the conventional wisdom of the programmers and advertisers who determine much of its content. Women watch more television than men, buy many more of the products advertised on television and, despite the popular stereotype regarding men and remote controls, tend to make more of the household viewing decisions. So it should come as no surprise that, following decades of progress on gender equality issues in America, female television characters have evolved from the compliant housewives, dutiful mothers, bespectacled secretaries, and childlike screwballs of 1950s and 1960s soap operas and sitcoms to the independent, proactive, self-assured heroines of our time. Though the road from Joanne Gardner (*Search for Tomorrow*) and Lucy Ricardo (*I Love Lucy*) to Buffy Summers (*Buffy the Vampire Slayer*) and Roseanne Connor (*Roseanne*) was filled with bumps and detours, if the rising number of female-centered series (*Bones, The Good Wife, Parks and Recreation, New Girl*) is any indication, now is a good time for women on television.[1]

That is one view. Another is that things have not changed all that much, and may even be getting worse. Though a record number of women currently hold executive positions at television and media companies, the number of active female television writers has dropped precipitously over the past half-dozen years, while the earnings gap between working male and female writers has continued to grow.[2] As for representations of women in television series, girls are being sexualized at younger and younger ages (*Gossip Girl; Glee*), female beauty is being fetishized to a degree never seen before, and with a few notable exceptions (Glenn Close, Jane Lynch, Jessica Walter), television seems increasingly ambivalent to women over the age of 45. In 2012, the five highest-paid female performers on television were either under-40–fashion-models-turned-actresses (Sophia Vergara, Eva Longoria) or reality show celebrities of dubious talent (Kim and Khloe Kardashian, Bethenny Frankel). The male list is topped by one under-50 (Ashton Kutcher, who also started as a fashion model), but the rest are over-50s with long, successful careers in film, television, and stage performance (Hugh Laurie, Ray Romano, Alec Baldwin, Tim Allen).

Other more troubling patterns have also begun to emerge. Take, for example, the rising tide of violence against women in contemporary television. A 2009 study conducted by the Parent's Television Council tracking television violence over a five-year period found that while overall incidents only increased by about 2 percent, violence against women grew by 120 percent, and violence against adolescent girls by 400 percent. Of these incidents, 92 percent were explicitly depicted rather than implied or described, 29 percent showed female characters being beaten and/or raped, and 19 percent ended in the death of the woman or girl involved.[3] While the study does not cite any specific reasons for this increase, there is plenty of room for speculation.

Perhaps this is simply the price of success. As more women occupy central roles in television series, and inherently violent genres like police, legal, forensic, and medical dramas occupy more of the television schedule, women are more likely to find themselves in violent situations. Perhaps it is tied to the moderate increase in real-life cases of domestic violence over the same time period, or to a growing indifference or antipathy regarding women's issues (the so-called "War on Women"). Perhaps we suffer from sympathy fatigue. Perhaps the real world has become so violent that we need popular culture to amplify it in order to feel anything at all. Or perhaps our attitudes about inter-gender violence have changed in more fundamental ways.

Another study found that viewers are far less likely to feel pity or concern for female characters who are victims of violence, if those characters are otherwise perceived as being strong and self-possessed: what the study refers to as "The Buffy Effect," after the hero of *Buffy the Vampire Slayer*.[4] But what about the many female characters who lack that strength and self-possession? What about all the non-Buffys among the countless victims of television violence? If Buffy is a symbol of girl power, what do they symbolize? Weakness? Vulnerability? Loss of Innocence?

The example of violence against female characters is meant to illustrate a larger point: that the place of women in television narrative cannot be understood simply as a straight line of progress from happy homemaker to vampire killer. While television may be a woman's medium, its stories tend to reflect the values of a man's world. This is precisely the criticism of many who disparage the "gross masculinity" of HBO series like *Deadwood, Rome,* and especially *The Sopranos,* in which all but a few women are relegated to the roles of lover, wife, or sex worker, and even the strongest women are defined by their relationships with powerful men.

Even Tony's therapist, Dr Jennifer Melfi, admits to being aroused by the animal magnetism of her sociopathic patient, and thrilled by her special access to his inner workings. When she is raped in Season Three, she makes the admirable choice *not* to tell Tony, and so unleash his wrath on the assailant, but confesses "a certain satisfaction in knowing that [she] could have that asshole squashed like a bug" ("Employee of the Month" 3:4). She draws the strength—to act or *not* to act—from a grossly masculine surrogate, making her not so different from Tony's wife Carmela, or his many *comari*. That is, until his power inevitably turns against them.[5] The case is still more evident among weaker women, like the 20–year-old stripper, Tracee who, two episodes after the rape of Dr Melfi, is beaten to death in the parking lot of the Bada Bing by Tony's psychotic underling, Ralph Cifaretto ("University" 3:6). Tracee is pregnant with Ralph's child at the time.

Though some critics have argued that such violent scenes actually bolster HBO's feminist credentials by compelling viewers to focus on "the economic and social roots of violence,"[6] the more common response has been to ask, Does HBO hate women? (Some critics have turned the question around: why does no one seem concerned about the extraordinary violence meted out to *men* in HBO series?) Are the countless acts of brutality against women, the gratuitous displays of female flesh, and the parade of strippers, prostitutes, and kept women the sum total of HBO's legacy to women in television, or just the surface?

These questions appear to go beyond the highly masculinized worlds of mob dramas (*The Sopranos; Boardwalk Empire*), frontier stories (*Deadwood; Carnivale*) and period epics (*Rome; Game of Thrones*). Even the strong, self-possessed women of series with a more explicit feminist subtext—*Six Feet*

Under's sexual expeditionary, Claire Fisher; *Big Love*'s rebel polygamist, Barbara Hendrickson—tend to shape their lives and identities around dominating and domineering men. Claire's lovers are psychologically abusive (Gabriel Dimas), obsessive (Russell Corwin), or psychotic (Billy Chenowith); and Barbara abandons the strict patriarchy of the Church of Jesus Christ of Latter Day Saints (aka: the Mormons) for an equally strict domestic one with her husband (Bill Hendrickson). They may restlessly search for their own identity, but compared to the female protagonists of Showtime series like *The L Word, Weeds, Nurse Jackie, The United States of Tara,* and *The Big C*—who *insist* that others recognize their singular worldviews and *refuse* to be defined or confined by men—HBO's women appear largely shaped by male expectations and assumptions (all of Claire's mentors are men, and Barbara only takes up the Mormon priesthood when her husband grants it to her with his dying breath).

And what is true of the dramas seems also to be true of many of HBO's female-centered comedies and dramedies, which focus particular attention to anxieties associated with age and desirability. In *Sex and the City*, sexually and financially independent women in their 30s and 40s worry about finding meaningful relationships with men; in *The Comeback*, an 40–year-old actress finds that she is no longer the "it" girl; in *Enlightened*, a 40–year-old woman has a nervous breakdown after being rejected by a lover; and in *Girls*, urban women in their 20s try to navigate increasingly complex gender politics. By contrast, the men in HBO comedies like *Entourage* and *Eastbound and Down* express little or no interest in gender politics, acceptance, or romance: they just want to get laid.

It is easy to be reductive when talking about HBO's representations of women. Some have taken the arch view that, under the "Golden Age" leadership of Chris Albrecht—whose history of domestic violence led to his firing in 2007—HBO's original programming "morphed into a testosterone-filled stronghold of blowhards (real and otherwise) like Bill Maher, Titus Pullo, and Ari Gold."[7] Others have argued that series such as *The Sopranos* are better examples of "women's television" than anything on the Lifetime network, because they offer more nuanced, realistic depictions of female choice.[8] And still others—especially feminist critics—have struggled to reconcile their ideological perspectives with their fandom.[9]

My intention here is not to debate the merits of these positions, but to consider how HBO has influenced representations of women on television, for good or ill. It is a question that poses significant problems, because casual connections can be difficult to trace when looking at such a broad subject. For example, how would one measure the cultural impact of the stripper, Tracee's brutal murder, beyond noting the number of hits the scene has received on YouTube (it is the second-most viewed, after the diner scene in the series finale), or offering a more elaborate critical survey than the one I have sketched above (and since when do critics speak for a culture)? While such "evidence" may enrich our understanding of the subject, it hardly makes sense of the bigger picture. To get that, we need to look more carefully at two underlying factors: where HBO's images of women come from, and how they have been disseminated.

Sex work

Despite Tracee's example, not all strippers end up dead in parking lots. Some move on to bigger and better things, including careers in movies (Carmen Electra; Diablo Cody) or the music business (Courtney Love; Lady Gaga). Some feather their nests with 401k plans, pay their rent and college tuition, find new jobs and new lives. Some even make their way onto HBO documentary series like *Real Sex* and *G-String Divas*, where they tell stories from the trenches and demonstrate their skills. These so-called "sex docs" have long been a mainstay of HBO's after-hours programming, despite the neglect of the television critics and awards committees who fawn over series like *Six Feet Under* and *The Sopranos*, but who tend to regard the sex doc as little more than softcore pornography posing as ethnography. While these programs are clearly of a different order from the prestige dramas and comedies—shown late at night, to mostly male audiences who seem far less interested in compelling narratives and characters than explicit content—they have a good deal to tell us about HBO's impact on contemporary images of women on television. Though the picture is not necessarily a pretty one.

In *Female Chauvinist Pigs*, Ariel Levy describes a type of woman who insists on defining the so-called "raunch culture" of pornography and sex work as empowering, who embraces the idea of sexual objectification for personal gain, and who desires the sort of power that can only be had through membership in the "boy's club." The most successful of these women gain admission by adopting the traditional "male" qualities of toughness, swagger, and easy humor, while flaunting their sexuality whenever it serves her advantage. But according to Levy, that success only gives credence to the most pernicious female stereotypes (the femme fatale, the flirt, the slut): pernicious because each plays into the notion that female sexuality is defined entirely by the desires of men. Levy's model for this so-called "female chauvinist pig" is Sheila Nevins, HBO's head of Documentary and Family Programming. Nevins has been responsible for more Emmys, Oscars, and Peabody Awards than anyone in the history of the network. She also happens to be its chief chronicler of "raunch culture."

Growing up in the Lower East Side of Manhattan, Sheila Nevins dreamed of a life in theater, not television. Thanks to the generosity of a wealthy uncle, she studied dance at the High School for Performing Arts in New York, and later earned a BA in English from Barnard College, and an MFA in theater directing at the Yale School of Drama. At Yale, she met and married a law student, who convinced her to give up her dream of a life in theater for a more 9–to-5 existence. This led her to take a job making English language instruction films for the United States Information Agency, then to a writing and producing gig with the Children's Television Workshop (home of *Sesame Street*), then to National Education Television, where she created *The Great American Dream Machine* and developed an interest in the *cinema verite* documentary style of Albert and David Maysles (*Salesman*; *Gimme Shelter*; *Grey Gardens*), whom she hired to direct segments of the show. That job led to several others producing stories for network "magazine" series, including *The Reasoner Report, 20/20*, and *Who's Who*. In 1979, shortly after turning down a spot at *60 Minutes*, she applied for the newly created position of Director of Documentaries at HBO, under the mistaken belief that she would be *directing* documentaries. Only after she was hired did she realize her role was administrative, not technical.

Her charge in those days was simple: come up with 14 hours of programming per year. The subject matter and style were up to her. Having only segment production experience, her first impulse was to create multi-part historical documentaries on the likes of Churchill and Hitler. So began the first HBO documentary series, *Time Was*. She also launched a consumer advocacy program in conjunction with *Consumer Reports* magazine. But it did not take Nevins long to realize that HBO subscribers tuned in expecting something edgier, darker, more adult in theme and content:

I started to do R rated documentaries... about things that were volatile, about drugs, about teenage pregnancy, but not in the way the networks were doing them.... I started to use the R [rating potential] of HBO to... create sort of limitless boundaries for what reality could do. And that meant we could do everything from a program about the Second World War and the women who had survived it, to something about hookers and prostitution.[10]

In an attempt to test the limits of "what reality could do," Nevins launched HBO's signature documentary series, *America Undercover* in 1983. With it, she hoped to "get underneath the American dream" and "show how we're struggling to live our lives."[11] It would become the umbrella for the majority of HBO's documentary projects, and quickly distinguish the network as a producer of high-quality programming.

From the start, *America Undercover* challenged conventional notions of television documentary, touching upon subjects that were either ignored by other networks or handled in the clinical manner of an educational film or travelogue. HBO documentaries focus on personal narratives, in order to create strong bonds of empathy between the viewer and the subject. This is especially true of the many that focus on social issues as they relate to women, from violence (*4 Little Girls*, 1997: *The Greatest Silence: Rape in the Congo*, 2007), to disease (*Three Sisters: Searching for a Cure*, 2004; *Sari's Mother*, 2006), to body image (*Breasts*, 1996; *Thin*, 2006), to political activism (*They Killed Sister Dorothy*, 2008; *Gloria: In Her Own Words*, 2011). These stories of voiceless, misrepresented or under-represented women strive for something beyond a fair hearing: they seek to move us.

HBO's sustained investment in documentary programming has earned the network a peerless reputation. But as Nevins learned early on, critical praise does not pay the bills. In order to subsidize these prestige projects, which tend to draw a faithful but limited audience, Nevins has long relied on a far more popular form of R-rated documentary often referred to as "sex docs." In 1992, she launched the first of a number of *American Undercover* sub-series: a half-hour magazine program exploring "sex 90's style," called *Real Sex*. It would continue to produce episodes off and on until 2009, and remains popular in late-night rotation. Over the course of its run, *Real Sex* would document any number of sexual practices and proclivities, explore the world of adult entertainment, and offer viewers a front-row seat at dozens of sex seminars. For all of that, *Real Sex* can be difficult to define. Was it meant to edify or arouse? Were viewers drawn to the naked flesh, or the sheer weirdness of watching "old women putting condoms on cucumbers," as a character from the popular CBS sitcom, *The Big Bang Theory*, put it ("The Adhesive Duck Deficiency," 3:08).

Whatever it was or is, the series owes a clear debt to the pioneering "sexology" work of Alfred Kinsey, William Masters, and Virginia Johnson. Yet it rejects the clinical view for the carnivalesque, and refuses to discriminate between prurient and academic interests. Though it shares a sense of fun with Hugh Hefner's *Playboy* magazine, *Real Sex* trades Hefner's dated sense of urbane sophistication for a brash, freewheeling attitude better suited to the age of Camille Paglia's *Sexual Personae* (1990), Madonna's *Sex* (1992), and Paul Verhoeven's *Basic Instinct* (1992): all of which appeared around the same time as the series. If Kinsey, Masters, and Johnson exposed, and Hefner exploited previously unspoken truths about human sexuality, *Real Sex* claimed only to reflect the sexual culture of its time: a culture defined in part by disease (AIDS) and scandal (Amy Fisher; Monica Lewinsky), but also by previously marginalized voices working their way into the mainstream,

FIGURE 6.1 German game show, *Tutti Frutti*, where ordinary people "strip for big prizes." *Real Sex: 4*, HBO

including sex-positive feminists, sex workers, pornographers, and the Lesbian, Gay, Bisexual, and Transgendered (LGBT) community. Despite its tendency to substitute verbal and visual exhibitionism for anything like socio-political commentary, *Real Sex* at least *pretended* to give these groups a forum.

In 1995, Nevins launched another sub-series from *America Undercover* that offered an even more compelling form of access: the hidden camera documentary, *Taxicab Confessions*. Here the chatter of sex therapists and the parade of un-retouched naked bodies familiar to viewers of *Real Sex* gives way to something far simpler: loquacious cab drivers with a talent for getting their customers to open up emotionally, and fares who seem surprisingly willing to reveal their deepest sexual desires, fears, . traumas, and triumphs to the hidden camera. Some seem driven by self-destructive inner exhibitionist impulses, but most pursue a perhaps more universal impulse: the need to reveal some basic truth about themselves, without concern for the larger implications. And where better to do so than in a cab, traveling alongside a complete stranger in that rare, privileged moment suspended between Where We Have Been and Where We Are Going? Through the camera, we share in that privileged moment, voyeuristic witnesses to lives that would otherwise remain invisible to us. If the subject of *Real Sex* is the way sex defines the boundaries of our social interactions, *Taxicab Confessions* is more about the way it helps us to understand who we are as individuals. It is the sort of reality one rarely sees in reality television: no doubt the reason the series won one Emmy award for Outstanding Informational Program, and was nominated for three others in the category of Outstanding Non-Fiction Reality Program.

The critical success of *Taxicab Confessions* is a testament to Nevins' and HBO's canny ability to draw clear distinctions between erotic programming and programming *about* erotic subjects: a distinction particularly well-served by its multiplexing strategy. HBO is not one channel, but many, each aimed at a different demography: families, Spanish-speaking viewers, comedy fans, etc. While there is a great deal of overlap between the audiences for these different channels, multiplexing helps to compartmentalize that audience. And where sexually explicit content is concerned, this strategy is especially important. Many viewers subscribe to premium services precisely for this content, but others—particularly those with young families—seek to contain and/or restrict access to it.

At the same time, premium channels like HBO and its longest-standing competitor, Showtime, make little or no effort to market their more adult-oriented programming, either externally (through advertisement, screener tapes, or home video releases) *or* internally (through coming attractions, behind-the-scenes programming, or presence on network web pages), because their audience knows precisely where to find it, and because it avoids the possibility of contaminating other aspects of their "quality" brands.[12] This policy of containment does not prevent HBO from showing sexually explicit material on its main channel. If anything, it liberates them to do so, provided that content is framed in ways that critical and popular audiences deem "legitimate." Want erotic content? Look to Cinemax—aka "Skinemax"—and the "Max After Dark" programming block for softcore movies and anthology series like *Scandals, Erotic Confessions,* and *Co-Ed Confidential.* Want documentaries about human sexual proclivities and practices? Go to HBO's main channel after the kids have gone to sleep.

Of course, the distinction between an "HBO show" and a "Cinemax show" may have more to do with perception than reality. Take for example the two HBO reality series, *G-String Divas* and *Pornucopia.* If *Real Sex* offers a survey of sexual subcultures that can be more amusing than erotic, and *Taxicab Confessions* teases surprisingly poignant moments from its voyeuristic premise, these latter series about women working in the sex industry play like "docuporn": a sub-genre of pornography that purports to reveal the "real" lives of adult entertainers, typically through behind-the-scenes interviews and "day-in-the-life" footage. The strippers of *G-String Divas* and the porn stars of *Pornucopia* present themselves to the documentary cameras as well-adjusted adults who happily participate in a consensual exchange of money for guilt-free pleasure. At least a part of that pleasure is being extended to HBO viewers, who are given access to the world of strip clubs and porn shoots under the guise of some more academic, or at least less salacious, purpose.

Maybe too academic, since neither series lasted more than a handful of episodes. Given the abundance and availability of Internet pornography, maybe such series no longer offered enough erotic interest. Maybe viewers jaded by primetime soap operas and reality television were unsatisfied with the level of drama in the lives of the strippers and porn stars. Or maybe the series failed to sustain an audience because they unwittingly exposed the Big Ugly Truth about strip shows and pornography: that they are actually mind-numbingly repetitive and dull stuff.

Far more successful is HBO's reality franchise, *Cathouse*, which has run since 2002 in various forms, from stand-alone documentaries, to a weekly series, to a musical. Set in Nevada's Moonlite Bunny Ranch brothel, and alternating between interviews and scenes of the prostitutes at work, *Cathouse* represents perhaps the most extreme example of HBO's effort to contain—but at the same time exploit—the limits of sexual content. Without the documentary frame, the sexually explicit scenes would be hard to defend as anything more than voyeuristic pornography. But by offsetting the sex work with conversations in which the women present themselves as well-adjusted, well-compensated professionals doing what they take pains to describe as a vital service for the community, it can easily be taken for a sex-positive feminist treatise on how prostitution can be rewarding for all involved, and need not be bound up in narratives of depravity, violence, disease, and dependency.[13] Not coincidentally, these claims also prop up the male fantasy that prostitutes are just horny women who enjoy having sex with strangers.

While *Cathouse* avoids the callow, romantic notions of prostitution that underlie popular Hollywood films from *Breakfast at Tiffany's* (1961) to *Pretty Woman* (1990)—not to mention Showtime's *Secret Diary of Call Girl* (2007)—it hardly reflects the poverty and social subjugation experienced by the vast majority of the world's estimated 40 million prostitutes. For that perspective, one must look to documentaries like *The Day My God Died* (2003), *Whore's Glory* (2011), or HBO's own *Hookers at the Point* (2002) and *Born into Brothels* (2004). Of course, *Cathouse*

FIGURE 6.2 Chatting up. *Cathouse*, HBO

is a reality show, and as such makes no more claim to describing the universal experience of prostitutes than *The Real Housewives* franchise does to reflecting the daily life of the average stay-at-home mom.

Like *Pornucopia*, *Cathouse* straddles the line between reality and fantasy, again mimicking docuporn. In pornography, the sex is real, but the emotions surrounding it are obviously, even deliberately fake, because the fantasy demands it. The ludicrous narrative arcs, the grotesque dialogue, the dull-eyed performances create a generic template upon which the (typically) male viewer may easily project himself (hence the largely unremarkable features of male actors in heterosexual porn). The sex depicted merely offers visual stimulation. Docuporn promises to cut through the artifice of standard pornography by injecting it with "reality," but all it really does is substitute a hollow story with a hollow character study, premised on the notion that porn stars are emotionally vulnerable and passionate about their work: qualities that help to sustain viewer fantasies about being desired by the female sexual surrogates on the screen.

The prostitutes of *Cathouse* certainly express these characteristics, but they never quite work as props in a viewer's fantasy because the "reality" of the series is insistent. From the interviews to the bedroom scenes, the camera constantly reminds us of its presence, and that we are *peering into* this world, rather than entering it. The interviews are in medium close-up, the women meeting our gaze, breeching the closed boundary necessary to maintain the illusion of fantasy. The scenes in the bedrooms are shot mostly at high angles, like a security camera feed. In many ways, *Cathouse* is not so different from "reality" shows like *Big Brother* and *The Real World*, which deliberately blur the lines between voyeurism and staged spectacle, intimacy and performance. And that confusion—along with the wide variety of interpersonal conflicts, character revelations, and clients that constitute the narrative of the series—is the source of drama, meaning, and pleasure.

The success of *Cathouse* and HBO's other sex docs also has a lot to do with the uniform style of the work. With the exception of *Taxicab Confessions* and *Pornucopia*, all of the sex doc series have been produced—and in most cases directed—by one person: Patti Kaplan. Like Nevins, Kaplan had her start at the Children's Television Workshop, where she directed segments of *3–2–1 Contact* for PBS and produced *Encyclopedia* for HBO. Whether due to shared backgrounds or shared interests, Nevins brought Kaplan in on the ground floor of *Real Sex* and has since given her reign over the bulk of HBO's sex doc empire.

Kaplan's unique production style defines the form to the same extent that it differs from the "quality" markers of the network's critically acclaimed productions. The editing is quick and playful, drawing attention to itself through bawdy musical punctuation and transitional effects (wipes, fills, cross-fades). Interviews are intercut with sexually explicit scenes meant to provoke the viewer, rather than probe the subjects, who tend to be more interested in exhibiting than revealing themselves. The camera works mostly in close-up and medium shots—straight on, or at high and low angles: part sympathetic listener, part Peeping Tom. The sort of objective tone we associate with documentary is absent. In its place we find some combination of the broad-minded confidante who refuses to pass judgment, and the winking carnival barker who bids the boardwalk passer-by to glance behind the curtain.

Kaplan's style has changed remarkably little over the decades. It is as though we are watching a single mosaic work on contemporary sexuality, imbued with a strong, sex-positive sense of fun: the lighter side of HBO's more serious documentaries about rape, abortion, sex trafficking, and prostitution. Though the sex docs may lack the gravitas of these other works—not to mention the sociological and narrative ambitions of HBO dramas like *The Wire* or *Game of Thrones*—no film or television work on human sexuality approaches their scope or scale. And whether the documentary frame serves a clinical or lascivious function, it forces the audience into a critical viewing position.

Kaplan's style may be shot through with good humor, but her subject matter is too serious and ungainly for mere burlesque. Reality is messy stuff. We cannot help but see that messiness in the imperfect bodies and unstudied gestures of the sex therapists, swingers, strippers, prostitutes, and johns; and in the self-conscious posturing and anxious affectations of the parade of exhibitionists, performers, and confidantes who trust the camera to express something vital about themselves, though they have no script or director to guide them. They work with what they have, and what they know, more or less aware of the expectations of their audience, and more or less willing and able to meet those expectations. The prostitutes in *Cathouse* are as aware of the television audience, generally, as they are of the johns specifically, and present themselves to both at once. The nature of those presentations may differ in important ways (one is actual, the other virtual; one is physical, the other psychological; one is immediate, the other remote), but in other ways they are similar. The women are paid to entertain us, to act as objects of desire, and to present a coherent image onto which we may impose both our critical and fantastical ideas of them.

Is the relationship reciprocal? If we are to believe what the prostitutes tell us, yes: the compensation they receive is adequate return for what they give the johns and premium channel viewers. Do the women have any control over our critical and fantastical view of them, beyond choosing to participate in the exchange? That is harder to say, especially given how entrenched are the almost exclusively male fantasies they play upon. But the documentary camera constitutes a viewer/subject relationship that seems to mimic the dynamics of sex itself: the give-and-take, the projection and interpretation of desires, and the complex interplay of physical satisfaction and self-image.

Have Real Sex, G-String Divas and Cathouse empowered their mostly female subjects, or fed into objectifying, mostly male fantasies. Or have they managed to straddle the line between liberation and exploitation? Sheila Nevins has long taken the view that the women in these series hold the real power because they are the engines of the fantasies: the source of erotic energy. Of G-String Divas, she says simply, "The women are beautiful and the men are fools."[14] But to Ariel Levy, HBO documentaries about strippers and prostitutes are nothing more than "raunch culture," subsidized and rewarded by a "female chauvinist pig," and the women who produce and participate in them trade in the worst sorts of stereotypes.

Perhaps Levy and Nevins merely reflect paired responses to the same reality. In a world in which the erotic discourses continue to be dominated by male perspectives and male desires, women can either find a way to make those desires work for them or demand an equal place for their own. Whichever HBO's sex docs do, they have certainly lifted the veil on sexuality—male and female—like nothing else in the history of television.

A significant relationship

In an early episode of Sex and the City, the series' main character, sex columnist Carrie Bradshaw, wakes up in a hotel room after a one-night stand with a French architect to find $1,000 waiting for her in an envelope on the nightstand, along with a note that reads, "Thanks for a beautiful day." Her first reaction at being mistaken for a prostitute is outrage, but by the time she welcomes her friends—Miranda Hobbes and Samantha Jones—into the same hotel room to have brunch (on the architect's expense account, though Carrie insists that they will pay for it themselves), she is no longer sure "whether to take it as an incredible compliment or as an incredible insult." The responses of her friends don't exactly clear up that ambivalence. While Miranda is adamant that the gesture is degrading, Samantha wonders why she is getting so uptight: "Money is power. Sex is power. Therefore, getting money for sex is simply an exchange of power." They go back and forth: Miranda calling Samantha a "dime store Camille Paglia," Samantha insisting that "men give and women receive." Finally, Carrie interrupts them to say that she has decided to "write the whole thing off as a bad date with a cash bonus," and the conversation turns quickly to the room service poached salmon ("The Power of Female Sex," 1:05).

This exchange is typical of *Sex and the City*: provocative without being too serious, opinionated without offering a consensus view, and meant to approximate—at least in spirit—the sort of conversation any contemporary group of 30- and 40–something women might have about sex, relationships, and power. True, many viewers find the conversation and

FIGURE 6.3 Girl talk over brunch. *Sex and the City*, HBO

the show shallow and frivolous: part gabfest, part vicarious shopping spree. One critic described it as "another example of television catching up with women's magazines, which have been blathering inanely about sex for years."[15]

But this "blathering" is an important part of the show's popular appeal *and* its cultural impact. *Sex and the City* delves into any number of taboo sexual subjects (abortion, masturbation, female orgasm) with a degree of candor and humor previously unseen on television. Women have been talking about sex on television since at least as far back as *Mary Tyler Moore*, but even the most outspoken—say, Peggy Bundy from *Married... With Children*—had almost nothing to say about female desire, other than the fact that men seem unwilling or unable to satisfy it. *Sex and the City* gets into the details, offering a "woman's perspective" unlike anything previously seen in female-centered television comedy, from *I Love Lucy* to *The Golden Girls*.

This new perspective is certainly limited. After all, *Sex and the City* is about four white, well-off, well-educated urban women, and was created by a gay man (Darren Star). But whatever those limitations, and whatever one's opinion of the show, it has certainly changed the way television characters—women *and* men—talk about sex, from Dwight Schrute of *The Office* asking his Human Resources representative the difference between the clitoris and the labia ("Sexual Harrassment," 2:02), to the endless string of vagina, cunnilingus, and vibrator jokes that constitute the dialogue of *2 Broke Girls*. And it has left an indelible mark on American popular culture.

To begin to understand that influence, let us look briefly at representations of women throughout the history of television comedy. In the 1950s and 1960s, women in comedic television series were restricted to two roles: the screwball (*The Burns and Allen Show*; *I Love Lucy*; *I Dream of Jeannie*) and the happy homemaker (*The Adventures of Ozzie and Harriet*; *Leave it to Beaver*; *The Donna Reed Show*). In the 1970s, the heyday of the Second Wave feminism of Betty Freidan (*The Feminine Mystique*, 1963) and Gloria Steinem (*Ms.* Magazine, which first appeared in 1971), sitcoms featured strong female characters who actively spoke out for women's liberation (*Mary Tyler Moore*; *Maude*), even in programs that centered on male characters (*All in the Family*; *M*A*S*H*), or focused less on gender than race and class (*The Jeffersons*; *Good Times*). Some of this rhetoric remained in the comedies of the 1980s and early 1990s, but the focus shifted from the political to the personal, as though the battle for equal rights had already been won, and women were simply adjusting to their status in the new order. These programs focus on professional women seemingly unencumbered by the "glass ceiling" (Julia Sugarbaker in *Designing Women*; Murphy Brown in *Murphy Brown*); and blue-collar moms balancing the challenges of work and domestic life with natural toughness and frank good humor (Roseanne Connor in *Roseanne*; Grace Kelly in *Grace Under Fire*). But by the late 1990s, these strong, self-assured women were being increasingly displaced by updated versions of two staples from 1950s and 1960s television comedy: the long-suffering wife in *Everybody Loves Raymond*, *King of Queens*, and *That 70s Show*, and the wacky, erratic screwball in *Suddenly Susan*, *Dharma and Greg*, and *Ally McBeal*.

Though there are no long-suffering wives on *Sex and the City*, it shares several things in common with the screwball series: most obviously their focus on romantically vulnerable women who struggle for some measure of control in their relationships. At the beginning of their respective series, Ally (*Ally McBeal*) and Susan (*Suddenly Susan*) have just broken off long-term relationships, and scramble to make sense of their professional and personal choices; while Dharma (*Dharma and Greg*) and Carrie (*Sex and the City*) embark on relationships that their closest friends and family warn them against. To meet these challenges, each series imbues its central character with an indomitable spirit that, despite the occasional low point, pushes her back into the fray, eager to turn every loss into a lesson (Ally: "I like being a mess. It's who I am"; Carrie: "Maybe our mistakes are what make our fate.").

Sex and the City even adopts the "battle of opposites" theme common to screwball comedy, in which seemingly incompatible characters are inevitably bound together. Only where the screwballs of *I Love Lucy* and *I Dream of Jeannie* find their opposite in straight-laced, paternalistic romantic partners (Ricky Ricardo; Major Nelson), here it is found in a menagerie of distinctive friends: "lusty, boiled Samantha; ditzy, doe-eyed Charlotte; Miranda, full of tart good sense; and Carrie, beguiling and plucky."[16] In other words, *Sex and the City* replaces the traditional dynamics of romantic conflict and resolution with an often revealing, frequently humorous, sometimes combative, but always supportive conversation between women.

Sex and the City's tone borrows largely from its source material: Candace Bushnell's advice column of the same name, which appeared in the *New York Observer* from 1994 to 1996, and was published as a single-volume collection in 1997. While the chirpy TV series glosses over the darker moments from Bushnell's column (Bushnell's Carrie deals with romantic disappointment by getting high and drinking herself sick), it shares her freewheeling, breezy wit and, at least in the early seasons, takes on the same rhetorical form. Episodes open with sex columnist Carrie posing a question (for example, "Do we need distance to get close?"), then take up the remaining time teasing revelations out of the personal experiences of herself and her friends. Much of Carrie's voice-over narration and the girls' dialogue is directly cribbed from Bushnell's column. The tone is conversational and irreverent, "girl talk" over cocktails and barely-eaten 30–something birthday cake. Like the most successful advice columns and self-help books, the series draws the viewer in with the promise of good-natured honesty and shared confidences ("Let's face it, ladies…"), and maintains the illusion of expertise by limiting and controlling the terms of the conversation: a few basic categories, a consistent point of view, and a limited range of perspectives.

This sort of anecdotal sexual wisdom was first made popular in the book that inspired Bushnell's column: Helen Gurley Brown's *Sex and the Single Girl* (1962). In the voice of a confidante, Brown offers practical advice for unmarried women, including how to identify and meet eligible partners, enhance one's sex appeal, maximize career opportunities, and navigate the various stages of an affair. The key themes are self-empowerment and personal satisfaction. Brown describes a woman who does for herself: dresses for success, but also to make herself happy; and pursues relationships that advance her goals, whatever they may be. She continues this idea in her *other* contribution to the history of female identity culture: *Cosmopolitan* magazine. Rather, her revamping of *Cosmopolitan* in the mid-1960s, from the American literary periodical it had been since its founding in 1886, to its current form as a sex-and-fashion magazine for women, distributed in 32 different languages, in more than 100 countries around the world. In a sense, the transformation has allowed the magazine to fulfill the meaning of its title, "one who is at home anywhere in the world." This notion of the "cosmopolitan" woman is a central tenet of Brown's notion of female sexual liberation: women should feel at home anywhere.

Sex and the City owes an extraordinary debt to *Sex and the Single Girl*, right down to its title. Even the breezy, light-hearted, winking tone of Carrie Bradshaw's/Candace Bushnell's columns sound like Brown. But if Brown's book takes the form of a how-to guide for women who have determined to live independent of men (though not necessarily without them), *Sex and the City* considers the merits of this choice. If Brown presents the theory, *Sex and the City* tests its limits. Carrie, Miranda, Samantha and Charlotte took Brown's advice to heart in their 20s, but now in their 30s and 40s they are forced to ask whether independence and sexual liberation are enough.

At one level, the series refocuses an issue that had plagued "feminist" television characters for decades: how to balance careers with relationships. *Sex and the City* takes a distinctly post-feminist view, in which women are free to choose whatever path suits them, rather than worrying over the social implications. Choosing between a career and a life of domestic bliss need not be seen as a compromise. And though professional and romantic failures are still painful, they need not be devastating. A similar attitude is evident in later comedic characters like Liz Lemon (*30 Rock*) and Jessica Day (*New Girl*), who refuse to wrap their identities around careers *or* relationships. But if personal choices are no longer driven by societal expectations, they do come with personal consequences. And though the women of *Sex and the City* meet the world with a combination of comic cynicism (Samantha: "The good ones screw you, the bad ones screw you, and the rest don't know how to screw you") and romantic optimism (Carrie: "Eventually all the pieces fall into place…. until then, laugh at the confusion, live for the moment, and know that everything happens for a reason"), their relationship anxieties become increasingly evident as the series sloughs off the advice column frame of early episodes for something closer to a conventional romantic comedy. Like a conventional romantic comedy, *Sex and the City* becomes less about *whether* the women will have lasting and meaningful relationships, than how much control they will have in them. Though they have tried to live self-contained lives, they continually threaten to spill out, especially as the women get older and independence begins to feel more and more like loneliness.

We see this shift clearly in Carrie's on-again, off-again relationship with Big, whom she often strategically puts off in order to gain leverage. Eventually they will come together: the only question is, under what— or whose—terms? We also see it in the relationship the four central characters have with Manhattan itself, which the series lays out in the very first sequence of the pilot episode. In it, Carrie describes a young English journalist who comes to New York in expectation of finding love. At first, we might think Carrie is speaking about herself (despite any pause the "English" part might give us). But as the story develops, we realize that the journalist has been introduced merely as an object lesson, to be discarded just as quickly as she is introduced. In the story, the journalist finds herself in the thrall of "one of the city's typically eligible bachelors," only to be jilted, and forced to come to terms with "the end of love in Manhattan," where relationships are about leverage, opportunism, and ambition, not romance. "Welcome to the age of un-innocence," Carrie proclaims in voice-over. "No one has breakfast at Tiffany's, and no one has affairs to remember. Instead, we have breakfast at seven a.m., and affairs we try to forget as quickly as possible. Self-protection and closing the deal are paramount. Cupid has flown the co-op!" ("Pilot," 1:01).

The journalist in the story returns to England, but Carrie and her friends stay in New York. Despite occasionally expressing ambivalence about relationships being negotiated like commodities on the New York Stock Exchange, they seem largely willing to accept those terms: partly because they have made their lives here (their careers, their meaningful friendships), partly because of all that New York has to offer (the nightlife, the shopping, the proximity to power and money), but mostly because their ideas of happiness are tied up in the place. In *Sex and the City*, as in Woody Allen's movies, Manhattan is a sort of urban ideal: a sacrosanct place, despite the unholy messes its inhabitants might find themselves in. But unlike Allen's films, the series views the city from the point of view of transplants, not native New Yorkers. These women were born elsewhere, and chose to live here. In fact, they seem largely content to let Manhattan define their entire existence. Though they have seen a bit of the world—even moved out of the city for brief periods of time— the only thing cosmopolitan about them is their signature drink. And regardless of where they travel, they always end up back in Manhattan. When Big comes to Paris to sweep Carrie off of her feet in the series finale, promising to take her wherever she wishes to go in the world, she puts it as bluntly: "I miss New York. Take me home" ("An American Girl in Paris: Part Deux," 6:20). Brown's women have no home, but the women of *Sex and the City* cling to theirs like a great love.

Of course, the primary relationship in the series is the friendship between the four women. While television comedy spotlighted iconic female friendships long before *Sex and the City*—Lucy and Ethel (*I Love Lucy*), Monica and Rachel (*Friends*)—never before had we seen a *community* of women so fully formed, with four strong personalities, four distinct points of view, and four overlapping storylines. Prior to *Sex and the City*, television women typically formed partnerships based on the pretext of proximity or past history. If Lucy hadn't moved in next to Ethel, she would have found some other bored housewife to go along with her hair-brained schemes. Rachel moves in with Monica after abandoning her fiancé at the altar because she is an old friend, and the only person she knows in the city. Even the four single senior women of The Golden Girls are brought together by circumstance and convenience. Three of them answer a "room for rent" advertisement posted by the fourth in a local supermarket. But the women of *Sex and the City* are more than just interlocking elements in a contrived social group: they are essential agents of mutual growth, change, and self-knowledge. Unlike the women of *Friends* (including Phoebe, who tends to serve as a quirky counterpoint to Rachel and Monica), the women of *Sex and the City* weather numerous marriages, affairs, relocations, diseases, births, and deaths while still drawing strength and sustenance from their evolving core community. By series end, none of the four women is where we would have expected. Charlotte converts to Judaism and adopts a Chinese baby after learning hard lessons about the hollowness of her patrician dream; Miranda is living in Brooklyn with her son, her bartender husband, and her invalid mother-in-law; Samantha has fallen in love with a younger man, not because of the sex, but because he stands with her through her treatments for breast cancer; and while Carrie ends up with Big, the terms of the relationship are very different from those when it began: he changes his life for her, rather than the other way around. The four friends remain strongly connected to each other.

What truly sets the series apart is the quality of that connection: their friendship is driven not by emotional co-dependency, but by a willingness to change and experience personal growth together. In the final lines of the series, Carrie sums it up neatly: "The most exciting, challenging and significant relationship of all is the one you have with yourself." She then adds, as a qualification rather than an afterthought, "And if you find someone to love the you *you* love, well, that's just fabulous." The hierarchy is clear: personal growth first, relationships second. Friends and lovers are the agents of change, and a "fabulous" gift. But the goal is self-knowledge, not the acquisition of intimates. Several earlier comedy series pretend to this sort of personal-transformation-through-female-bonding, but they are invariably secondary to other goals. *Friends* confronts Rachel and Monica with plenty of reversals and revelations, but despite career changes, babies, romantic pairings and re-pairings, they end up right where viewers expected they would all along, making the show read more like farce than a truly evolving serial narrative.

Since *Sex and the City*, we have seen a new sort of bonding among female television characters, where friends are supportive, but are not afraid to be critical, or to make the relationship and each other vulnerable by exposing the hard truths that make personal growth possible. We see it in dramas like *Grey's Anatomy* (Meredith and Christina), *The Good Wife* (Alicia and Kalinda), and *Pretty Little Liars* (Aria, Hanna, Spencer and Emily), as well as in comedies such as *Parks and Recreation* (Leslie and Ann), *30 Rock* (Liz and Jenna), and *2 Broke Girls* (Max and Caroline). At the same time, we are seeing fewer and fewer series built around easy female friendships.[17] Though there are still a few that build on the successful formulas of such classic series as *Cagney and Lacey* (*Rizzoli and Isles*) and *The Golden Girls* (*Hot in Cleveland*), the heavy emphasis contemporary television places upon driven professional women more often than not puts them at odds with one other. And even where friendship does exist, women struggle to make time to sustain it (with her work schedule, Alicia barely has time to eat, let alone bond; and if Ann and Leslie didn't work in the same building, they might never see each other). It seems the days of Lucy, Ethel, Monica, and Rachel are long past.

Five months after *Sex and the City* took its final bow in 2004 (though the ladies would live on in syndication and through a highly-profitable movie franchise), HBO filled *Sex and the City*'s vaunted Sunday night timeslot with a new series called *Entourage*, which clearly attempted to capitalize on *Sex and the City*'s winning formula: the story of a small group of friends filling their Big City days and nights with conspicuous consumption, casual sex, and candid conversation. Even the series core characters seemed to parallel each other, from the generically likeable protagonists (Carrie Bradshaw and Vince Grenier) to the well-connected power brokers (Samantha Jones and Ari Gold), level headed cynics (Miranda Hobbes and Turtle), and romantic commitment-seekers (Charlotte York and Eric Murphy). But instead of haunting the clubs, gallery openings, and fashion shows of Manhattan with four successful 30- and 40-something single women, *Entourage* follows a group of 20-something playboys through the funhouse of Hollywood celebrity culture. And unlike *Sex and the City*, *Entourage* seems contented to simply display, rather than investigate the dynamics of same-sex friendship. It is a show about little more than getting laid and hanging out with the boys.

This is perhaps an overstatement, but it does raise questions about our assumptions regarding male and female notions of friendship, and helps to explain why *Sex and the City* was so successful. For regardless of how narrow the world view *Sex* offered (Manhattan yuppiedom), it reflected perhaps a more realistic view of female friendship than had previously been seen on television.

Contemporary gender research tends to suggest that, while men and women have similar emotional needs (intimacy, trust, open communication), they serve those needs very differently, especially when same-gender friendships are concerned.[18] Women's friendships tend to be built around the sharing of intimate feelings, openness, and one-on-one, face-to-face interactions that often result in strong, though not necessarily lasting attachments. Sustaining them takes hard work and commitment. As Carrie puts it, "Friendships don't magically last 40 years. You have to invest in them. It's like your savings. You don't expect to wake up one day, old and find a big bucket of money waiting there" ("Luck Be an Old Lady," 5:03). For women, friendships are often intense, even volatile and psychologically competitive. In the clichéd figuration, women praise each other up close, but curse each other at a distance. *Sex and the City* popularized the term, "frenemy," to describe this phenomenon.[19] And in many cases, women's most trusted companions are men: spouses, boyfriends, or "platonic" friends whose motives they do not suspect. For the women of *Sex and the City*, these companions are often gay men like Carrie's friend, Stanford Blatch, or "gay straight men": Carrie's term for the "passive, self-absorbed… soft-spoken, fashionable object of affection" often referred to as a metrosexual.[20] In other words, male versions of themselves, who love to shop and haunt the best restaurants and clubs, are obsessed with appearances, and offer no immediate competition in the romantic realm.

Men also tend to share their insecurities and concerns with trusted companions of the opposite sex, but unlike women, those companions tend to be parental figures or paid professionals rather than platonic friends. In *Entourage*, Vince's publicist, Shauna Roberts is a brutally honest and trustworthy confidante, who refers to herself as his "West-Coast mother." But perhaps the starkest contrast between male and female friendships is the role community plays in shoring up bonds of intimacy. Women tend to maintain and strengthen those bonds through acts of emotional exposure: sharing personal feelings and experiences. Carrie and her friends are open books with each other. But young men like those in *Entourage* tend to express their connections through casual social activities (sports, nightclubbing), prescribed social rituals having to do with shared adventures (going to the Playboy Mansion, or Las Vegas, or back home to Queens), competitions (bragging about the number and quality of their sexual conquests), and "shooting the shit" (discussing random, inconsequential things), rather than sharing the sort of intimate feelings and secrets that might expose them to ridicule. Of course, verbal insults and minor humiliations are all part of the male social ritual, but in the sort of guy culture described by *Entourage*, they are an expression of affection rather than cruelty. There are no "frenemies," only friends: when together they think well of each other, and when apart they speak well of each other.

These gender dynamics certainly offer insight into the highly masculinized worlds of HBO dramas like *The Sopranos* and *Deadwood*, in which men rely on professional female listeners to deal with their anxieties (the psychiatrist Dr Jennifer Melfi in *The Sopranos*; the prostitute Trixie in *Deadwood*) and male communities are forged through fierce competition; or to the frailties of masculinity revealed in comedies like *The Larry Sanders Show* and *Bored to Death*, where men are *only* able to reveal their deepest insecurities to male friends. But *Entourage* reflects only the simplest rituals of male bonding: the affectionate teasing, the sexual conquests, and the drunken nights on the town. A "bromance" mixed with an adolescent fantasy of supermodels, high performance cars, and movie stardom, *Entourage* is remarkably un-self-critical for an HBO series. That is precisely why it offers such a valuable point of comparison to *Sex and the City*.

For all of the charges of shallow "blathering," *Sex and the City* is about questioning assumptions, looking at other points of view, and pushing personal limits: that is what the conversations are all about. The series may present a privileged, glossy, hermetically-sealed world, but at least its characters are critically aware, and willing to express themselves honestly. And of all the ways *Sex and the City* has impacted popular culture—the fashions (Manolo Blahniks), the catch phrases ("woulda, coulda, shoulda"), the re-glamorization of New York City—its most enduring contribution may simply be the way it has allowed for more honest conversations about what women know, don't know, expect, desire, and fear about sex.

What they're worth

Given the extraordinary success of *Sex and the City*, it is hardly surprising that HBO would attempt to exploit the formula with *Entourage*. What might be more surprising is that the network seemed unable to develop another successful female-centered series until nearly a decade after the *Sex* finale in 2004. While Showtime was scoring popular and critical success with *The L Word* and *Weeds*, HBO's *The Comeback* and *No. 1 Ladies' Detective Agency* didn't even make it to a second season. Granted, the network's highest-performing series in those years featured some of the most compelling female characters on television, from Atia of the Julii (*Rome*) to Sookie Stackhouse (*True Blood*). But only recently has the network found renewed success with series about women, and those successes speak directly, though not always kindly, to the legacy of *Sex and the City*.

Near the end of an early episode of HBO's *Girls* titled "Hannah's Diary" (1:4), the series' main character—a 24–year-old, under-employed aspiring writer named Hannah Horvath, played by the show's creator, writer, and sometime director, Lena Dunham—shows up at the door of her not-boyfriend, Adam, to not-break up with him. Hannah has had a rough day, which began with her receiving a nude photo text from Adam that was clearly meant for another woman. It only got worse after she allowed her workmates to pluck and paint her eyebrows. She arrives at Adam's apartment—ragged lines of eye pencil making her look like what he describes as a "Mexican teenager"—and launches into an epic, rambling, but deeply moving kiss-off-cum-rationalization. She begins by outlining her needs clearly, honestly, and in language we might imagine Carrie using with Big in *Sex and the City* (though Carrie would never leave the house with those eyebrows): "I just want someone who wants to hang out all of the time, who thinks I'm the best person in the world and wants to have sex with only me." But then Hannah's speech veers in a decidedly un-Carrie direction:

> It makes me feel very stupid to tell you this because it makes me sound like a girl who wants to, like, go to brunch. And I really don't want to go to brunch, and I don't want you to sit on the couch while I shop or even meet my friends.

No *brunch*? No *shopping*? No *meeting her friends*? This clearly isn't Carrie Bradshaw's idea of a relationship. But then, Hannah is no Carrie: she is tough, but untried; articulate, but unsure of her footing. Carrie is living *la dolce vita*, while Hannah is struggling to get by, and to be seen and heard.

Perhaps Hannah's words do compel Adam to see and hear her, or maybe he just wants to shut her up. In any case, he reaches across the threshold to pull her toward him. It is a surprisingly tender, passionate moment, given his previous disdainful or indifferent attitude toward her. And it dovetails neatly into another, equally tender one in which Hannah asks Adam to give some honest assessment of the nude photo she sent him in return. When he remarks that he found it "strange," she offers that taking a "serious naked picture" of herself is "just not who I am." Again drawing her close to him, he says without affect, "Then just be who you are." These are precisely the words she has longed to hear, at precisely her most vulnerable moment. Suddenly we find ourselves back in *Sex and the City* territory. The perfect ending, a mix of mutual understanding and fulfillment of desire.

But this is not *Sex and the City*, and we are nowhere near the end. The next time they meet, Adam is deliberately cold to Hannah, apparently still stinging from the earlier doorway speech. But rather than talking about those feelings, Adam enlists Hannah in a fantasy of sexual humiliation: he masturbates while she rains insults down on him. At first he seems into it, but as the energy begins to flag, she shifts from generic abuse to more pointed comments about his personal deficiencies. As her tones of distain and disgust amplify, so does his excitement. She demands money, intimating that it is for services rendered, and as she takes $100 from Adam's bureau drawer, he is brought to orgasm.

FIGURE 6.4 The perfect ending. *Girls*, HBO

In the moments following, it is clear that Hannah struggles to understand what she has just seen and done. The scene is clearly some sort of turning point in their relationship: for the first time, he has made himself vulnerable to her. But what is that relationship, really? Who are these two to each other, in this moment or any to follow? At their core, these questions are not so different from the ones Carrie raises in countless episodes of *Sex and the City* (though it would be hard to imagine Carrie participating in Adam's fantasy): What do men want, and what does it have to do with what she wants? What is she willing to do for a relationship?

Of course, when the architect pays Carrie for sex, all she can think to do is ask whether it is a compliment or an insult: a question she is never willing to answer, because either would be unbearable to her. But not to Hannah. She is fearless and engaged, while Carrie is clever and circumspect. Where Carrie poses provocative, never-truly-answered questions in a sex advice column in order to make sense of her relationships, Hannah forges ahead with her own story and goes willingly and honestly where it takes her. The $100 Hannah takes from Adam is not the value she has placed on bearing witness to Adam's humiliation, but her contribution to the fantasy itself. As several critics have pointed out, this is Hannah the fiction writer "writing herself into" the narrative, claiming co-authorship of Adam's fantasy.

For a show that claims to spring from an admiration for *Sex and the City*, *Girls* is in many ways a rebuttal to its predecessor. As Dunham puts it, "Here's the life that you set up for us, and here are the ways that we are failing."[21] Observers of *Girls* are often quick to note parallels between the four women in both series: Carrie, Miranda, Samantha, and Charlotte York in *Sex and the City*, and Hannah, Marnie, Shoshanna, and Jessa in *Girls*. But those parallels merely amplify their differences, and the narrowness of the original characterizations. The naïve Shoshanna, who is an avowed fan of *Sex and the City*, is perhaps most like Charlotte: plucky, romantic, conservative, and devoted to *The Rules*.[22] But when the series begins Shoshanna is an emotionally stunted ingénue obsessed with losing her virginity: possibly out of a sense of shame, possibly to unlock some power she expects to find by accessing her sexuality. Rather than a prelapsarian Charlotte, Shoshanna is a critique of her predecessor's shallow values: the social registry wedding and the home in Connecticut with Mr Right. On the surface, Marnie looks to be *Girls'* Miranda. Though she shares some social characteristics with Charlotte (she comes from a blue blood family, she is a control freak, and in the first season she works at an art gallery), like Miranda she imagines herself to be a hardened pragmatist (each fancies herself the voice of reason in her group), seeks a more compatible, less compliant lover (both reject men for being "too good"), and plays the role of best friend to the lead character. But while Miranda weathers one crisis after another with self-confidence and a sharp wit, Marnie turns out to be the most vulnerable member of the group, thrown into an existential crisis after miscalculating a relationship and unexpectedly losing her job. Jessa resembles Samantha, in that both are very loyal to friends, sexually liberated, and promiscuous. But while Samantha squeezes all she can out of life, Jessa is sexually reckless (in a less hermetically sealed story world, she would be the one to get AIDS or be raped) and erratic (she marries a near-stranger suddenly—and unbelievably—at the end of Season One). The would-be *femme fatale* turns out to be a lost child. As for Hannah and Carrie, the only thing they seem to share is a vocation: both are writers. But Carrie writes a chirpy sex column, while Hannah, the fiction writer and essayist, struggles to be "the voice of my generation, or at least *a* voice of *a* generation," as she tells her parents in the opening scene of the series. Physically, socially, and psychologically, they could not be more different. One is petite, fashion-obsessed, successful and self-assured; the other full-figured, a fashion nightmare, barely able to pay the rent and cut adrift.

In a sense the white, urban, upper middle-class girls of *Girls* are the women of *Sex and the City* not yet fully formed: or more accurately, developmentally stunted by a new set of realities and a deep generational divide. Carrie's generation is self-assured because they have already achieved career success. When they graduated from college in the yuppie heyday of the late 1980s, opportunities were everywhere. Hannah's generation was also promised success, but in the wake of changes in the global economy, they have been left struggling to find a foothold. *Girls* represents "a recession-era adjustment" to *Sex and the City*: "The gloss of Manhattan is traded for the mild grit of Brooklyn's more affordable neighborhoods. The anxieties are as much economic as erotic. The colors are duller, the mood is dourer and the clothes aren't much. It's *Sex and the City* in a charcoal gray Salvation Army overcoat."[23]

Hannah belongs to what has been variously described as Generation Y, the Millennial Generation, the Internet Generation, the MTV Generation, Generation 9/11, and in Britain, the Jilted Generation. Over-protected by helicopter parents, hyper-connected to the digital world, and excessively served in a consumer economy that places youth above all other values, this generation came of age with a strong sense of entitlement, self-confidence, and assertiveness—not to mention a natural impatience toward the values and conventions of previous generations—only to reach their 20s to face desperate economic conditions (the Great Recession), dissipated revolutions (Occupy Wall Street), and the depressing realization that Twitter and Facebook may actually make one less capable of finding meaningful relationships. In other words, this is a generation woefully unprepared for the "real" world, but with just enough naïve confidence and technical acuity to fumble through grown-up life choices. That is, once they have worn out the patience and consumed the discretionary savings of their parents, as Hannah has by the time the first scene of *Girls* begins.

These economic circumstances amplify key themes in each series. *Sex and the City* is about women who seem to have it all: career, fulfilling relationships (or at least friendships), great sex, and unlimited credit. *Girls*, on the other hand, is about women who, according to Dunham, don't yet "know what they're worth":

It's about that moment when you know you should form your idea of what you want, but you don't know enough to know what you want yet... . The depiction of women [in film and television] tends to be sexy confident slut, or anxious girl who's obsessed with work and pleasing other people, and can't get it together sexually. And I think the idea of the sweet vulnerable person who is also interested in danger and has some perversions: that's the kind of complex character you meet in life and don't often meet on television.[24]

While both series present fairly self-involved characters, Carrie and Co. are glamorous narcissists at the peak of their powers, while Hannah and Co. are self-conscious and self-centered in the way 20–somethings tend to be. The *Girls* narrative is driven by awkward, uncomfortable, not-okay moments: groping bosses, naked parents, cruel betrayals, and abandonment. It is a catalog of humiliations used to reveal moments of emotional honesty. And *Girls* attempts to "normalize" such moments because they speak to real experience rather than fantasies of unlimited pleasure and contentment, without sparing, or wallowing in the suffering. Again, Dunham: "I always thought the saddest feeling in life is when you're dancing in a really joyful way and then you hit your head on something. It's sad and embarrassing and I feel like Hannah's entire life is like dancing and then hitting her head on something."[25]

Of course, embarrassment and discomfort are not only reserved for the characters. The audience shares in them, too, especially during the sex scenes, which tend to be lengthy, explicit, presented directly (no music, few cuts, mostly medium close-ups), and built around moments ranging from the awkward to the creepy.

The second episode of *Girls* opens with a particularly troubling scene, in which Hannah attempts to play along with a role-playing fantasy Adam springs on her during sex: he imagines her as an 11–year-old junkie prostitute he has picked up on the street. It is the sort of scene one might expect to find in the films of Catherine Brelliat (*Fat Girl; Sex is Comedy*) or Todd Solondz (*Welcome to the Dollhouse; Happiness*), but not on television, and certainly not in a half-hour comedy. So it should hardly be surprising that the scene drew the attention of many television critics, who struggled to reconcile the content of the fantasy with the quiet humor and pathos of Hannah's willing response. Most saw the scene as a sort of metaphor for the kinds of humiliations a young woman often endures along the path to sexual maturity and self-possession. While Hannah consents to participate in Adam's fantasy, she seems subordinated into it. Others read the scene along lines similar to Adam's humiliation fantasy two episodes later: an exercise in participatory story-telling, where Hannah is not subjugated, but critically present. She seems to understand that Adam is merely mimicking behavior he has seen while trolling porn on the Internet. Though the content of the fantasy raises disturbing questions about what sort of pornography Adam is watching.

Sex is rarely pretty, and almost never erotic in *Girls*: it is a groping, fumbling adventure into unknown and untried areas of pleasure, marked by fear and doubt. But for all of the humiliation and shame these scenes evoke, they are also remarkably honest about what it is to be young and to explore one's sexual identity. In other words, *Girls* uses sex as a form of knowing. Dunham puts it best:

[F]or me and for a lot of people I know, sex has been this battleground on

which you're playing out a lot of identity issues beyond just getting off.… . We were really trying to make each sex scene be a real moment of education about that character and what they want, and what the two want from each other.[26]

These scenes can be troubling, sad, or infuriating, partly because Dunham refuses to cap them with fake-pithy Carrie-isms about how failed relationships are like crashed computers ("The best we can do is breathe and reboot"), or men are like drugs ("Sometimes they bring you down...sometimes they get you so high").

Does *Girls* reject *Sex and the City*'s simplistic, overly-romantic way of looking at contemporary sexual mores to expose the lie, or simply because it doesn't work in real life? Hard to say. But *Girls* certainly reflects a more realistic—if just as narrowly defined (white, well-educated, urban)—female perspective. According to *Girls*, being a woman—or at least a young woman—is less about achieving self-actualization through the fulfillment of one's desires than testing the limits of those desires in the always unsettled, often unsettling moment. And this is ultimately why the series matters: it is truly subjective. Hannah is "*a* voice of *a* generation." Though the pop cultural feminism of generations past has taught us to think of women in terms of social roles, or as a composite of personal and professional accomplishments, the girls of *Girls* are uniquely themselves: not demographic samples, not personality types, not pithy sentiments. Their problems are messy, their failures are many, and their lives are never simple. Because that's the way it is for girls (and for that matter, boys).

A similar sentiment runs through other contemporary HBO series focused on female characters, most notably *Enlightened*, which was co-created by series star Laura Dern (*Blue Velvet*; *Jurassic Park*) and co-star Mike White (*Chuck and Buck*; *School of Rock*). If *Girls* revisits the basic premise of *Sex and the City* through the lens of a younger, far less self-possessed generation, *Enlightened* inverts it. The main character of *Enlightened*, Amy Jellicoe, is the same age as the women of *Sex and the City*—40—but she is a product of a very different time. Carrie embodies the entitled, mostly contented Manhattan yuppie of the 1990s, while Amy's story reflects "a common cultural apathy we were all feeling over the last decade in this country. And Amy, like so many of us, is as mad as hell and she's not going to take it any more."[27] If *Sex and the City* is about looking for love in a postcard of New York, *Enlightened* is about looking for spiritual truth and karmic justice in the sprawl of Riverside, California. Carrie Bradshaw is a successful columnist for the *New York Star*, and a fashionista who manages to live well beyond her means. Amy does data entry for the faceless Abbaddon corporation, and dresses like "she's having to live out of a closet she had from age 14 to 22," because hard financial times have forced her to move back into her mother's suburban home.[28] While Carrie struts her stuff among the elite of Manhattan, Amy thrusts New Age platitudes at her uninterested co-workers, her emotionally shattered ex-husband, and her distant mother. For all of their romantic woes, Carrie, Samantha, Miranda, and Charlotte are highly successful women, navigating the Manhattan dating scene with all of the advantages available to women of their age. As women, the deck may be stacked against them, but they know how to "play the hand [they've] been dealt, and accessorize what [they've] got." Amy, on the other hand, spent her 30s using her sex appeal to climb the corporate ladder. But at 40 that appeal has faded, and her last lover and boss, Damon, has pushed her aside.

In the opening shot of the series, we find Amy sobbing on a ladies' room toilet in Abbaddon's Health and Beauty division. Damon has apparently had her moved to the Cleaning Supplies division in order to put some distance between them. Moments later, two female co-workers enter and, unaware of Amy's presence, begin mocking her for breaking the golden rule: "You don't shit where you eat." Her indignation and grief boil over into an epic bout of rage that begins with her cursing out her co-workers and ends with her loudly and publicly threatening Damon, after prying open his elevator doors with her bare hands.

And that's just the opening scene. The second presents a montage of images from her month-long stay at a New Age recovery center in

FIGURE 6.5 A woman on the verge. *Enlightened*, HBO)

Hawaii, with Amy's voice-over expressing—in her tone as much as her language—a profound transformation of mind and spirit:

> I'm speaking with my true voice now, without bitterness or fear and I'm here to tell you, you can walk out of hell and into the light. You can wake up to your higher self and when you do, the world is suddenly full of the possibility of wonder and deep connection. ("Pilot," 1.01)

Through a strict regimen of meditation, group therapy sessions, and self-help books, Amy has come to realize that the future is hers to make, just as the past was a result of her own choices. After all, she knew Damon was a married man. Her only wish is to return to her old life carrying the light of this knowledge with her, and to set everything to right. But what she doesn't see is that her recent public breakdown has made her a pariah.

Until recently, Amy had the career and the sexual satisfaction of her Manhattan compatriots. But here the story is about having those things taken away, and how she responds to that loss. If the girls of *Girls* don't yet know "what they are worth," Amy is learning that she only thought she did. She thinks she has found a deeper spiritual truth, but doubts do surface, especially when the world does not reflect back her beatific grin. Has she really transcended the traps of careerism and sexual diminution that confront so many women as they cross the threshold into their 40s, or is she only fooling herself? Has she seen past the limitations of "conventional" notions of success—career advancement, sexual satisfaction, a clearly-defined role in one's community—or does losing those things simply reinvigorate the need for them? Amy is an emblem of another sort of "new" woman: casualty of lipstick feminism, new age spiritualism, and consumer nihilism. Like earlier versions of the "hysterical" woman (Bertha Mason in *Jane Eyre*; Mabel Longhetti in *A Woman Under the Influence*), she struggles to make others acknowledge her point of view. And though that point of view often strikes one as misguided, flaky, or naïve (for example, her effort to influence Abbaddon's polluting practices by printing some unflattering news stories from the web and presenting them to her corporate bosses), it is uniquely, distinctly, proudly hers.

Which is no guarantee of success, either in life or on television. After two seasons, HBO cancelled *Enlightened*, citing low viewership. Why did *Enlightened* fail to draw a sufficient audience to merit its continuation, while *Girls* quickly established itself as a cultural phenomenon? Perhaps it has something to do with the ages of the central characters. Are those 40–something men who make up so much of *Girls'* audience watching, at least in part, to sublimate some sort of mid-life crisis? Are the girls of *Girls* part of some virtual "fling," while Amy reminds them of the women in their long-term relationships? *Girls* also offers far more nudity, sex, and humor. Perhaps viewers are uncomfortable with women prone to nervous breakdowns, and would rather watch women struggling to form and reform their sexual identities than women engaged in New Age-y soul-searching.

Perhaps Amy Jelllicoe is simply the wrong kind of a mess. The women of series produced by Showtime (Cathy Jameson, *The Big C*; Jackie Peyton, *Nurse Jackie*) and Lifetime (Jane Bingum, *Drop Dead Diva*; Denise Sherwood, *Army Wives*) are lithely self-confident, even in the worst of crises. They don't have nervous breakdowns, only external changes of circumstance. And contemporary female characters on broadcast and basic cable tend to wear easy labels like "adorkable" (Claudia Donovan, *Warehouse 13*; Jessica Day, *New Girl*) and "ruthless" (Patty Hewes, *Damages*; Sue Sylvester, *Glee*). Not so Amy, whose motives and actions seem alternatively transparent and inscrutable (does she want to change the world, or merely get others to see it through her eyes?), and whose mask of serenity is so obviously a mask that we don't know whether to feel pity, annoyance, or amusement toward her. Is that mask meant primarily to protect, or to project? Is her need to be heard driven my a sense of powerlessness, exhibitionism, or true revelation?

Like Hannah, Amy trusts her instincts—however dubious—to direct her through the dissonance of the moment. We see this quality in several contemporary female television characters, from Maeby Bluth (*Arrested Development*) and Virginia Chance (*Raising Hope*) to Kara "Starbuck" Thrace (*Battlestar Gallactica*) and Carrie Mathison (*Homeland*), though in most cases it expresses itself as preternatural competence. Not so Amy or Hannah. And Amy distinguishes herself from most others, including Hannah, by committing so deeply to something so untenable, even ridiculous. Amy herself seems to grasp this. In the final episode, "Agent of Change" (2.08), she asks herself, "Am I the fool, the goat, the witch...or am I enlightened?"; but this question runs through the whole series. The great virtue of *Enlightened* is that it refuses to simply laugh her off as yet another acolyte to whatever New Age philosophy happens to be selling in the self-help section this week. The series recognizes how vulnerable we all are to such illusions (hence the enormous revenues generated by self-help books), and that their appeal reveals something more than our folly. It reveals what we want, and how far we are willing to go to get it.

****

The problem with discussing representations of gender is that one risks assuming half of the human population can be reduced to a series of shared character criteria. This is, of course, ridiculous. But for many years, television has done precisely that with its female television characters, reducing all women to a tidy set of characteristics and stereotypes: the nag, the help-mate, the selfless mother, the trophy wife, the bitter ex-wife, the temptress, the wizened widow. True, male characters are also subject to stereotyping and caricature (the working stiff; the dirty cop), but the patterns are much more pervasive with women. Over the past few decades, those rigid structures have begun to give way, and HBO has been an important part of that change. Whether populating grossly masculine story worlds with strong, willful women (Carmela Soprano, *The Sopranos*; Kima Greggs, *The Wire*), or introducing a more frank dialogue about female sexuality (*Real Sex*; *Sex and the City*), or injecting more authentic female voices into that dialogue (*Girls*; *Enlightened*), HBO has sought to present women not as types, but as unique individuals, with their own desires, problems, and points of view. Have series like *Cathouse* and *G-String Divas* perpetuated notions of women as objects of male fantasy? Sure. Does Carmela Soprano's unwillingness to give up the lifestyle her mobster husband Tony provides make her a hypocrite? Certainly. Can the women of *Sex and the City* be perceived as shallow opportunists? Absolutely. But the strippers and prostitutes of HBO's sex docs also insist on defining themselves. And at the very least, Carmela Soprano and Carrie Bradshaw *ask* themselves whether they are hypocrites or opportunists (though neither seems especially willing to probe for an answer).

HBO series are willing to put aside many of the trite notions of women perpetuated by television over the decades: the happy homemakers and harmless screwballs; the derelict hookers and femmes fatale; the "right on" feminists and super women who effortlessly balance career and family. In their place, they offer complex characters, with their own flaws and irresolvable internal conflicts. They cannot be quantified in easy categories—their virtues measured against their vices, their ambitions against their successes and failures—because no such quantities exist in real life. Though HBO series may not succeed in expressing that "real life," it has certainly moved television closer to it. And if recent series like *Girls* and *Enlightened* indicate a trend toward more HBO programs by and about women, we may soon find that women have become the primary producers, not only the primary consumers of television. Then we may get a better sense of how women are viewed, how they view themselves, and "what they're worth."

7 WIN OR DIE

When you play the game of thrones, you win or you die. There is no middle ground.

CERSEI LANNISTER, *GAME OF THRONES*

In his best-selling business guide, *The Innovator's Dilemma*, Clayton Christensen describes the problem of successful companies confronted by disruptive innovations: new ideas that threaten to undermine the values of the existing marketplace. The digital age has seen many such innovations emerge, from the filmless cameras that put Kodak out of business, to the shareable music files that left record companies reeling, to the Internet itself, which began as a system for connecting scientists and engineers, and has since reshaped all manner of human interactions, from retail sales and entertainment to social networking and surveillance. Unlike sustaining innovations, which merely bolster existing market values (think Folgers flavored coffees), disruptive innovations open up new markets, and eventually change the way we think about how and what we consume (think Starbucks coffeehouses).

Provided they reach a point of critical mass. Take Christensen's example of the automobile. Few inventions have had a more transformative effect on modern life, yet in its early days it was seen as little more than a "horseless carriage": a noisy, lumbering novelty enjoyed by the same wealthy class who kept liverymen and carriage makers employed. The automobile did not truly disrupt the marketplace until Henry Ford devised a system for mass-producing the inexpensive Model T in 1908, making cars available to a wide range of consumers, and transforming "horse and buggy" into a phrase of distain for outmoded ways of thinking. In Ford's case, the disruptive innovation was not the automobile *per se*, but the cheap, mass-producible automobile, which changed the values of the marketplace, making speedy, efficient personal transportation available to the masses and putting carriage makers out of business.

Like the Ford Motor Company, many of the most successful enterprises have been born of disruptive innovations, from the Sears mail order catalog to the Google search engine. But these disruptions hardly appear from thin air. Often they emerge from an existing idea or ideas. Richard Warren Sears' catalog owed a great debt to his knowledge of late nineteenth-century farm journal advertising and railroad delivery routes; Google drew upon every digital library project since Ted Nelson's *Project Xanadu* (1960). As we have seen in previous chapters, HBO has had a disruptive impact on the television and media marketplace. It did so not by reinventing the form, but by exploiting existing technologies, most notably cable and satellite. While broadcast networks saw these technologies as little more than a means to extend signal range, HBO used them to reinvogorate the starry-eyed visions of pay television pioneers and Blue Sky idealists into the model for exclusive global content services, so changing the way we think about television in general. Before HBO, few imagined a world where the average consumer would willingly pay for television, much less uncensored, commercial-free television beamed around the world via satellite. But that is the way with disruptive innovations: they redefine our values, open up entirely new possibilities—some constructive (vaccines, integrated circuits), some destructive (nuclear weapons, AK-47s)—and so pose an enormous threat to the status quo. Of course successful enterprises that spring from disruptive innovations eventually *become* the status quo, and face the challenge of new disruptive innovations that threaten the conditions of the market into which they have grown. Some, like DuPont, are agile enough to survive, adapting to those innovations and investing in new markets. DuPont began as a gunpowder producer, but has since been a driving force in areas ranging from plastics to bioscience to healthcare. Others, like Blockbuster, stagnate, struggle, and eventually die. While Netflix set the standard for through-the-mail and streaming home video, Blockbuster redoubled its investment in bricks-and-mortar video stores.

But what about HBO? After four decades of unprecedented success built upon disruptive innovations from cable and satellite to home video and streaming, has it become too big, too successful, and too deeply entrenched in existing market values to adapt to the next wave of disruptive innovations? In the age of media convergence, in which telephone, cable, and satellite companies bundle media services, and phones, cameras, computers, and music players have morphed into multimedia devices, what will "television" become, and what part will HBO play in it? Over the past several years, HBO has made a great show of preparations for the coming of this brave new world, with flashy experiments in interactive multiplatform programming (The HBO Voyeur Project), stand-alone content streaming services (HBO Nordic), video-on-demand systems that exploit new media technologies (HBO 3D On Demand; HBO Go), and "360-degree programming" that offers interactive features and web-only content through popular series blogs and websites. As a content provider, HBO seems uniquely suited for the age of media convergence: in theory, its programming can be consumed using virtually any media device or platform. But HBO is also deeply invested in cable, where the vast majority of consumers *still* go for their television. Just how freely will the service move from the cable to the cloud, and will subscribers follow? And are HBO's gestures toward the new media environment *only* gestures, or are they part of a long-standing policy to embrace disruption? To answer these questions, we must look for clues in HBO's recent programming and distribution strategies.

Winter is coming

The world of television has certainly changed over the four decades of HBO's existence. In the early years, "build-out" was the by-word around the offices of Time, Inc.: how to make the premium service available to more potential subscribers. As domestic cable systems neared market saturation in the 1980s, and new cable networks sprang up by the dozens, HBO shifted its growth strategy by investing heavily in the sort of original content other networks could not produce: profane, political, uncensored. Thanks to enormous capital investments by CEOs Jeff Bewkes and Chris Albrecht in the 1990s and 2000s, HBO established itself as the premiere venue for "quality" television, which accounted for a 20 percent rise in domestic subscribers from the premiere of *Oz* in 1997 to the bow-out of *The Sopranos* in 2007. HBO domestic subscription actually peaked a year after *The Sopranos* finale, with 29.11 million in 2008. But over the past half-dozen years or so, domestic subscriptions have stalled, even slid backward. Whether this is due to a temporary economic lull in the wake of the Great Recession, or to a natural market correction following the big number gains of HBO's "Golden Age," or to increased competition from other premium and basic cable networks, HBO subscription numbers in the U.S. market remain stubbornly below 30 million (Time Warner reports 40 million, but their numbers include Cinemax subscribers), and for the first time in its history, HBO is now only the second largest premium service in America (lagging behind Encore, which in 2012 boasted 35 million domestic subscribers). HBO's annual revenues continue to shatter records, exceeding $14 billion in 2012, but to achieve these results the network has had to rely increasingly on the development of international markets (accounting for more than 50 million viewers and over a $1 billion in revenues in 2012), and home video (HBO recouped the entire budget for Season One of *Thrones* in the first week of DVD sales). Yet despite this steady stream of cash, some media watchers are beginning to wonder whether HBO's best days are behind them.

Much of this criticism focuses on HBO's "wait-and-see" approach to the emerging media environment. Though the network claims to be prepared for whatever may come, it has so far shown no signs of giving up the cable/satellite infrastructure for a web-based distribution model. And that is too bad, say some media critics, who think that by remaining loyal to cable and satellite companies and refusing to launch a stand-alone web-based service, HBO is missing an enormous opportunity to gain access to a generation of viewers accustomed to media environments like iTunes and Amazon Instant Video, where programming decisions reflect individual consumer choice rather than the arcane bundling deals of companies like Comcast and DirectTV. HBO's retort is simple: the vast majority of American viewers get their television via cable subscription, and it makes no sense at this time to alienate their 30 million domestic subscribers, or the cable companies who sell and provide customer service to those subscribers, to satisfy a few eager cable cutters (who are currently increasing at a rate of about 1.5 million per year). But critics and bloggers eagerly point out that the Internet, and more specifically the most recent generation of mobile broadband networks (4G), has the potential to disrupt the cable and satellite ecosystem in cataclysmic ways. Unlike the three previous generations, 4G offers integrated telephony, Internet, gaming, and streaming multimedia; and while few media watchers are willing to claim that it works *as well as*, say, a hard line cable connection, most expect the next generation (5G) to meet or exceed cable speeds.

Several other factors currently prevent mobile broadband services from providing television viewers with the same quality of experience (QoE) as cable. The biggest is lack of capacity, but just as important is the absence of a system for mobile carriers to share in the profits with over-the-top carriers. Currently, the carriers supply the bandwidth, while HBOGo and Hulu make the money.[1] But this is an essential step in realizing the sort of web-based TV that liberates viewers from the constraints of set-top boxes and cable modems, while allowing content providers more direct access to them. Services like TV Everywhere and Hulu extend the reach of cable companies and broadcast networks into the web. TV Everywhere is a joint venture of Comcast and Time Warner. It allows web-based access to the same content available over their cable systems, but *only* for existing cable subscribers. Hulu is owned by a large group of media partners—including NBCUniversal Television Group, Fox Broadcasting, and the Disney-ABC Television Group—who use it primarily to recycle their own content, and draw added advertising and subscription revenue (with the premium service, Hulu Plus).

But true web-based TV might allow content creators to directly access consumers, potentially cutting out the big media companies entirely. Though, as we have seen in the example of the music industry, this may be easier said than done. While several big-name recording artists and a few unknowns have had success self-releasing material over the Internet, most still require the marketing and public relations support of major record labels to get their work in front of enough potential listeners.

Whether television as we know it actually *is* dying, or merely being integrated into a new hybrid media paradigm where both cable and broadband have their place, few doubt that change is coming. And if the history of disruptive technologies teaches us anything, it is that the agents of change thrive, while those who wait on the change end up like Blockbuster.

Of course, it is easy to confuse strategizing with standing around. Take, for example, HBO's apparent lack of response to the issue of piracy. Much of the hue and cry concerning the creation of a stand-alone HBO service has come from young cable cutters: those unwilling or unable to pay for premium cable, many of whom have resorted to stealing popular HBO series like *Game of Thrones* and *True Blood* through such torrent sites as The Pirate Bay and ISOHunt. In fact, the second season of *Thrones* averaged 4 million illegal downloads per episode, exceeding the average number of legal first-broadcast viewers in the U.S. market, and continuing its reign as the most pirated series in the history of television. The vast majority of those downloads occurred outside the U.S.. According to TorrentFreak.com, the U.S. market accounts for only 20 percent of *all* illegal downloads.[2] Still, some media critics and bloggers wonder whether this trend prophesies HBO's demise—why buy the milk if you can steal the cow?—but HBO's response has been more sober and measured, diminishing the impact by comparing the numbers to total global viewership, and insisting that the theft is just a temporary by-product of hard economic times. Once conditions improve, they claim, viewers will sign up again, because the product is just that good. And as more viewers get a taste for HBO programming—legally or illegally—the incentive to subscribe will only increase.

This is the same "first hit is free" logic that informed HBO's popular "free weekend" promotions of the 1980 and 1990s, and its decision to post early episodes of *Veep, Girls* and *The Newsroom* for free on YouTube. It also explains HBO's apparent lack of concern over the illegal sharing of HBO Go passwords. In fact, HBO Go reveals a great deal about the network's digital age strategy. Besides enhancing subscribers' sense of value by offering more consumption options (a la multiplexing and On Demand), HBO Go also helps to acclimate viewers to the emerging media environment. Similarly, pirated HBO Go—especially in the hands of young tech-saavy cable cutters—may serve as enough of an enticement for them eventually to pay for the service, once they have grown tired of stealing it. And as television integrates itself more fully into the media convergence paradigm, it only benefits HBO to ensure that legal and illegal users are familiar with its service, since the key to HBO's future is inviting existing and potential subscribers into this new media environment.

Concerns over HBO's future also extend to the programming itself. HBO's value is and always has been measured by the quality and exclusivity of its content, but in the post-*Sopranos* age, HBO may be a victim of its own effect. Though the network still has its fair share of hit series— especially mega-budget productions like *True Blood, Boardwalk Empire*, and *Game of Thrones*—they are harder to come by. This is partly due to the impossibly high standard HBO has set for itself. Despite all of the critical good will shown toward David Milch's *Luck* and David Simon's *Treme*, both series were doomed to fall short in comparisons to their earlier HBO series, *Deadwood* and *The Wire* (even the anemic viewing numbers for *The Wire* exceeded those of the later series).

FIGURE 7.1 This scene from the pilot episode of *Luck* proved prescient: HBO cancelled the series after several horses died during production

Also, the recent up-tick in "quality" television programs on broadcast and basic cable channels has made it harder for HBO to remain in the vanguard. If quirky HBO comedies like *The No. 1 Ladies Detective Agency* or *Bored to Death* had appeared a decade earlier, they might have stirred the same sort of critical and popular passions as *The Singing Detective* or *Northern Exposure* once did, but in the shadow of well-crafted broadcast fare like *House* and *30 Rock*, they went largely unnoticed.

No longer the only game in town, HBO appears to have retreated from the sort of daring experiments that made its reputation, instead trading off of its legacy by reprising popular narratives (the New Jersey Mob Story from *The Sopranos* to *Boardwalk Empire*; the Decline of an American City in *The Wire* and *Treme*), developing new projects with alumni producers (David Milch; Alan Ball), and inviting Hollywood auteurs (Martin Scorsese; Darren Aronosky) and bastions of "quality" broadcast television from both sides of the Atlantic (Aaron Sorkin; Armando Iannucci) to bring their unique sensibilities to HBO's signature dramas of moral ambivalence (*Boardwalk Empire*; *Reds*) and behind-the-curtain social satires (*The Newsroom*; *Veep*). Similarly, HBO has been cultivating series that plug into younger viewers' identification with their programming. *Girls* focuses on a group of young women who—like the show's creator and star, Lena Dunham—grew up watching *Sex and the City* in re-runs, while *Eastbound and Down* and *Funny or Die Presents* ratchet up the celebrity fishbowl cringe humor of *Curb Your Enthusiasm* for the viral video generation. And if these series prove popular with other demographics—such as *Girls*, which is very popular with men in their 40s and 50s—all the better.[3] HBO has also significantly expanded its genre spectrum to include melodrama (*Mildred Pierce*), hardboiled noir (*True Detective*), espionage (*The Missionary*), hipster comedy (*The Life and Times of Tim*), and the news magazine (*Vice*). But perhaps the most surprising development in recent HBO programming has been the proliferation of fantasy and horror series, beginning with Alan Ball's *True Blood,* and including a spate of shows currently being developed by Michael Chabon (*Hobgoblin*), Neil Gaiman (*American Gods*), Tom Perrotta (*The Leftovers*), and Stephen King (*The Dark Tower*). Though HBO has traversed this generic territory before (recall the uneven *Tales from the Crypt* in the 1980s, and the ill-fated *Carnivale* in the early 2000s), the scale of investment in new fantasy and horror programming suggests a significant shift in generic emphasis.

Nowhere is this more apparent than in its most ambitious series to date, *Game of Thrones*: an adaptation of George R.R. Martin's wildly popular book series, *The Song of Ice and Fire*. It is also arguably HBO's most lucrative series to date, shattering the DVD/BluRay sales records of *True Blood* and *Boardwalk Empire*, and commanding more than twice the international licensing fees of *The Sopranos*. In many ways, *Thrones* is a typical HBO series. The brutal violence and misogyny of its story world would be familiar to any fan of *Deadwood*, and its rendering of social hierarchies through the richly detailed, interlocking narratives of its sprawling cast of characters reminds one of *The Wire*. Like *Rome*, *Thrones* analyzes the roles of class, gender, race, and religion in the getting, keeping, and losing of power. Like *The Sopranos*, it explores the limits of self-actualization, self-deception, and self-awareness. And like virtually all HBO programs, it uses genre as a mere point of entry, rather than an absolute boundary. *Thrones* is a fantasy only insomuch as *Six Feet Under* is a domestic melodrama, or *Sex and the City* a romantic comedy. Despite outward appearances, George R.R. Martin's sprawling saga of war set in a fictional Middle Age kingdom shares little in common with J. R. R. Tolkien's Middle Earth adventures. Even the show's co-creator, David Benioff, half-jokingly refers to it as "*The Sopranos* in Middle Earth." But *Thrones* is different from these earlier series in at least one way that has drawn the attention, and in some cases the ire of media critics: it represents HBO's first clear shift from "real world" stories to the realm of pure fantasy.

When the network announced plans to shoot a pilot for the series in 2008, most fans of Martin's books were thrilled at the prospect of HBO bringing its high production values and storytelling patience to the material, but many non-Martinites expressed confusion, even alarm at what appeared to be HBO's decision to forsake the high-minded realism of its best dramas for the mythical landscapes and mystical creatures of this "airport fiction." When *Game of Thrones* eventually aired in April 2011, reviews were generally very positive, most drawing favorable comparisons to older HBO series. Others were not so flattering in their comparisons. In her *New York Times* review, Ginia Bellafante chastised HBO for abandoning the "real-world sociology" of *The Sopranos* and *Big Love* for a series that "serves up a lot of confusion in the name of no larger or really relevant idea beyond sketchily fleshed-out notions that war is ugly, families are insidious and power is hot."[4]

Bellafante's review drew a good deal of criticism, mostly for another passage in which she made the bizarre claim that women only watch the series for the graphic sex. Women, who consume the majority of fantasy fiction, were especially loud in their outrage. But she was not alone in her condemnation of *Thrones*: not even at the *New York Times*, which a year later published an equally scornful review by Neil Genzlinger, claiming that *Thrones'* convoluted plots, gruesome decapitations, and "regular helpings of bare breasts and buttocks" were clearly meant to pander to "Dungeons and Dragons types." Nancy DeWolf Smith of the *Wall Street Journal* made a similar claim, suggesting that *Thrones* would likely *only* appeal to role-playing gamers.[5] Meanwhile, Phillip Maciak at *Slate* took exception to the series' depictions of violence, gender, and race, where "[e]very act of brutality, every assaulted woman, every exoticized barbarian is presented for the delectation of the audience."[6] Maciak's criticism was similar to *Time* critic James Poniewozik's rebuke of *True Blood* a few years earlier, in which he wondered how "a show about prejudice" could be so "free with stereotypes," including a "sassy black friend... flaming gay cook and sundry racist Juh-hee-sus-fearing rednecks."[7] Whether chastening the network for slackening social conscience or characterizing its new programs as blood-and-balls soap opera, the subtext of these negative comments is clear enough: in an appeal to the popular and the prurient, HBO had begun to turn its back on "serious" drama.

All in the game

There are at least two problems with this supposition. The first is that HBO has never tried to *avoid* the popular, or the prurient. Leaving aside the countless programming hours HBO filled with gratuitous R-rated movies and sex documentaries—not to mention its reputation as the home of America's favorite blood sport, boxing—even "serious" programs like *The Sopranos* feature plenty of brutal violence, convoluted plots, and "regular helpings of bare breasts and buttocks." This is precisely why they draw such large audiences: some come for stimulation of the mind, some for the flesh and the blood. The same could be said for *Game of Thrones*, which often finds ingenious ways of using graphic sex and violence to develop character and advance sophisticated plotlines. Perhaps the best example is a device that has come to be known as "sexplication," where characters reveal key elements of backstory during coital conversation: often for no other reason than to give flesh-seeking viewers something to look at. *Game of Thrones* attracts all sorts of audiences, from fans of political history and epic storytelling to folks who just can't get enough of brothels and blood-letting.

The second problem with this critique is that it equates an appeal to "Dungeons and Dragons types" with pandering. Of course, *Thrones does* appeal to this group, along with fantasy enthusiasts, and the many consumers and authors of the enormous body of fan fiction that has grown around Martin's books, and now the HBO series. The popular site, FanFiction.net, currently lists more than 2,000 examples in these two categories alone, despite the fact that Martin has expressed disapproval of fan fiction loudly and often, and has several times requested that this and other sites take down any work connected with his books. But in exploiting that appeal, HBO is looking toward a much bigger picture.

Though fantasy fiction has long inspired a passionate following, the past decade has seen the form explode in popularity, thanks in large part to the spectacular success of the *Harry Potter* book and film series and Peter Jackson's *Lord of the Rings* films. Fantasy is escapism, reflecting a desire to dislocate oneself from the "real" world. Like pornography, its pleasure requires affective distance. In pornography, that distance is created through the flimsy artifice of the "story" and the mechanical "passions" of the performers. In fantasy narrative, that distance is created by making the story remote in time (e.g.: the Middle Ages) and place (e.g.: Middle Earth), by drawing upon stereotypical characters (e.g.: dark lords and fairies in white), and by pursuing conventional narrative lines (e.g.: the journey and the return). The worlds of fantasy offer parallels and alternatives to our own, making it possible to "place" ourselves in them without their reality threatening or overlapping with ours. The Middle Earth of Tolkien's *Lord of the Rings* trilogy evokes the darkness of the Middle Ages, but as a diabolical supernatural force rather than a legacy of ignorance, social inequity, and epidemic; just as the "lost world" narratives of Edgar Rice Burroughs and H. P. Lovecraft allow readers to export the real-life twentieth- and twenty-first-century problems of crime, violence, and xenophobia to adventure stories set in remote and exotic locales that never quite touch our own "fallen world." Fantasy offers a sort of thought experiment, in which we test our values and limitations within the protective confines of escapist fiction. On the other hand, science fiction, which often overlaps with fantasy (see *Star Wars* for example), also speculates on human values, motivations, and anxieties. The primary difference between the two is that fantasy tends to focus on what we have always been, where sci-fi tends to focus on what we might become: one typically looks backward in the form of a quasi-history, while the other tends to look forward, at the legacy of human advancement (esp. technological advancement).

Of course, *all* narrative offers some sort of affective distance and escape, but in fantasy it takes the form of a heightened experience, where beauty, horror, love, and pain are felt more acutely; where wills are tested through almost unimaginable extremes, victories are won by extraordinary sacrifice, and losses threaten to rock the very foundations of the fantasy world. Fantasy is visceral in its intensity, perhaps to bridge the affective distance it creates. It is also goal-oriented, eschewing psychological complexity and hard personal truths for amulets of power, acts of courage, and the destruction of foes. And finally, fantasy offers a sense of community. In some ways, the renewed popularity of the form owes as much to the social networking opportunities afforded by the Internet as to the work of any one author of filmmaker. Fantasy fans tend to be closeted, perhaps to avoid long-standing associations with "geekdom." But the Internet has created strong virtual (and at least semi-anonymous) communities that help to propagate beloved fantasy works, and to build upon them through fan fiction. In fact, many of these communities take on the spirit of that most common of fantasy story subjects: the building and mobilizing of coteries or fraternities, from Frodo's traveling companions to Harry Potter's Hogwarts classmates.

A *Song of Ice and Fire* has not come close to the sales of J.K. Rowling's or J. R. R. Tolkien's books. Total sales for the Martin series so far have been 15 million copies. Rowling's *Potter* books have sold over 450 million, and *The Lord of the Rings* and *The Hobbit* have sold a combined 250 million. But it was a formidable franchise when HBO signed on for the series: so much so that Martin reportedly begged HBO not to produce the series, fearing that a flopped production would be a detriment to future book sales. More importantly, it represented a new direction in the genre. If J. K. Rowling's stories drew on the tradition of C. S. Lewis' magical tales of children in peril, and J. R. R. Tolkien's belong to the tradition of "high" fantasy, where writ large good and evil characters enjoin in supernatural battles, Martin's epic eschews simplistic morality and magical powers for characters who are all-too-human, fallible, and mortal, and he protects no one—not even children—from peril. In one of the series' opening scenes, for example, seven-year-old Bran Stark is pushed out of a tower window after witnessing Jaime and Cersei Lannister having incestuous relations. The fall puts him into a coma and cripples him.

Although technically fantasy, Martin's story is primarily concerned with politics, military strategy, and interpersonal drama. His Seven Kingdoms reflect the cultures of Europe as they emerge from and through the brutality and ignorance of the Middle Ages, rather than the enchanted lands of elves and wizards so familiar to readers of the genre. It is a world transitioning between the Age of Magic and the Age of Reason through acts of will, valor, wisdom, and cruelty. Though *Time* magazine dubbed Martin "the American Tolkien," he writes in a style more in line with Geoffrey of Monmouth's *History of the Kings of Britain* (1136) than *The Hobbit* (1937), and the scale of his work makes *The Lord of the Rings* look like a brisk hike up a mountain. His characters come across as real people with real flaws and virtues, rather than allegorical symbols, yet their stories exist only in the service of a far larger narrative campaign, the likes and limits of which can hardly be seen by studying individual motives and deeds. Characters come and go, live, love, hate, and die, and even the ones we most identify with are dispatched with shocking swiftness, when their deaths serve the needs of the story. Those needs are often hard to determine, since a central conceit of the narrative is that character choices lead to unintended consequences, because it is difficult, if not impossible, to see how they will play out against the choices of so many others. And that is finally what the narratives of each succeeding book come down to: a series of discrete moves in an ongoing game built on a foundation of political intrigue (*A Game of Thrones*), savage warfare (*A Clash of Kings*; *A Storm of Swords*), and chaos theory (*A Feast for Crows*; *A Dance with Dragons*).

Martin has been fascinated with games—especially strategy role-playing games (RPGs)—since discovering *Dungeons and Dragons* in the 1970s, and that fascination is displayed in his work. It also helps to explain part of the appeal of his books, and the HBO series, which reflect many of the qualities and values of an RPG. But before getting to those qualities and values, it is worth talking a bit about why games—and especially RPGs—have become so popular in recent years. It would be hard to overstate the importance of games, not only to the digital age economy (on-line and console video games accounted for nearly $70 billion in global sales in 2012[8]), but also on our sense of story. This includes everything from shooters (*Call of Duty*; *Halo*) and platform games (*Super Mario Bros.*; *Tomb Raider*) to strategy and war games (*Age of Empires*; *Warcraft*), but it is particularly true of RPGs.

In many ways, RPGs function similarly to fantasy fictions. They are narrative in structure (one plays to create compelling scenarios and rise to ever higher levels of play, not to "win" in any concrete sense), establish parameters of a virtual reality for the express purpose of giving us a "safe" place to play out an assumed role, and are guided by strict conventions or rules (character attributes; appropriate obstacles; "turns" in the action). But RPGs also offer structural advantages to more traditional forms of narrative: we imagine ourselves as active participants—agents of our characters' fates—rather than mere readers taking our cues from the text itself. Decision points allow us to vary the direction of the narrative, as well as the outcome. Of course, these directions are limited by the options available (like lines on a flowchart, they present us with a series of binaries that eventually establish links to a set of pre-determined conclusions), but the affect can be empowering, at least in the short term. Moreover, narrative games—especially RPGs like *Pathfinder* and *Dark Heresy*—present players with the opportunity to adopt another identity. While more traditional forms of fictional narrative require us to identify with the plight of the protagonist, role playing games go a step beyond that, demanding we embody them. This may serve both as a means of wish fulfillment ("I always wanted to be a wizard / assassin / hero") *and* disguise.

Of course, every liberty comes with its own natural limits. Though traditional works of fiction are constrained by the monologic flow of the author's narrative, the reader is free to impose meaning and value on it, constrained only by the evidence of the text. Indeed, we often read against, or around, or beyond the intentions of the author: what pedagogical theorists Paolo Friere and John Dewey called "critical literacy." Otherwise, we would simply reject out of hand D. W. Griffith's *The Birth of a Nation* (1915) or the comedy of W. C. Fields as racist, without ever engaging their particular genius. But with RPGs, the goal is not critical but constructive: to fashion a sequence of events that abides by the rules and conventions of the game. Though RPGs take on the formal structures of narrative, with rising and falling action, conflict, climax, and resolution, they focus on only two areas of concern: the achievement of pre-determined goals (meeting a challenge; acquiring status points) and creating a sense of agency. But only a sense. As Michael Mateas points out, RPG players are "not able to form any real intentions within the dramatic world that actually matter."[9] There is a large, though limited number of directions one might take the narrative in service of whatever goals the players and/or game have set. But this interaction, this active series of choices is the sum total of the narrative's meaning. While not a valueless enterprise, the reduction of narrative to a series of "turns" and choices denies the player the opportunity to experience the text at a deeper emotional, psychological, and philosophical layer.

Take, for example, narrative empathy and catharsis. To truly feel empathy for fictional characters, one must feel *with* them. RPGs require only that we exploit their characteristics to advance our position. And in the absence of empathy, we are incapable of experiencing catharsis. Catharsis can be understood as both a form of purgation (getting rid of an excess of feeling to bring emotions back into balance) and understanding (we "know" something through the experience that we did not "know" before). When Oedipus discovers the horrible import of his actions (unwittingly murdering his father and marrying his mother), the audience is sickened and horrified, but at the same time enlightened about the folly of good intentions, and the cruel consequences that come to those who attempt to defy their fates. A similar effect occurs in comedy: when the insensible fool slips on the banana peel, we laugh at the gap between what we know and he does not (that there is a banana peel lying in wait on the sidewalk), at the same time realizing that we might as easily be taken down by what we do not perceive (where are our banana peels?). Catharsis *requires* this critical sense, this reactive ability to draw meaning from experience. To recoil from Oedipus's fate or laugh at a joke, we must not only comprehend it, but also contemplate it. That is what draws us to the theater in the first place. From the safety of our seats, we are given the liberty to observe and consider. But RPGs belong to the Coliseum: in place of catharsis and revelation, they offer spectacle and thrills. RPGs allow few, if any opportunities for contemplation, as one "turn" quickly and inevitably follows upon another; and regardless of how sophisticated or variable those "turns" are, they never achieve real "meaning," but simply come to an end, to be played again and again.

This brings us back to HBO's *Game of Thrones*. It goes without saying that *Thrones* is *not* an RPG. It lacks interactivity or agency. Viewers identify with characters, but have no real or perceived control over their actions (in fact, Martin refuses to read fan blogs, because he worries that plot suggestions made therein might have undue influence on his writing). Furthermore, while RPGs are primarily interested in character attributes (what they are capable of doing in a given situation), *Thrones*, like any traditional narrative, is far more interested in what characters' actions tell us about them, and what they reflect about human nature in a dangerous universe. And of course, there is plenty of empathy and catharsis. For example, King Joffrey's unexpected and unjust execution of Ned Stark is a devastating finale to Season One. But in many telling ways, HBO's *Thrones* and Martin's books mirror the underlying theory of RPG narrative: that stories are a series of causal events played to a logical conclusion, rather than a process of emotional, psychological and spiritual revelation. So, shocking as it is, Ned's death reveals nothing more than the capriciousness of power, and the hazards of identifying with any character subject to that caprice.

In the realm of RPGs, certain actions determine certain results. Typically, these results directly correspond to and follow upon the actions. For example: a character passes a test of strength, and a portal is open to him. But in some cases, the desired result requires several actions in series, and may be less predictable. For example: a character passes a test of strength in order to open a portal, but before passing through it he must determine whether attackers lay in wait on the other side. The most successful players are often those with the best predictive skills: those able to see the danger in the opportunity. While heroes in traditional narrative draw strength from their passions and emotions, the best game players—whether engaged in a chess tournament or a bloody game of thrones—are objective and circumspect, measuring risk against reward, and ready to take action as soon as the measure has been made. In *Thrones*, these qualities are key to the survival and success of all characters, especially outcasts like Tyrion Lannister and Daenerys Targaryen, who may initially lack many of the attributes that impel others (high position, warrior strength, the respect of peers).

Thrones also identifies itself with gaming in more explicit ways, from its title (which sounds like a version of *Risk* set in Medieval Europe) and title sequence (which presents the map of the Seven Kingdoms of Westeros as an enormous, mechanically animated game board), to the ways it sacrifices character to plot (Martin's books are notorious for dispatching favorite characters), favors deeds over words (even the crisp, often humorous dialogue is more often than not spoken in tones of conflict, or as a provocation to conflict), and puts strategy above all other concerns (winning or losing are finally all that matters). Little wonder the book and television series have spawned several card and board games, on- and off-line role-playing games, and several game-based parodies, including one posted on the popular CollegeHumor website that reduces the plots and characters of *Thrones* to a series of simple turns in an early PC-based RPG similar to *Ultima* (1981) or *Wizardry* (1981).[10] *Thrones* merely builds the *concept* of the game into the story, but in so doing liberates the narrative from several constraints, such as the sustenance of heroes (in gaming, characters live or die as a result of the agency of play, not because they "deserve" it) and the resolution of plot points (in gaming, one chooses a path, rather than worrying about how each path might connect).

FIGURE 7.2 The game-board title sequence: King's Landing. *Game of Thrones*, HBO

As a long-form dramatic narrative that exploits and undercuts the conventions of fantasy and RPGs, *Thrones* shares something else in common with such "groundbreaking" and successful HBO series as *The Sopranos*, which refuses to play straight with the rules of gangster stories and domestic dramas, and *Deadwood*, which eschews the typical conventions of western and frontier narrative (the journey, the vastness of the wilderness, the outcast hero, etc.) for a sort of primordial politics. By deconstructing and combining familiar forms, these series inject their stories with a sense of ambivalence and mystery that makes them seem new and vital. If genres and character types degrade the more commonplace and predictable they become, the best HBO series force us to see them with new eyes. *The Larry Sanders Show* uses the culturally debased form of the late-night talk show to poke fun at the pettiness and fear that drives the entertainment industry; *Oz* trades prison movie platitudes about punishment and redemption for brutal nightmares of revenge and rape; *Sex and the City* lets women speak to their own desires; and *Six Feet Under* lets the dead speak for the living. Like these earlier HBO series, *Thrones* intentionally flaunts common assumptions about how stories are made, and what we expect from them. Take character for example. Our identification with Tyrion Lannister is as ambivalent as that with Tony Soprano, Nate Fischer, or Al Swearengen: we like them, but are never allowed to get past their failings, and just as we begin to connect with them, their behavior turns monstrous or inscrutable. Their stories don't merely zig and zag: they dislocate, break off, rupture. Who achieves self-actualization? Who finds true love? Who gets what they want, or even what they deserve? By challenging our sense of character, of right and wrong, and of meaningful resolution, the most successful HBO series—of which *Thrones* is undoubtedly one—recreate the necessary conditions for empathy and catharsis: the ability to truly see ourselves in these all-too-human figures, and to be truly surprised, shocked, and moved by their fates. HBO's decision to produce a series that appeals to fantasy fans and gamers might be viewed as opportunism at a time when these groups have such a significant impact on the media economy, but *Thrones* also reflects HBO's unique talent for combining the familiar with the new: a morally ambiguous, narratively ambitious, gorgeously-made piece of pop culture that manages to bridge the gap between traditional television narrative and digital age culture. And it is precisely this talent that has made HBO so successful, for so long.

The end is near

Of course, successes can be unreliable sources of information. We tend to see them as auguries of greatness, even when they owe more to serendipity or foolish consistency than to hard work or vision. Failures, on the other hand, naturally expose truths to any who hope to learn from them. So what better way to round out this discussion of HBO's prospects than to mine their failures and false starts? While HBO certainly has produced some mediocre shows (*Arli$$*; *Mind of a Married Man*), even a few truly bad ones (*Spicy City*; *Dane Cook's Tourgasm*), the most revealing ones are those that began boldly, then faltered, whether due to market miscalculations, poor execution, or going too far out on a creative limb. In the end, our aspirations may say more about us than our achievements.

Take, for example, *The High Life*, which aired briefly on HBO in 1996, before sinking into obscurity. An edgy sitcom set in 1950s Pittsburgh, created by Adam Resnick (*Get a Life*; *Cabin Boy*) and produced by David Letterman's Worldwide Pants company, *The High Life* is like *The Honeymooners* without the sentimentality. Here characters battle with depression and pursue doomed schemes to cover crippling insecurities and personal failings. And here the cringe-worthy, surreal humor is built around real social problems of the 1950s, including racism and the Red Scare. In one episode the main characters, Emmett and Earl, unwittingly rent out space in their failing storage business to a Ku Klux Klan chapter; in another, Emmett and his wife sidestep accusations of communist sympathy by bribing a politician with the services of a prostitute. In its dark tone and subject matter, *The High Life* predicted the new directions the sitcom would go in series like *It's Always Sunny in Philadelphia* and *Workaholics*, not to mention HBO's *Curb Your Enthusiasm* and *East Bound and Down*. But in 1996 it barely attracted an audience, and critics split between measured praise and wholesale condemnation (the *New York Times* approvingly referred to it as the "evil twin of Nick and Nite,"[11] while *Variety* condemned it for being "as phony as the Wonder Bread sitcoms...that it means to turn on their ears"[12]). In the end, HBO proved unwilling to take a long-term risk on the oddball amalgam of farce and *film noir*, and cancelled the show after only a handful of episodes had aired. It has since all but disappeared from cultural memory. No DVD releases, no network re-runs, no YouTube clips: all that remains are a few fading VHS copies recorded by fans during its initial run.

A slightly kinder fate met other failed series, including HBO's second foray into mock-documentary political comedy, following Robert Altman's *Tanner '88* (1988). Steven Soderberg's *K Street* (2003) starred real-life husband-and-wife political consultants James Carville and Mary Matalin, playing only slightly fictionalized versions of themselves in a narrative ripped from the daily headlines. Spontaneous, ambitious, and largely unscripted, *K Street* also had an unfortunate tendency to sprawl, then grasp for moments of narrative poignancy, and it failed to draw much of an audience beyond beltway political junkies. While critics admired the effort, few could be persuaded to go beyond calling it a noble experiment, and it fizzled out after one ten-episode season. Soderberg's second effort at this style of storytelling for HBO, *Unscripted* (2005), suffered a similar fate. On the other hand, *The Comeback* (2005)—created by Michael Patrick King (*Murphy Brown, Will & Grace, Sex and the City*) and series star Lisa Kudrow on the heels of her decade-long run on *Friends*—received more enthusiastic critical praise for its inventive structure, its sharp-edged entertainment industry humor, and especially Kudrow's brilliantly dark, against-type performance as a washed-up television actress making one last desperate grasp at celebrity by letting her life be turned into a reality television show. But despite earning three Primetime Emmy nominations (including best actress for Kudrow), the series struggled to draw an audience, and it too was dropped by HBO after just one season.

Low numbers are, of course, a common reason to cancel a series, even at a network like HBO, where ratings are not the only consideration. But some critics have speculated that HBO cancelled *The Comeback* because it mercilessly bit the hand that fed it, attacking not only the vice and folly of Hollywood, but also the stupidity of the average television viewer.[13] While *The Larry Sanders Show* and *Curb Your Enthusiasm* send up the pretensions of celebrities and industry types (with the winking participation of those celebrities and industry types), *The Comeback* was perhaps *too* acerbic in its criticism of Hollywood culture, not to mention viewers of reality TV and sitcoms like, say, *Friends*.

It is easy to poke fun at these genres because their deficits are so apparent, but their popularity also suggests that the familiarity and amusement we draw from them is worth a great deal to us.

Perhaps this is why audiences were not drawn to the darkness of *The High Life*, or Louis CK's effort to revisit the domestic sitcom in *Lucky Louie* (2006: though Louis CK claims that they often beat out *Deadwood*

FIGURE 7.3 Too real? *The Comeback*, HBO

in the ratings[14]). Or maybe they just did not respond to CK's decision to shoot the series live in front of a studio audience, or the stiff performances, or the raunchy dialogue, or the blue-collar storylines. Or maybe *Lucky Louie*, and *The High Life*, and *The Comeback* simply committed the ultimate sitcom sin: they failed to make enough people laugh. Whatever the individual reasons, each of these series was both a benefactor and victim of HBO's success. Thanks to the legacy of *Tanner '88*, *The Larry Sanders Show*, and *Curb Your Enthusiasm*, Resnick, Soderberg, King, and CK were granted an opportunity to experiment with form and content, to push out further from the shores of mediocrity in the hopes of charting some new territory. But the fates of these series also reveal HBO's growing impatience with projects that do not immediately prove themselves. With expectations and competition ever on the rise, the days of letting audiences "find" a series may be over. While HBO seems to remain willing to take a chance on new projects, second chances are getting more and more scarce.

Nowhere is this truth more self-evident than in the case of David Milch's much-hyped flop, *John from Cincinnati* (2007). The series arose out of conversations between Milch and then-CEO of HBO, Chris Albrecht, about the fate of *Deadwood*, which had lost significant ground in its third season ratings. HBO was looking to develop a series about surfers, which Albrecht hoped would appeal to younger viewers, and wondered whether Milch would be interested. In the end, his collaboration with "surf-noir" novelist, Kem Nunn, would prove to have some appeal for young viewers, but perhaps not in the way HBO originally intended. The network had hoped for an edgy show to replace *The Sopranos* on Sunday nights, and to encourage Milch to bring *Deadwood* to a tidy close. What HBO got was neither *The Sopranos*, nor *Deadwood*, nor a youth-oriented meditation on surfing, but a manic combination of mysticism, gnosticism, and nihilism that made the frontier philosophizing of *Deadwood* look like paint-by-numbers. And though *John from Cincinnati* pulled down low, but still respectable viewer numbers (nowhere near those of *The Sopranos*, but better than those of *The Wire*, and occasionally better than those of *Deadwood*), the network cancelled it the day after running the season finale.

The failure of the series resulted from several factors, not least of which was its connections to *The Sopranos* and *Deadwood*. Premiering immediately after the smash-to-black final scene of *The Sopranos*, *John from Cincinnati* was given the unenviable task of trying to draw in an audience reeling with frustration—even anger—at the unwillingness of David Chase to answer the many looming questions posed by *The Sopranos*: most notably, "What happens to Tony?" Only about a third of *The Sopranos'* viewers stuck around for the premiere of *John from Cincinnati*, and those who did were immediately confronted with a whole new set of questions like, "Why is this guy levitating six inches off the ground?" and "Why does this other guy keep repeating everything everyone says?" and "Why did the cop have the bird kiss the kid in the coma?"

Faced with such questions, only half the number of viewers returned the following week (probably realizing that they were not going to be answered), and reviewers began piling on: some offering guarded admiration for Milch's grand experiment, but most condemning it as pretentious, obtuse, and painful to watch. Little wonder HBO executives started getting skittish about the show's future. Add to that the perception among *Deadwood* fans that *John from Cincinnati* had been the reason for the sudden cancellation of their beloved program, and you have the ingredients for a fatal cocktail: anger, indifference, and confusion. And the greatest of these is confusion.

John from Cincinnati focuses on the Yosts, a Southern California surfing dynasty fallen on hard times following years of drug addiction, betrayal, and unresolved trauma. The Yosts are visited by a mysterious, perhaps autistic, apparently divine being named John Monad ("monad" meaning "The One" or God in gnostic philosophy). John is, according to Milch, "a variable creature of enormous energy and power, and very little understanding" who, through a series of cryptic words and miraculous deeds, "reorients [the Yosts'] understanding of the life that they've been living." But has he come, like John the Baptist, to harken a new beginning, (he repeatedly tells the family patriarch, Mitch Yost, that he needs to "get back in the game"), or like John the Revelator, to announce the final judgment (his first words, and the first words in the series are, "The end is near")?

The answer is never quite clear. In a story with so many oddball surfers and star-struck hangers-on, ex-cops and criminals, war veterans and walking wounded, one struggles to make sense of who is who, much less what is going on. Then there are the patterns of speech: more profane and convoluted than anything in *Deadwood*, and peppered with surfer idioms. Perhaps most challenging of all is the manner in which the title character communicates: through a combination of overheard phrases ("I'm shy about doing my business"; "See God, Kai") and obscure references to "the word" and "my father" ("The word on the wall hears my father"; "If my words are yours, can you hear my father?"). After watching a single episode, it is easy to understand why many viewers abandoned the show early on. This was a pity, since they missed out on some pretty astounding moments, such as a scene in the sixth episode,

FIGURE 7.4 The face of God? *John from Cincinnati*, HBO

in which John weaves many of these phrases into a stunning sermon on the power of faith and revelation, and the immanence of God. Yet even in these moments, the series remains irreducibly strange. Or as one reviewer put it, *John from Cincinnati* "makes *Twin Peaks* seem like *Mayberry RFD*."[15]

Perhaps this strangeness accounts for HBO's decision to cancel the show. After all, the success of any series requires the cultivation of a loyal audience, and audiences typically return for a sense of continuity, familiarity, and belonging. But *John* keeps the viewer at arm's length, presenting itself less as an entertainment than a philosophical challenge. Even *Twin Peaks* shrouded its eccentricities in the conventions of a whodunit, and a seductive combination of comedy, thriller, and soap opera. Perhaps HBO had no faith in the series' ability to keep audiences coming back. But the fact that HBO gave *John from Cincinnati* a chance at all, and has since continued to develop projects with its idiosyncratic creator, David Milch, is both a testament to the network's continued willingness to go out on a limb, and a measure of the risk involved. For what good is clearing a new path if your audience is unwilling or unable to follow? This problem is only compounded with each new success, because success demands emulation: from *Band of Brothers* to *The Pacific*; from *Sex and the City* to *Girls*. And as those successes begin to track with popular genres and tastes (mob dramas; fantasy series), those demands only grow stronger. While it may be true that HBO subscribers tune in expecting to find something unavailable everywhere else, they also come with preconceived notions of what constitutes "an HBO show."

Given this essential truth, it should come as little surprise that HBO often abandons projects, when the network thinks they have failed to meet that standard. A good example is Linda Bloodworth-Thomason's soapy satire, *12 Miles of Bad Road* (2007), which HBO decided to shelve after assembling an impressive ensemble cast led by Lily Tomlin, and spending $25 million dollars to shoot six episodes. HBO dropped it before airing a single episode, claiming simply that the result did not meet its initial expectations. In other words, the story of a dysfunctional family of Texas real estate tycoons, which one reviewer described as "*Dallas* meets *Designing Women*,"[16] turned out not to be "an HBO show." Perhaps a similar logic was at work when HBO recently decided not to move forward with a series adaptation of Jonathan Franzen's *The Corrections*, after shooting a pilot starring Ewan McGregor, Maggie Gylennhaal, Chris Cooper, and Dianne Wiest in 2012. It may also explain why a number of high-profile in-development series—Doug Ellin's *40*, Spike Lee's *Da Brick*, Alan Ball's *All Signs of Death*, Neil LaBute's *The Member Guest*, and Kathryn Bigelow's *The Miraculous Year* to name a few—never made it past the pilot stage.

HBO has cultivated an image of itself as a place where "important" cultural work can still be done on television: where talent finds the freedom necessary to create unique, and uniquely compelling programming. The network has spent decades cultivating that talent and developing that programming. Along the way, it has chosen to produce (and *not* produce) many extraordinary films and series, contracted with many of the best writers, directors, and producers working in film and television, and optioned the rights to a veritable canon of modern and contemporary fiction, including the recent acquisition of the complete fiction of William Faulkner, which David Milch has agreed to produce in some form or other. But holding all of that cultural ground inevitably drains resources that might be used to advance in new directions: a strategy that has so far been essential to HBO's growth [what?]. Inevitably, HBO has had to make choices about what will work, and what will not. For if failure teaches us anything, it is that failure sucks, and that an advance made at the expense of ground already held is really just another form of retreat. Are HBO's abandoned and cancelled projects evidence that the network may be losing its stomach for new and innovative programming, choosing instead to thumb through its old playbook, trying to make something new from bits and pieces of the old? Or is HBO simply the New York Yankees of television content providers: rich and powerful enough to absorb a few unproductive contracts, but so big that it is expected to field a winning line-up, year after year? Maybe a bit of both. But HBO's dominant position owes to a philosophy of big risk, big reward. Turning its back on that philosophy—now or at any time in the future—would surely undermine the value of the HBO brand, and threaten HBO's very existence.

****

In *The Innovator's Dilemma*, Christensen notes that the seeds of an enterprise's failure spring from the heights of its success, meaning its investment in the status quo is never greater than when it is most successful. This is partly due to the fact that success breeds fear (we become more conservative as we have more to lose). But it is mostly due to the increasing demands of customers and shareholders, who hold a greater stake in decision-making as enterprises grow, and tend to favor predictable gains—even standing still—over risky innovation and change. Many critics have predicted HBO's coming demise for just this reason: it is too beholden to its stakeholders, and too invested in its distribution and programming models to prosper in the evolving media environment, or to resist more agile competitors who have already thumbed through, and borrowed heavily from HBO's playbook. But so far, HBO has modeled the timeless dictum: those who do not embrace change are eventually swept away. By leveraging past successes and continually cultivating new ones, by growing existing markets and making conscious preparations for emerging and future ones, and by continuing to successfully brand its service as both ubiquitous and unique, exclusive and inviting, familiar and novel, luxurious and essential, HBO continues its four-decade, uninterrupted advance. Strong enough to absorb losses and take risks, HBO's survival is not guaranteed, but the extraordinary effect it has had so far on how we watch and what we watch suggests that HBO will continue to have a significant impact on the future of television, whatever form the medium might take.

NOTES

The visible effect

1   See for example the I.B. Tauris *Reading Contemporary Television* series volumes on *Sex and the City*, *The Sopranos*, *Six Feet Under*, and *Deadwood*; and Gary Edgerton and Jeffrey Jones (eds), *The Essential HBO Reader* (Lexington: University of Kentucky Press, 2008), which offers brief surveys of individual series, sports, feature films, and documentaries.

2   See for example, Marc Leverette, Brian L. Ott, and Cara Louise Buckley (eds), *It's Not T.V.: Watching HBO in the Post-Television Age* (New York: Routledge, 2008).

3   Parents Television Council, "Habitat for Profanity" (2010), http://www.parentstv.org/PTC/publications/reports/2010ProfanityStudy/study.pdf (accessed March 15, 2013).

4   For a neat summary of perspectives, see Toby Miller and Linda J. Kim, "It Isn't TV, It's the 'Real King of the Ring'," in *The Essential HBO Reader*, 217–36.

5   See esp. Janet McCabe and Kim Akass, *Quality TV* (New York: I. B. Tauris, 2007).

6   Kristen Thomson, *Storytelling in Film and Television* (Cambridge: Harvard University Press, 2003).

7   See esp. Avi Santos, "Paratelevision and the Discourses of Distinction: The Culture of Production at HBO," and Tony Kelso, "And Now No Word From Our Sponsor: How HBO Put the Risk Back Into Television," in Leverette, Ott and Buckley (eds), *It's Not T.V.: Watching HBO in the Post-Television Age* (New York: Routledge, 2008).

8   Erik Adams, "Is Television a Medium Without a Past?" *The AV Club*, March 8, 2012, http://www.avclub.com/articles/is-television-a-medium-without-a-past,70520/ (accessed March 15, 2013).

9   Carl Sagan, *Pale Blue Dot: A Vision of the Human Future in Space* (New York: Random House, 1994), xv–xvi.

A great notion

1 Earl Mazo, *Richard Nixon, a Political and Personal Portrait* (New York: Avon, 1960), 141.

2 Michael Medved, *The Shadow Presidents* (New York: Times Books, 1979): 329.

3 J. C. R. Licklider, "Man-Computer Symbiosis," *IRE Transactions on Human Factors in Electronics* (March 1960): 4–11.

4 M. Mitchell Waldrop's fine Licklider biography, *The Dream Machine: J.C.R. Licklider and the Revolution That Made Computing Personal* (New York: Viking, 2001), was a welcome resource for understanding the early history of the Internet, and Licklider's role in it.

5 Ralph Lee Smith, "The Wired Nation," *Nation* (May 19, 1970): 582.

6 For a more complete history of cable television in America, see Thomas P. Southwick's *Distant Signals: How Cable TV Changed the World of Telecommunications* (Overland Park, KS: Primedia Intertec, 1998); Megan Mullen's *The Rise of Cable Programming in the United States* (Austin: University of Texas Press, 2003) and *Television in the Multichannel Age* (Malden, MA: Blackwell, 2008); Patrick R. Parsons' *Blue Skies: A History of Cable Television* (Philadelphia: Temple University Press, 2008); and the invaluable interviews and histories posted on The Cable Center website (www.cablecenter.org). These have been enormously useful resources in filling in my own knowledge gaps.

7 Donald R. LeDuc, *Cable Television and the FCC: A Crisis in Media Control* (Philadelphia: Temple University Press): viii.

8 President's Task Force on Communications Policy, *Final Report* (Washington, DC: U.S. Printing Office, 1968), 4.

9 Davidson Gigliotti, "A Brief History of Raindance," *Radical Software*, 2003, http://www.radicalsoftware.org/e/history.html (accessed March 15, 2013).

10 Michael Shamberg and Raindance Corporation. *Guerilla Television* (New York: Holt, Rinehart and Winston, 1971), back cover.

11 Charles A. Reich, *The Greening of America* (New York: Random House, 1970).

12 Steve Jobs, Stanford University Commencement Address, June 12, 2005.

13 See Brand, "We Owe It All to the Hippies" (*Time*, Spring 1995, 145:12); Hafner and Lyon, *Where the Wizards Stay Up Late* (Simon and Schuster, 1995); Markoff, *What the Dormouse Said* (Viking: 2005); and Turner, *From Counterculture to Cyberculture* (University of Chicago Press, 2006).

14 Marshall McLuhan, *Understanding Media: The Extensions of Man* (New York: Mentor, 1964).

15 "HBO: the First Twenty Years."

16 J. C. R. Licklider, "Televistas," in *Public Television, a Program for Action: The Report and Recommendations of the Carnegie Commission on Educational Television* (New York: Harper and Row, 1967), 212.

17 *On the Cable: The Television of Abundance*, 54.

18 "Televistas," 212.

19 Two particularly useful sources of information on the early history of subscription television are H. H. Howard and S. L. Carroll's *Subscription Television: History, Current Status, and Economic Projections* (Knoxville: University of Tennessee, 1980); and Robert V. Bellamy Jr, "Constraints on a Broadcast Innovation: Zenith's Phonevision System, 1931–1972," in *Journal of Communication* 38:4 (Autumn 1988), 8–20

20 John McMurria, "A Taste of Class: Pay-TV and the Commodification of Television in Postwar America," in *Cable Visions: Television Beyond Broadcasting*, eds. Sarah Banet-Weiser, Cynthia Chris and Anthony Freitas (New York: New York University Press, 2007), 45.

21 Ibid., 48.

22 Ibid., 58.

23 "Death of STV," *Time* 84:21 (November 13, 1964), 82.

24 Ibid., 46.

25 *HBO v. FCC* (1977)

26 "Will Vote Halt Pay TV's Growth?," *Broadcasting* (November 9, 1964): 22.

27 Whiteside, Thomas. " 'Onward and Upward With the Arts: Cable – III." *The New Yorker* (June 3, 1985): 82–105.

28 Raymond Williams, *Television: Technology and Cultural Form* (London: Collins, 1974).

29 Jerry Mander, *Four Arguments for the Elimination og Television* (New York: Morrow, 1978).

30 George Mair, *Inside HBO: The Billion Dollar War Between HBO, Hollywood, and the Home Video Revolution* (New York: Dodd Mead, 1988): 25–6.

31 Arthur C. Clarke, "Extra-terrestrial Relays," *Wireless World* (October 1945): 306.

32 Eisenhower used the term in his televised farewell address from the White House on January 17, 1961.

The caterpillar

1 Miller and Kim, "It Isn't TV, It's the 'Real King of the Ring'," *Essential HBO Reader*: 223.

2 James Sullivan, *Seven Dirty Words: The Life and Crimes of George Carlin* (Cambridge, MA: Da Capo, 2010): 169.

3 Richard Zoglin, *Comedy at the Edge* (New York: Bloomsbury, 2008): 80.

4 *Lenny Bruce Live at the Curran Theater* (Fantasy Records, 1971: recorded November 19, 1961)

5 "Notebook 18 (February–September 1879)" in *Mark Twain's Notebooks & Journals*, Vol. 2 (1975), ed. Frederick Anderson: 304.

6 Jerry Seinfeld, "Dying is Hard, Comedy is Harder," *New York Times* (June 24, 2008).

7 Pryor recounts these circumstances in his many stage performances, as well as his more sober and circumspect autobiography, *Pryor Convictions* (London: Revolver Books, 2005).

8 Lenny Bruce, *The Essential Lenny Bruce* (New York: Ballantine, 1967): 42.

9 Marc Cooper, "*The Progressive* Interview: George Carlin," *The Progressive* 65:7 (July 2001): 33.

10 George Carlin, *Class Clown* (Little David/Atlantic, 1972).

11 *On Location: George Carlin at USC* (Home Box Office, 1977).

12 Bill Carter, "Seriously, Michael Fuchs Moves HBO into Comedy," *New York Times* (November 5, 1989).

13 George Carlin, *A Place for My Stuff* (Atlantic Records, 1981).

14 The Canadian series, which aired between 1996 and 2004, not the recent HBO series of the same title.

15 David Gillota, "Negotiating Jewishness and the Schlemiel Tradition," *Journal of Popular Film and Television* 38:4: 152–61.

16 Richard Butsch, "Five Decades and Three Hundred Sitcoms about Class and Gender," *Thinking Outside the Box*, eds. Edgerton and Rose (Lexington: University of Kentucky Press, 2005): 111–35.

Everything. Everyone. Everywhere. Ends.

1 Karen Anderson and Jake Harwood, "The Presence and Portrayal of Social Groups on Prime-Time Television," *Communication Reports* (15:2, Summer 2002).

2 Dorothy Collins Swanson, *The Story of Viewers for Quality Television* (Syracuse, NY: Syracuse University Press, 2000).

3 David Marc and Robert Thompson, *Prime Time, Prime Movers: From I Love Lucy to L.A. Law—America's Greatest TV Shows and The People Who Create Them* (Boston, MA: Little, Brown, 1992).

4 Bill Carter, "HBO as a Modern-Day Dickens," *New York Times* (November 1, 1992).

5 Joy DeLyria and Sean Michael Robinson, *Down in the Hole* (Brooklyn, NY: Powerhouse Books, 2012): 31.

6 Greg Metcalf's *The DVD Novel* (Santa Barbara, CA: Praeger/ABC-CLIO, 2012) offers an excellent analysis of the powerful impact of these modes of viewing on how television is viewed and made.

7 Jeremy Wilson, "Gorging on *House of Cards*: How Netflix has turned binge TV viewing mainstream," *The Telegraph* (February 7, 2013).

8 DeLyria and Robinson, 31–2.

9 Ibid., 32.

10 David Simon, Foreward to Humphrey Cobb's *Paths of Glory* (New York: Penguin, 2010).

11 Nick Hornby, Interview with David Simon. *The Believer* (August 2007).

12 "A-Hunting We Will Go" was originally written for John Gay's *Beggar's Opera* (1728) to be sung by the highwayman, Macheath (a.k.a., Mack the Knife in the Bertolt Brecht's twentieth-century musical adaptation, *The Threepenny Opera*, 1928).

13 It was, in fact, made by the same production company responsible for *Hill Street Blues* and *St Elsewhere*: MTM.

14 Quoted in Rafael Alvarez, *The Wire: Truth Be Told* (New York: Grove, 2009): 283.

Changing the conversation

1 "The Politics of *The Sopranos*," *The Brian Lehrer Show*. WNYC New York Public Radio (New York: New York, June 5, 2007).

2 See for example, Gordon Hodson and Michael A. Busseri, "Bright Minds and Dark Attitudes" (*Psychological Science*, 23:187, January 5, 2012) and Scott Eidelman et. al., "Low-Effort Thought Promotes Political Conservatism" (*Personality and Social Psychology Bulletin*, March 16, 2012).

3 See for example, Dana R. Carney et. al., "The Secret Lives of Liberals and Conservatives: Personality Profiles, Interaction Styles, and the Things They Leave Behind" (*Political Psychology*, 29:6, 2008).

4 James Hibberd, "Republicans vs. Democrats TV: Lefties Want Comedy, Right Wingers Like Work." *EW.com*, posted December 6, 2011, http://insidetv.ew.com/2011/12/06/republican-vs-democrat-tv/ (accessed March 15, 2013).

5 John Podhoretz, "The Liberal Imagination." *The Weekly Standard* (March 27, 2000), 23.

6   See for example Chris Lehmann, "The Feel-Good Presidency." *Atlantic Monthly* 287:3 (March 2001), 93–6.

7   See for example, Tim Groseclose, *Left Turn: How Liberal Media Bias Distorts the American Mind* (New York: St Martin's Press, 2011).

8   See for example, Steven J. Ross, *Hollywood Left and Right: How Movie Stars Shaped American Politics* (New York: Oxford University Press, 2011).

9   See for example, Ben Shapiro, *Primetime Propaganda: The True Hollywood Story of How the Left Took Over Your TV* (New York: Broadside Books, 2011)

10 Ginia Bellafante, "Feminism: It's all About Me," *Time* 151:25 (June 29, 1998), 54–60.

11 Todd Gitlin, *Inside Prime Time* (New York: Pantheon, 1983).

12 James Truslow Adams, *The Epic of America* (New York: Blue Ribbon Books, 1931), 214.

13 Thorstein Veblen, *The Theory of the Leisure Class* (1899).

14 Robert Warshow, "The Gangster as Tragic Hero," *Partisan Review* (February 1948); reprinted in *The Immediate Experience* (Garden City, NY: Doubleday, 1962).

15 Discussed at length in *Eichmann in Jerusalem: A Report on the Banality of Evil* (New York: Viking, 1963), which reports on the 1961 trial of Adolph Eichmann: former officer in the Nazi SS, and chief engineer of the Holocaust.

16 Josh Vasquez, "DVD Review: *The West Wing: The Complete Fourth Season*," *Slant* (posted April 4, 2005), http://www.slantmagazine.com/dvd/review/the-west-wing-the-complete-fourth-season/597 (accessed March 15, 2013).

17 In late 1919 and early 1920, United States Attorney General A. Mitchell Palmer organized a series of raids, with the intention of rounding up and deporting known anarchists and leftists. With the resources of the Department of Justice, and the enthusiastic assistance of his young deputy, J. Edgar Hoover, Palmer made more than 10,000 arrests in 23 states over a three-month period.

18 Amanda Marcotte, "How to Make a Critically Acclaimed TV Show About Masculinity," *Jezebel* (posted September 7, 2011), http://jezebel.com/5837945/how-to-make-a-critically-acclaimed-tv-show-about-masculinity (accessed March 15, 2013).

19 Maurice Yacowar, *The Sopranos on the Couch* (New York: Continuum, 2006).

20 Richard Green and Peter Vernezze (eds), *The Sopranos and Philosophy: I Kill, Therefore I Am* (Peru, IL: Open Court, 2004).

21 Anthony Schneider, *Tony Soprano on Management* (New York: Berkley/Penguin, 2004).

22 Bob Ingle and Sandy McClure, *The Soprano State: New Jersey's Culture of Corruption* (New York: St Martin's Griffin, 2010).

23 Chris Seay, *The Gospel According to Tony Soprano* (New York: Tarcher/Putnam, 2002).

24 See for example, David R. Simon, *Tony Soprano's America: The Criminal Side of the American Dream* (Boulder, CO: Westview Press, 2002).

25 Carmela Soprano et. al., *Entertaining with the Sopranos* (New York: Grand Central Publishing, 2006).

Serious naked pictures

1 Here I mean *representations* of women, not necessarily female audiences. The thorny issue of why certain shows skew toward certain genders is a complex one that I will not try to engage here.

2 Maureen Ryan, "Why is Television Losing Women Writers?" *Huffington Post*, November 4, 2012, http://www.huffingtonpost.com/2011/09/08/women-writers-television_n_1418584.html (accessed March 15, 2013).

3 Parents Television Council, "Women in Peril: a Look at TV's Disturbing New Storyline Trend," *Parents Television Council* Special Report (October 2009).

4 Christopher Ferguson, "Positive Female Role-Models Eliminate Negative Effects of Sexually Violent Media," *Journal of Communication* 62:5 (Oct 2012): 888–99.

5 Tony's preferred form of assault –on both men and women—is choking, which not only leaves the victims helpless and flailing, but robs them of their voice. It is the ultimate act of domination. Over the course of the series, he chokes Carmela, Dr Melfi, and his bipolar girlfriend, Gloria Trillo; not to mention strangling Ralph Cifaretto and Christopher Moltisante to death, and attempting to smother is mother with a pillow.

6 Henry Jenkins et. al., "The Culture that Sticks to your Skin," in *Hop on Pop: The Politicals and Pleasures of Popular Culture* (Duke UP, 2002: 11), quoted in Johnson "Gangster Feminism: The Feminist Cultural Work of HBO's *The Sopranos*" *Feminist Studies* 33:2 (Summer 2007): 269–96.

7 Anna Holmes, "HBO Honcho Beats Up Girlfriend: We Blame Floyd Mayweather, Tony Soprano," *Jezebel* (posted May 8, 2007), http://jezebel.com/258594/hbo-honcho-beats-up-girlfriend-we-blame-floyd-mayweather-tony-soprano?tag=gossipbigpussy (accessed March 15, 2013).

8 Rebecca Traister, "Is *The Sopranos* a Chick Show?" *Salon* (posted March 6, 2004), http://www.salon.com/2004/03/07/carmela_soprano/ (accessed March 15, 2013).

9 *The Scholar and Feminist On-Line* devoted an entire issue to "The Case of HBO" in 2004 (3:1), inviting a number of high-profile feminist media scholars to address this concern head-on, and offering what editors Janet Jakobsen and David Hopson describe as "a balance between appreciation and skepticism, between pleasure and danger."

10 Robin Finn, "Want Pathos, Pain and Courage? Get Real" *New York Times* (April 15, 2001).

11 Ibid.

12 James Hibberd, "*Cathouse* Not a Secret to Viewers," *Television Week* 24:28 (July 11, 2005).

13 Jennifer Dunn largely endorses this perspective in "It's Not Just Sex, It's a Profession": Reframing Prostitution through Text and Context," *Communications Studies* 63:3 (July/August, 2012).

14 Levy 92.

15 Hoggart 2.

16 Margo Jeffeson, "Finding Refuge in Pop Culture's Version of Friendship," *New York Times* (July 23, 2002).

17 Sheila Moeschen, "Where the Girls Aren't: What the Absence of Female Friendships on Network TV Reveals," *Huffington Post* (posted October 1, 2012). http://www.huffingtonpost.com/sheila-moeschen/female-friendship_b_1919511.html (accessed March 15, 2013).

18 See, for example, Shelley E. Taylor, *The Tending Instinct* (New York: Henry Holt, 2002); Geoffrey Grief, *Buddy System* (New York: Oxford University Press USA, 2008); and Kelly Valen, *The Twisted Sisterhood* (New York: Ballantine, 2010).

19 The term actually dates back to a 1953 Walter Winchell quip referring to the Soviet Union.

20 Mark Simpson, "Meet the Metrosexual" *Salon* (posted July 22, 2002), http://www.salon.com/2002/07/22/metrosexual/ (accessed March 15, 2013).

21 "A Conversation with Lena Dunham and Judd Apatow," Disc 2, *Girls: The Complete First Season* (New York: HBO Home Entertainment, 2012). In this passage, Dunham also remarks that a working title for the series was *Degradation in the City*.

22 A relationship guide offering "Time-Tested Secrets for Capturing the Heart of Mr Right" by Ellen Fein and Sherrie Schneider, including "Don't Stare at Men or Talk Too Much" and "Be Honest but Mysterious."

23 Frank Bruni, "The Bleaker Sex," *New York Times* (April 1, 2012).

24 "A Conversation with Lena Dunham and Judd Apatow."

25 Alan Sepinwall, "Interview: *Girls* Producers Lena Dunham and Jenni Konner," *HitFlix* (posted April 7, 2012), http://www.hitfix.com/blogs/

whats-alan-watching/posts/interview-girls-producers-lena-dunham-jenni-konner (accessed March 15, 2013).

26 "A Conversation with Lena Dunham and Judd Apatow."

27 "Q & A with Laura Dern," *HBO Connect* http://connect.hbo.com/events/enlightened/laura-dern/

28 Ibid.

Win or die

1 Mate Prgin, "Why the Future of Video Depends on the Mobile Carriers," *Forbes.com* (posted March 30, 2012), http://www.forbes.com/sites/ciocentral/2012/03/30/why-the-future-of-video-depends-on-the-mobile-carriers/ (accessed March 15, 2013).

2 Ernesto, "*Game of Thrones* Most Pirated TV-Show of 2012," *Torrent Freak* (posted December 23, 2012), http://torrentfreak.com/game-of-thrones-most-pirated-tv-show-of-2012–121223/ (accessed March 15, 2013).

3 Josef Adalian, "More Boys Watch *Girls* Than Girls," *Vulture* (posted June 14, 2012), http://www.vulture.com/2012/06/more-boys-watch-girls-than-girls.html (accessed March 15, 2013).

4 Ginia Bellafante, "A Fantasy World of Strange Feuding Kingdoms," *New York Times* (April 15, 2011).

5 Nancy Dewolf Smith, "Servants, Swords and Sad Sex," *Wall Street Journal* (April 8, 2011).

6 Phillip Maciak, "*Game of Thrones*: Season One" (Review) *Slate* (posted April 14, 2011), http://www.slantmagazine.com/tv/review/game-of-thrones-season-one/248 (accessed March 15, 2013).

7 James Poniewozik, "Undead on Arrival," *Time* 172:11 (September 15, 2008): 62–3.

8 John Gaudiosi, "New Reports Forecast Global Video Game Industry Will Reach $82 Billion By 2017," *Forbes* (posted July 18, 2012), http://www.forbes.com/sites/johngaudiosi/2012/07/18/new-reports-forecasts-global-video-game-industry-will-reach-82–billion-by-2017/ (accessed March 15, 2013).

9 Michael Mateus, "A Preliminary Poetics for Interactive Drama and Games," in *First Person: New Media as Story* (Wardrip-Fruin and Harrigan (eds). Cambridge: MIT Press, 2004).

10 "Animation/ *Game of Thrones* Season 2 RPG" *College Humor* (posted July 3, 2012), http://www.collegehumor.com/video/6791810/game-of-thrones-season-2–rpg (accessed March 15, 2013).

11 Caryn James, "America's Dreams of the '50s, Seen Darkly," *New York Times* (November 11, 1996).

12 Jeremy Gerard, "*The High Life*" (Review) *Variety* (November 4–10, 1996): 40.

13 Gillian Flynn, "Ego Trips," *Entertainment Weekly* Issue 824 (June 10, 2005): 91–2.

14 Joel Keller, "Louis C.K. on the Words You Can't Say on FX." *Huffpost Television* (posted June 26, 2010), http://www.aoltv.com/2010/06/25/louis-ck-on-the-words-you-cant-say-on-fx/ (accessed March 15, 2013). In the same interview, CK claimed that one of the HBO executives had a particular distain for working-class comedy, and saw to it that the series did not survive.

15 Brian Lowry, "*John from Cincinnati*" (Review) *Daily Variety* (June 7, 2007): 6.

16 Rob Salem, "Hot Box: Television to Talk About," *The Star* (posted March 31, 2008), http://www.thestar.com/news/2008/03/31/hot_box_television_to_talk_about.html (accessed March 15, 2013).

BIBLIOGRAPHY

Adalian, Josef. "More Boys Watch *Girls* Than Girls." *Vulture*, entry posted June 14, 2012, http://www.vulture.com/2012/06/more-boys-watch-girls-than-girls.html (accessed March 15, 2013).

Adams, Erik. "Is Television a Medium Without a Past?" *The A.V. Club*, entry posted March 8, 2012, http://www.avclub.com/articles/is-television-a-medium-without-a-past,70520/ (accessed March 15, 2013).

Adams, James Truslow. *The Epic of America*. New York: Blue Ribbon Books, 1931.

Akass, Kim and Janet McCabe (eds), *Reading Six Feet Under: TV to Die For*. New York: I. B. Tauris, 2005.

Alvarez, Rafael. *The Wire: Truth Be Told*. New York: Grove, 2009.

Anderson, Karen and Jake Harwood. "The Presence and Portrayal of Social Groups on Prime-Time Television." *Communication Reports* 15:2 (Summer 2002): 81–97.

Arendt, Hannah. *Eichmann in Jerusalem: A Report on the Banality of Evil*. New York: Viking, 1963.

Bellafante, Ginia. "A Fantasy World of Strange Feuding Kingdoms," *New York Times* (April 15, 2011), C:O, p. 4.

—"Feminism: It's all About Me." *Time* 151:25 (June 29, 1998): 54–60.

Bellamy Jr, Robert V. "Constraints on a Broadcast Innovation: Zenith's Phonevision System, 1931–1972." *Journal of Communication* 38:4 (Autumn 1988): 8–20.

Brand, Stewart. "We Owe It All to the Hippies." *Time* 145:12 (Spring 1995): 54–6.

—*Whole Earth Catalog*. San Francisco: Whole Earth (1968–1972).

Bruce, Lenny. *The Essential Lenny Bruce*. Edited by John Cohen. New York: Ballantine, 1967.

—*Lenny Bruce Live at the Curran Theater*. Fantasy. LP. 1971 (recorded November 19, 1961).

Bruni, Frank. "The Bleaker Sex." *New York Times*, April 1, 2012.

Butsch, Richard. "Five Decades and Three Hundred Sitcoms about Class and Gender." In *Thinking Outside the Box*, Gary R. Edgerton and Brian G. Rose (eds), 111–35. Lexington: University of Kentucky Press, 2005.

Carlin, George. *Class Clown*. Little David/Atlantic. LP. 1972.

—*A Place for My Stuff*. Atlantic. LP. 1981.

Carney, Dana R., John T. Jost, Samuel D. Gosling, and Jeff Potter. "The Secret

Lives of Liberals and Conservatives: Personality Profiles, Interaction Styles, and the Things They Leave Behind." *Political Psychology* 29:6 (2008): 807–40.

Carter, Bill. "HBO as a Modern-Day Dickens." *New York Times*, November 1, 1992.

—"Seriously, Michael Fuchs Moves HBO into Comedy." *New York Times*, November 5, 1989.

Christensen, Clayton M. *The Innovator's Dilemma*. New York: HarperBusiness, 2003.

Clarke, Arthur C. "Extra-terrestrial Relays." *Wireless World* (October 1945): 305–8.

"A Conversation with Lena Dunham and Judd Apatow." Disc 2. *Girls: The Complete First Season*. DVD. New York: HBO Home Entertainment, 2012.

Cooper, Marc. "*The Progressive* Interview: George Carlin." *The Progressive* 65:7 (July 2001): 32–7.

Creeber, Glen. *Serial Television: Big Drama on the Small Screen*. London: BFI Publishing, 2004.

"Death of STV." *Time* 84:21 (November 13, 1964): 82.

DeLyria, Joy and Sean Michael Robinson. *Down in the Hole: The unWired World of H.B. Ogden*. Brooklyn, NY: Powerhouse Books, 2012.

Dunn, Jennifer. "'It's Not Just Sex, It's a Profession': Reframing Prostitution through Text and Context," *Communications Studies* 63:3 (July/August, 2012): 345–63.

Edgerton, Gary R. and Jeffrey P. Jones (eds), *The Essential HBO Reader*. Lexington: University of Kentucky Press, 2008.

Eidelman, Scott, Christian S. Crandall, Jeffrey A. Goodman, and John C. Blanchar. "Low-Effort Thought Promotes Political Conservatism." *Personality and Social Psychology Bulletin* 38:8 (March 16, 2012): 808–20.

Ernesto. "*Game of Thrones* Most Pirated TV-Show of 2012." *Torrent Freak*, posted December 23, 2012, http://torrentfreak.com/game-of-thrones-most-pirated-tv-show-of-2012–121223/ (accessed March 15, 2013).

Fein, Ellen. *The Rules*. New York: Warner, 1995.

Ferguson, Christopher. "Positive Female Role-Models Eliminate Negative Effects of Sexually Violent Media." *Journal of Communication* 62:5 (October 2012): 888–99.

Finn, Robin. "Want Pathos, Pain and Courage? Get Real." *New York Times*, April 15, 2001.

Flynn, Gillian. "Ego Trips." *Entertainment Weekly* Issue 824 (June 10, 2005): 91–2.

"*Game of Thrones* Season 2 RPG," *College Humor*, entry posted July 3, 2012, http://www.collegehumor.com/video/6791810/game-of-thrones-season-2–rpg (accessed March 15, 2013).

Gaudiosi, John. "New Reports Forecast Global Video Game Industry Will Reach $82 Billion by 2017." *Forbes.com*, posted July 18, 2012, http://www.forbes.com/sites/johngaudiosi/2012/07/18/new-reports-forecasts-global-video-game-industry-will-reach-82–billion-by-2017/ (accessed March 15, 2013).

Gerard, Jeremy. "*The High Life*." Review. *Variety* (November 4–10, 1996): 40.

Gigliotti, Davidson. "A Brief History of Raindance." *Radical Software*, posted

2003, http://www.radicalsoftware.org/e/history.html (accessed March 15, 2013).

Gillota, David. "Negotiating Jewishness and the Schlemiel Tradition." *Journal of Popular Film and Television* 38:4 (December 4, 2010): 152–61.

Gitlin, Todd. *Inside Prime Time*. New York: Pantheon, 1983.

Green, Richard and Peter Vernezze (eds), *The Sopranos and Philosophy: I Kill, Therefore I Am*. Peru, IL: Open Court, 2004.

Grief, Geoffrey. *Buddy System: Understanding Male Friendships*. New York: Oxford University Press, 2008.

Groseclose, Tim. *Left Turn: How Liberal Media Bias Distorts the American Mind*. New York: St Martin's Press, 2011.

Hafner, Katie and Matthew Lyon. *Where the Wizards Stay Up Late*. New York: Simon and Schuster, 1995.

Hibberd, James. "Republicans vs. Democrats TV: Lefties Want Comedy, Right Wingers Like Work." *EW.com*, posted December 6, 2011, http://insidetv. ew.com/2011/12/06/republican-vs-democrat-tv/ (accessed March 15, 2013).

Hodson, Gordon, and Michael A. Busseri. "Bright Minds and Dark Attitudes: Lower Cognitive Ability Predicts Greater Prejudice Through Right-Wing Ideology and Low Intergroup Contact." *Psychological Science*, 23:2 (January 5, 2012): 187–95.

Holmes, Anna. "HBO Honcho Beats Up Girlfriend: We Blame Floyd Mayweather, Tony Soprano." *Jezebel*, posted May 8, 2007, http://jezebel. com/258594/hbo-honcho-beats-up-girlfriend-we-blame-floyd-mayweather-tony-soprano?tag=gossipbigpussy (accessed March 15, 2013).

Hornby, Nick. "David Simon." Interview. *The Believer* 5:6 (August 2007).

Howard, H.H. and S.L. Carroll. *Subscription Television: History, Current Status, and Economic Projections*. Knoxville: University of Tennessee Press, 1980.

Ingle, Bob and Sandy McClure. *The Soprano State: New Jersey's Culture of Corruption*. New York: St Martin's Griffin, 2010.

James, Caryn. "America's Dreams of the '50s, Seen Darkly." *New York Times*, November 11, 1996.

Jancovich, Mark and James Lyons. *Quality Popular Television*. London: BFI Publishing, 2003.

Jeffeson, Margo. "Finding Refuge in Pop Culture's Version of Friendship," *New York Times*, July 23, 2002.

Jenkins, Henry, Tara McPherson, and Jane Shattuc. "The Culture that Sticks to your Skin: A Manifesto for a New Cultural Studies." In *Hop on Pop: The Politics and Pleasures of Popular Culture*. Durham, NC: Duke University Press, 2002.

Jobs, Steve. "Stanford University Commencement Address," delivered June 12, 2005.

Johnson, Catherine. *Branding Television*. New York: Routledge, 2012.

Johnson, Lisa. "Feminist Television Studies: The Case of HBO." *The Scholar and Feminist On-Line* 3:1 (Fall 2004), http://sfonline.barnard.edu/hbo/ (accessed March 15, 2013)

Johnson, Merri Lisa. "Gangster Feminism: The Feminist Cultural Work of HBO's *The Sopranos*." *Feminist Studies* 33:2 (Summer 2007): 269–96.

Keller, Joel. "Louis C.K. on the Words You Can't Say on FX." *Huffpost Television*, posted June 26, 2010, http://www.aoltv.com/2010/06/25/louis-ck-on-the-words-you-cant-say-on-fx/ (accessed March 15, 2013)

Kelso, Tony. "And Now No Word From Our Sponsor: How HBO Put the Risk Back Into Television." In Marc Leverette, Brian L. Ott, and Cara Louise Buckley (eds), *It's Not T.V.: Watching HBO in the Post-Television Age* (New York: Routledge, 2008): 46–64.

Lavery, David (ed.), *Reading Deadwood: A Western to Swear By.* New York: I. B. Tauris, 2006.

—(ed.), *Reading The Sopranos: Hit TV from HBO.* New York: I. B. Tauris, 2006.

LeDuc, Donald R. *Cable Television and the FCC: A Crisis in Media Control* Philadelphia: Temple University Press, 1973.

Lehmann, Chris. "The Feel-Good Presidency." *Atlantic Monthly* 287:3 (March 2001): 93–6.

Leverette, Marc, Brian L. Ott, and Cara Louise Buckley (eds), *It's Not T.V.: Watching HBO in the Post-Television Age.* New York: Routledge, 2008.

—"Man-Computer Symbiosis." *IRE Transactions on Human Factors in Electronics* (March 1960): 4–11.

Lotz, Amanda D. *The Television Will Be Revolutionized.* New York: New York University Press, 2007.

Lowry, Brian. "*John from Cincinnati.*" Review. *Daily Variety,* June 7, 2007: 6.

Maciak, Phillip, "*Game of Thrones:* Season One." Review. *Slate,* posted April 14, 2011, http://www.slantmagazine.com/tv/review/game-of-thrones-season-one/248 (accessed March 15, 2013).

Mair, George. *Inside HBO: The Billion Dollar War Between HBO, Hollywood, and the Home Video Revolution.* New York: Dodd Mead, 1988.

Mander, Jerry. *Four Arguments for the Elimination of Television.* New York: Morrow, 1978.

Marc, David, and Robert Thompson. *Prime Time, Prime Movers: From I Love Lucy to L.A. Law—America's Greatest TV Shows and The People Who Create Them.* Boston, MA: Little, Brown, 1992.

Marcotte, Amanda. "How to Make a Critically Acclaimed TV Show About Masculinity" *Jezebel,* posted September 7, 2011, http://jezebel.com/5837945/how-to-make-a-critically-acclaimed-tv-show-about-masculinity (accessed March 15, 2013).

Markoff, John. *What the Dormouse Said: How the Sixties Counterculture Shaped the Personal Computer Industry.* New York: Viking, 2005.

Mateas, Matthew. "A Preliminary Poetics for Interactive Drama and Games." *First Person: New Media as Story.* Edited by Noah Wardrip-Fruin & Pat Harrigan. Cambridge: MIT Press, 2004.

Mazo, Earl. *Richard Nixon, a Political and Personal Portrait.* New York: Avon, 1960.

McCabe, Janet and Kim Akass (eds), *Quality TV: Contemporary American Television and Beyond.* New York: I. B. Tauris, 2007.

McLuhan, Marshall. *Understanding Media: The Extensions of Man.* New York: Mentor, 1964.

McMurria, John. "A Taste of Class: Pay-TV and the Commodification of Television in Postwar America." In *Cable Visions: Television Beyond*

Broadcasting. Edited by Sarah Banet-Weiser, Cynthia Chris, and Anthony Freitas (New York: New York University Press, 2007).

Medved, Michael. *The Shadow Presidents*. New York: Times Books, 1979.

Metcalf, Greg. *The DVD Novel: How the Way We Watch Television Changed the Television We Watch*. Santa Barbara, CA: Praeger/ABC-CLIO, 2012.

Miller, Toby and Linda J. Kim. "It Isn't TV, It's the 'Real King of the Ring.'" In Gary R. Edgerton and Jeffrey P. Jones (eds), *The Essential HBO Reader* (Lexington: University of Kentucky Press, 2008): 217–36.

Moeschen, Sheila. "Where the Girls Aren't: What the Absence of Female Friendships on Network TV Reveals." *Huffington Post*, posted on October 1, 2012, http://www.huffingtonpost.com/sheila-moeschen/female-friendship_b_1919511.html (accessed March 15, 2013).

Mullen, Megan. *Television in the Multichannel Age*. Malden, MA: Blackwell, 2008.

—*The Rise of Cable Programming in the United States*. Austin: University of Texas Press, 2003.

On Location: George Carlin at USC. DVD. Orland Park, IL: MPI Home Video, 2001 (originally aired on Home Box Office September 1, 1977).

Parents Television Council. "Habitat for Profanity: Broadcast Television's Sharp Increase in Foul Language." *Parents Television Council*, posted November 9, 2010, http://www.parentstv.org/PTC/publications/reports/2010Profanity Study/study.pdf (accessed March 15, 2013).

—"Women in Peril: a Look at TV's Disturbing New Storyline Trend." *Parents Television Council*, posted November 2009, http://www.parentstv.org/PTC/publications/reports/womeninperil/study.pdf (accessed March 15, 2013).

Parsons, Patrick R. *Blue Skies: A History of Cable Television*. Philadelphia: Temple University Press, 2008.

Pew Research Center for the People and the Press. *Beyond Red vs. Blue Political Typology*. Washington, DC: Pew Research Center, 2011.

—*Trends in American Values: 1987–2012*. Washington D.C.: Pew Research Center, 2012.

Podhoretz, John. "The Liberal Imagination." *The Weekly Standard* (March 27, 2000): 23–8.

Poniewozik, James. "Undead on Arrival." *Time* 172: 11 (Sept 15, 2008): 53–63.

"The Politics of *The Sopranos*." *The Brian Lehrer Show*. WNYC New York Public Radio. New York: New York, June 5, 2007.

President's Task Force on Communications Policy. *Final Report*. Washington, DC: U.S. Printing Office, 1968.

Prgin, Mate. "Why the Future of Video Depends on the Mobile Carriers." *Forbes.com*, posted March 30, 2012, http://www.forbes.com/sites/ciocentral/2012/03/30/why-the-future-of-video-depends-on-the-mobile-carriers/ (accessed March 15, 2013).

Pryor, Richard (with Todd Gold). *Pryor Convictions: And Other Life Sentences*. London: Revolver Books, 2005.

"Q & A with Laura Dern." *HBO Connect*, http://connect.hbo.com/events/enlightened/laura-dern/ (accessed March 15, 2013)

Reich, Charles A. *The Greening of America*. New York: Random House, 1970.

Ross, Steven J. *Hollywood Left and Right: How Movie Stars Shaped American Politics*. New York, Oxford University Press, 2011.

Ryan, Maureen. "Why is Television Losing Women Writers?" *Huffington Post*, posted April 11, 2012, http://www.huffingtonpost.com/2011/09/08/women-writers-television_n_1418584.html (accessed March 15, 2013).

Sagan, Carl. *Pale Blue Dot: A Vision of the Human Future in Space*. New York: Random House, 1994.

Salem, Rob. "Hot Box: Television to Talk About." *The Star*, posted March 31, 2008, http://www.thestar.com/news/2008/03/31/hot_box_television_to_talk_about.html (accessed March 15, 2013).

Santos, Avi. "Paratelevision and the Discourses of Distinction: The Culture of Production at HBO." In Marc Leverette, Brian L. Ott, and Cara Louise Buckley (eds) *It's Not T.V.: Watching HBO in the Post-Television Age* (New York: Routledge, 2008): 19–45.

Schneider, Anthony. *Tony Soprano on Management*. New York: Berkley/Penguin, 2004.

Seay, Chris. *The Gospel According to Tony Soprano*. New York: Tarcher/Putnam, 2002.

Seinfeld, Jerry. "Dying is Hard, Comedy is Harder." *New York Times*, June 24, 2008.

Sepinwall, Alan. "Interview: *Girls* Producers Lena Dunham and Jenni Konner." *HitFlix*, posted April 7, 2012, http://www.hitfix.com/blogs/whats-alan-watching/posts/interview-girls-producers-lena-dunham-jenni-konner (accessed March 15, 2013).

Shamberg, Michael and Raindance Corporation. *Guerilla Television*. New York: Holt, Rinehart and Winston, 1971.

Shapiro, Ben. *Primetime Propaganda: The True Hollywood Story of How the Left Took Over Your TV*. New York: Broadside Books, 2011.

Simon, David. Foreward to *Paths of Glory*, by Humphrey Cobb. New York: Penguin, 2010.

Simon, David R. *Tony Soprano's America: The Criminal Side of the American Dream*. Boulder, CO: Westview Press, 2002.

Simpson, Mark. "Meet the Metrosexual." *Salon*, posted July 22, 2002, http://www.salon.com/2002/07/22/metrosexual/ (accessed March 15, 2013).

Sloan Commission on Cable Communications. *On the Cable: The Television of Abundance*. New York: McGraw-Hill, 1971.

Smith, Nancy Dewolf. "Servants, Swords and Sad Sex." *Wall Street Journal*, April 8, 2011.

Smith, Ralph Lee. "The Wired Nation." *The Nation* 210:19 (May 19, 1970): 582–606.

Soprano, Carmela, Allen Rucker, Michele Scicolone and David Chase. *Entertaining with the Sopranos*. New York: Grand Central Publishing, 2006.

Southwick, Thomas P. *Distant Signals: How Cable TV Changed the World of Telecommunications*. Overland Park, KS: Primedia Intertec, 1998.

Sullivan, James. *Seven Dirty Words: The Life and Crimes of George Carlin*. Cambridge, MA: Da Capo, 2010.

Swanson, Dorothy Collins. *The Story of Viewers for Quality Television: From*

Grassroots to Primetime. Syracuse, New York: Syracuse University Press, 2000.

Taylor, Shelley E. *The Tending Instinct.* New York: Henry Holt, 2002.

Thomson, Kristen. *Storytelling in Film and Television.* Cambridge: Harvard University Press, 2003.

Traister, Rebecca. "Is *The Sopranos* a Chick Show?" *Salon,* posted March 6, 2004, http://www.salon.com/2004/03/07/carmela_soprano/ (accessed March 15, 2013).

Turner, Fred. *From Counterculture to Cyberculture: Stewart Brand, the Whole Earth Network, and the Rise of Digital Utopianism.* University of Chicago Press, 2006.

Twain, Mark. "Notebook 18 (February–September 1879)." In *Mark Twain's Notebooks & Journals, Volume II: 1877–1883.* Edited by Frederick Anderson. Berkeley: University of California Press, 1976.

Valen, Kelly. *The Twisted Sisterhood.* New York: Ballantine, 2010.

Vasquez, Josh. "DVD Review: *The West Wing: The Complete Fourth Season.*" *Slant,* posted April 4, 2005, http://www.slantmagazine.com/dvd/review/the-west-wing-the-complete-fourth-season/597 (accessed March 15, 2013).

Veblen, Thorstein. *The Theory of the Leisure Class* (1899). New York: Oxford University Press, 2009.

Waldrop, M. Mitchell. *The Dream Machine: J.C.R. Licklider and the Revolution That Made Computing Personal.* New York: Viking, 2001.

Warshow, Robert. "The Gangster as Tragic Hero." *Partisan Review* 15: 2 (February 1948). Reprinted in Warshow, *The Immediate Experience* (New York: Doubleday, 1962).

Whiteside, Thomas. "'Onward and Upward With the Arts: Cable Television-Part III." *The New Yorker,* June 3, 1985: 82–105.

"Will Vote Halt Pay TV's Growth?" *Broadcasting,* November 9, 1964: 22.

Williams, Raymond. *Television: Technology and Cultural Form.* London: Collins, 1974.

Wilson, Jeremy. "Gorging on House of Cards: How Netflix has turned binge TV viewing mainstream." *The Telegraph,* February 7, 2013.

Yacowar, Maurice. *The Sopranos on the Couch.* New York: Continuum, 2006.

Zoglin, Richard. *Comedy at the Edge.* New York: Bloomsbury, 2008.

INDEX